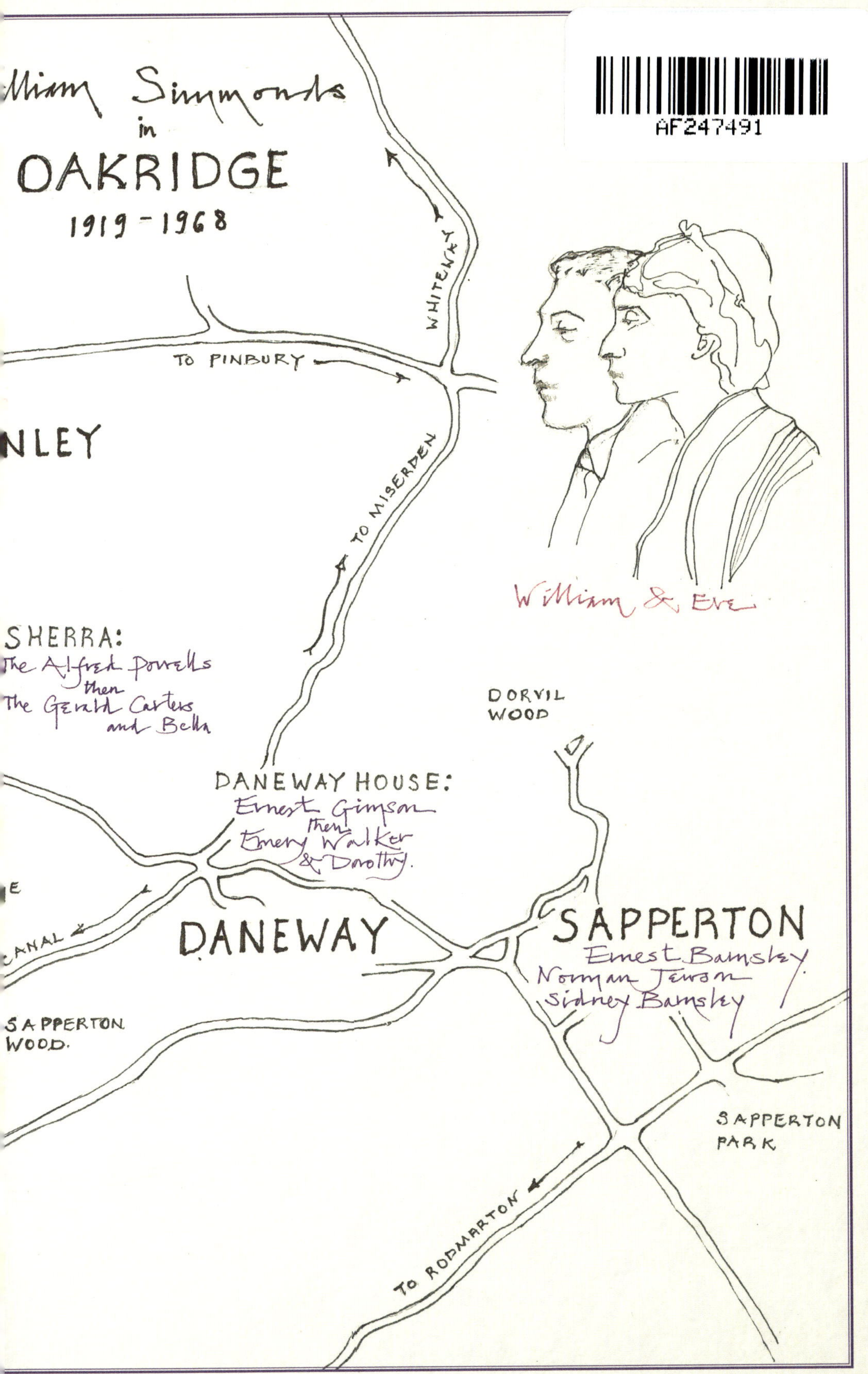
William Simmonds
in
OAKRIDGE
1919 - 1968
WHITENEY
TO PINBURY
TO MISERDEN
NLEY
William & Eve
SHERRA:
The Alfred Powells
then
The Gerald Carters
and Bella
DORVIL
WOOD
DANEWAY HOUSE:
Ernest Gimson
then
Emery Walker
& Dorothy.
DANEWAY
SAPPERTON
Ernest Barnsley.
Norman Jewson
Sidney Barnsley
CANAL
SAPPERTON
WOOD.
SAPPERTON
PARK
TO RODMARTON

WILLIAM
SIMMONDS

WILLIAM SIMMONDS

The Silent Heart of the Arts and Crafts Movement

JESSICA DOUGLAS-HOME

Published in 2018 by Unicorn,
an imprint of Unicorn Publishing Group LLP
5 Newburgh Street
London
W1F 7RG

www.unicornpublishing.org

A catalogue record for this book is available from the British Library.

ISBN 978-1-911604-75-4

Edited by Caroline Brooke Johnson
Proofread by Ramona Lamport
Index by Nicola King
Designed by Ocky Murray
Printed in Poland for Latitude Press Ltd

Front cover: William in his Oakridge workshop, c. 1930 (page 135)
Back cover: *Portrait of William* by William Rothenstein, 1920s (plate 28)
Endpapers: Maps by Jessica Douglas-Home based on an ARP (Air Raid
Precautions) map, 1939, by William Simmonds

Contents

Prologue

When I was six, my father inherited a house in the Cotswolds, Nether Lypiatt Manor, from his aunt, the musician Violet Gordon Woodhouse. Its interior had been kept entirely unchanged, exactly as she had left it, like a shrine to Violet's memory. On entering the front door for the first time, my eyes lit on animals settled happily on cushions on the drawing- and sitting-room floors: a cat stretched its claws to play with a marble, another bunched up by the fire slept peacefully; a Pekinese gazed soulfully upwards with jet-black eyes (see plate 23); and under the harpsichord there was a hedgehog which, if prodded, waddled along from side to side. All these, I was told later, were carvings by Violet's close friend, the sculptor and puppetmaster William Simmonds.

Other smaller objects were housed in glass cabinets. I found a tiny ivory duck, an inch long, and a wren sitting on a chestnut-tree leaf painted in gilt. The most intriguing was a 22-inch high puppet of the Archangel Gabriel (see plate 25). The locks that crowned his head were flicks of curly wood shavings, framing intense, happy eyes of deep blue. His mouth was open, as if he were singing to the heavenly multitude; his body was clothed in a tight-fitting garment made of little leather flaps cut like leaves; his wooden wings could be stretched out to a span of almost three feet. Apart from his face, what struck me most was the detail of the carving: the delicacy of the hands and fingers, the feet and toes. Decades later, when I understood more of William Simmonds's character, this puppet seemed like an unwitting self-portrait. Music and song were as much part of his life as his sculpture.

I used to think it was my mother who led me to become a painter. Lonely in smog-ridden London, where I was taken after my parents' divorce, she gave me a box of charcoal sticks with which to draw. I experimented with thick lines, shading and smudging with

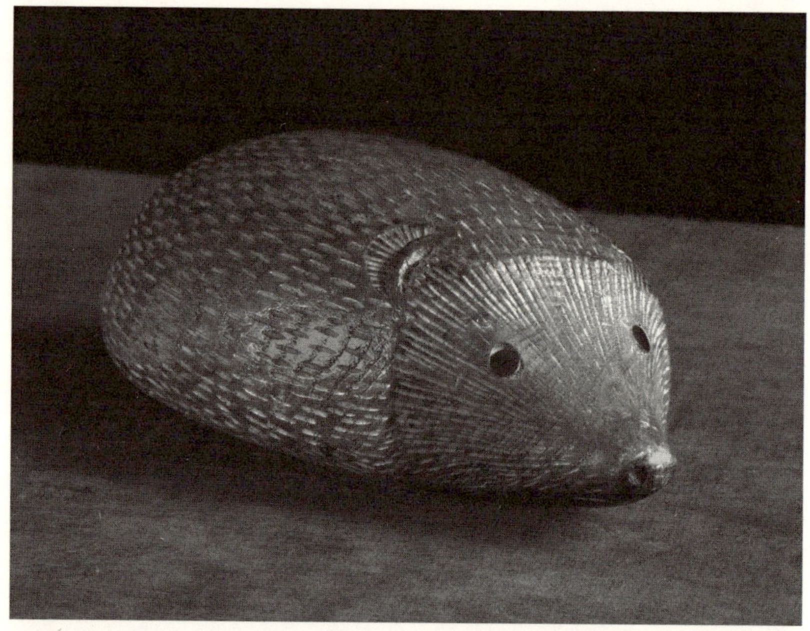

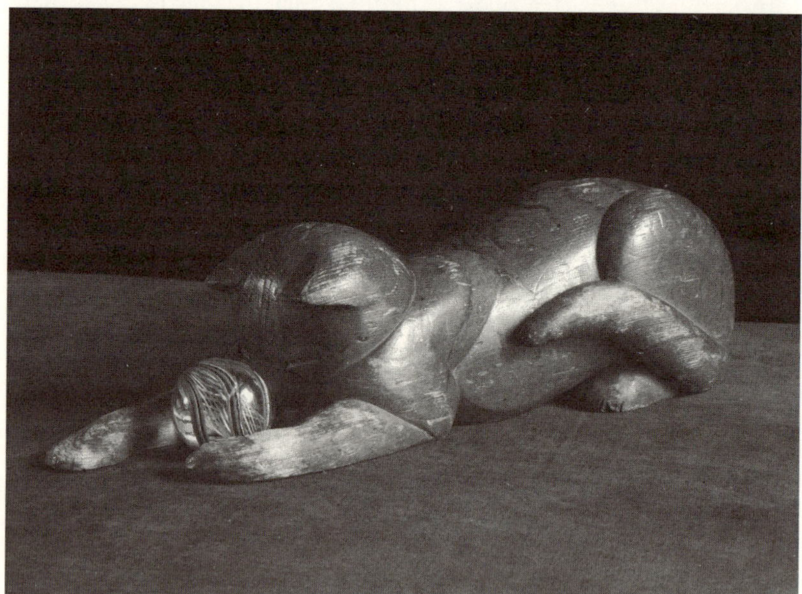

Above: *Hedgehog*, designed to amble along when gently pushed
Below: *Cat with Marble* that permanently settled on the carpet in the
Nether Lypiatt Manor's drawing room

cloth or fingers. I was excited and somehow liberated by this new method of drawing. But now, as I look further back, I think it must have been my father who started me on the track, with more purpose.

One late morning in the heat of an early summer sun, he announced we were off for a 'ten-minute drive' to the Simmondses' cottage, The Frith, in Far Oakridge. We left the car on a verge in a lane, scrambled out and pushed through a small gate into a steep field, leaving behind us hedges of roses and honeysuckle, foxglove, bramble and rabbits. As I padded behind my father down the narrow path, I met a head-high wall of ripening green meadow grasses, big as a forest, green as a moving sea, stems supple and billowing in the summer breeze. Through gaps I saw more flowers: willow-herb, cinquefoil, moon daisies, speedwell, eyebright, pimpernel and pink orchid with spotted leaves – all these and others. My father loved flowers and taught me their names. But he would not let me run among them and pressed on – we were always late it seemed – pointing down at the house beyond and urging me with his strong voice and dark-eyed glance to 'come along'.

There, halfway down the valley, on the edge of the hill stood a mottled grey stone house. It had a moss-covered tiled roof and a chimney, upright, steep and sharp as a child's drawing. For no traceable reason the first sight of William Simmonds and his wife Eve in their garden, the memory of the sharp meadow grass about my chin and the moon daisies level with my eyes, has stayed with me since.

That morning I had my first lessons in drawing. I know this from William's pocket diary, in which he had also recorded a far earlier encounter when my father, on leave from Special Operations in Greece towards the end of the war, had brought me to my great aunt Violet's house. I was then a few days old, my brother aged two.

Drawing lessons with William became a central part of my child-hood. His studio in the barn was a world apart: a wounded owl discovered in the woods, perched recovering in the rafters; there was a magnificent workbench, and near the wall a crowd of puppets clipped on to a line of rope. But William had long stopped performing in the barn; it was in The Frith's sitting room that my brother and I saw the dolls at work. Each school holidays, spring, summer and winter, I would be dropped off to draw with William in the garden, in the fields or, if it was raining, in his studio. Without spelling it out, he conveyed the message that nothing could be achieved without a visual language, which meant a proper study in drawing. Charcoal was a beautiful medium in a dexterous hand, he said, but more adaptable to mass blocks and shapes than to line drawing. To mark the end of our sessions, Eve would look in, remark charmingly on what I had done, and summon us back to the house for scones with jam and cream.

William was convinced that, to be a true artist, inspiration is not enough: there must always be a properly developed craftsmanship. He went through eight years of training, according to a method that originated with the French atelier and the German artists' guilds, and which had evolved over centuries. This practice had produced some of the great artists of our civilisation, as well as those unassuming artists like William, whose work neither professes to rival the works of genius nor fears the challenge of perfection. William was one of the last graduates of a method that was able to develop natural gifts into a disciplined artistic identity. He became a master of anatomy, science, woodcarving, plaster-modelling, stone carving, watercolours, canvas-preparation and oil painting. He learned all the traditional crafts including the art of mixing his own pigments, plaster-cast drawing and drawing from life.

This exacting training of hand, eye and mind, far from being a constraint on creativity, endowed him with both competence and the freedom to exercise it. He was convinced ever afterwards that true discipline is also a liberation, and that artistic licence without skill leads only to anarchic repetition. In addition to absorbing all those practical skills, he was able to enjoy the benefits of attending weekly lectures on ancient and medieval European art, and on the art and literature of the civilisations of Egypt, Greece and Rome.

In the decades that followed the First World War, William's puppets gathered a cult following – their design, songs, words, sets and music all his own creation. Many leading musicians, writers, theatre directors, poets, critics and politicians of the day were spellbound by them, such as the Suffragette and composer Ethel Smyth, Bernard Shaw, John Masefield, Thomas Hardy and Winston Churchill. So, too, were local villagers and children from all over the English countryside – all succumbed to their charm, although 'charm' would be too platitudinous a term for Ethel Smyth, who wrote to William about the 'strange haunting absolutely unique impression your art leaves in one's life … as for "The Woodland" … I long dreadfully to see that scene again'.

But all this was of secondary importance to William; it was his serious sculpture above all that really mattered to him, and where his true genius lay. He worked slowly. Early in his career he acquired a following of serious art collectors, museums and patrons who snapped up everything he could produce. As a result his work seldom came on the market. In 2017 two pieces appeared in the saleroom: the collectors and cognoscenti of the Arts and Crafts world entered a bidding war, proof of Simmonds's enduring achievement as an artist.

CHAPTER I

Beginnings

1876–1892

'William's father released him, enabling William to take up a scholarship at London's National Art Training School.'

William Simmonds was the son of John Simmonds, a poor builder who started life in the tiny hamlet of Eton Wick on the outskirts of Windsor, eventually becoming a respected District Councillor of Works. Like many who rise to fame in later life, William romanticised his childhood, attributing to his parents a situation rather more elevated than they had in fact enjoyed. John had lost his own parents at a young age and had been forced to support his three sisters and younger brother by working in the pub that his parents had run, the Grapes Beer House. He also worked as a carpenter and, thanks to this skill, was able to obtain a position in Windsor Castle's Office of Works. His chance for promotion came in 1872 when the castle's resident architect, John Lessels, asked him to help him survey and reconstruct the British Embassy in Turkey, in Constantinople's Galata district, on the European side of the Golden Horn. It was the second time that century that the British Embassy had gone up in flames.

Lessels's choice of an inexperienced 26-year-old carpenter was risky but inspired. John was an able draughtsman and proved resourceful, determined, industrious and full of artistic talent (the Royal Archives have an accomplished Simmonds drawing of buildings inside the precincts of the castle). Lessels, still negotiating his own contract's terms, would arrive later in the year, leaving John to undertake the preparatory work single-handed. Living expenses were to be covered by the Embassy and John calculated that within a year he could save enough to get married. He was leaving behind his sweetheart, Martha Walker, a London girl, stalwart and sensible. She had promised to wait.

John set out in January 1872 on the SS *Timsah* to take on the role of Assistant Clerk to the Office of Works. It was a far larger job than his title and slender salary suggested. Besides the Embassy mansion, he would be supervising the rebuilding in stone of the English Church at Kadiköy, the British Seamen's Hospital and Institute, the British Consular building, the Ambassador's Residence, the coach house at Tarabya, the post office and the Jewesses' College in Galata. Much of the old Ottoman city had been transformed two decades earlier into a relatively modern metropolis, but in its heart it remained a medieval labyrinth. The houses were virtually all built of wood and the city was constantly ravaged by fire.

Unprepared for the fierce intensity of the summer heat, he found the twelve-hour working day exhausting and in July went down with a fever. He recovered in five days and from then on allowed himself a day off a week; after that, as if inoculated, he was never ill again.

As a member of the Embassy staff, he went to most of the official national parties from the staid American Feast Day to the exotic Greek one with its regatta on the Sea of Marmara and the Islamic bayram for which mosques were illuminated all over the city. He went on expeditions, to see the Sultan's new mosque, an eclectic mix of different styles, built for the Sultan's mother in Aksaray, to sketch the Galata Tower on the hill below the Embassy or to bathe in the Marmara. Constantinople's vivid cosmopolitan world opened up before him. He took lessons in Turkish, bought a French dictionary (the city had a large French-speaking community), and began recording the ancient city's way of life and its minutest architectural details.

When news came that Lessels was arriving by ship with a Captain Galton on 30 September, John, who was becoming a hard taskmaster, pressed his men in the August heat. He finished a sketch for the Porter's Lodge. Large deliveries of cement were ordered – 100 caskets for the post office, the Embassy and the British Seamen's Hospital.

The day after Lessels's arrival, they were all on site. John orchestrated a tour of the Embassy and its outbuildings – stables, coach house, grooms' quarters, the nearly completed servants' hall – and

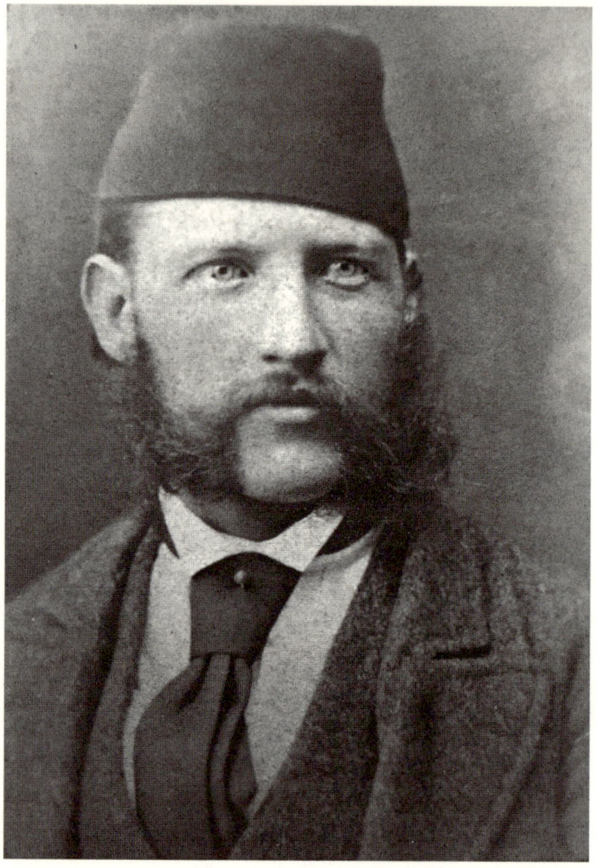

William's father, John Simmonds, was in charge of the restorations of the British Embassy in Constantinople after its destruction by fire in 1872

Lessels made a final decision on the design for the Embassy's grand staircase. More than content with John's work, Lessels agreed to his request for a pay rise and returned to England in December, taking with him a letter from John proposing marriage to Martha.

Although William encouraged his mother in old age to talk about life in Turkey, there are no details about her north London background nor how she and John actually met. Now twenty-three and a fiancée, the intrepid Martha Walker arrived in Constantinople on 13 September 1873. John took a small boat out into the Bosphorus to meet her ship, which, he found to his intense disappointment, had been put into quarantine for ten days. He would have to make the preparations for the wedding in two weeks' time on his own – particularly trying since he and the rest of the Embassy staff had been enlisted for extra work: Queen Victoria's second son, Prince Alfred, was due to stay en route for Russia. Having narrowly escaped an assassination attempt in Australia, he would need protection in Constantinople's far more dangerous environment. John managed a half-day holiday to buy things on 26 September, dined that evening with a male colleague and the following morning married Martha in the Embassy chapel.

Martha settled in well enough, and was to some extent captivated by the glamour and colour of the city. But she never came to terms with Turkish brutality and mayhem. To the end of her life one incident remained vividly in her mind: crossing the Bosphorus with her friend in the Embassy, Mrs Meekins, she had noticed a strangely disquieting object beside their small boat. 'Whatever is that large black thing in the water?' she asked. Mrs Meekins told her to look away. There had been an attempted rising among the Greeks. Forty *papaz*, as the priests were called, suspected of leading the insurgence, had been taken out on the Bosphorus and beheaded. 'And serve them right', said the boatman.

Violence was so prevalent that John never let his wife out alone and hardly dared walk about the streets himself after dark; if he did, he made sure he carried a paper lantern (on sale in every street) with his pistol, so that he could see where he was shooting. It was certainly not the ideal place to have children but within a year Martha gave birth to a daughter Annie and, eighteen months later, on 3 March 1876, to William.

At the time of William's birth, life in the city was becoming increasingly alarming. The previous year some Christian peasants in Herzegovina and Bosnia, two small mountainous provinces on the western front of Turkey's Empire, had rebelled against their Muslim landlords and the Turkish Sultan Abdülaziz. By the spring of 1876 isolated skirmishes had turned into full-scale war, with vicious battles in the hills, woods and valleys of the region, and many dead. The disruption was felt in Turkey itself, with turmoil spreading to Constantinople.

Soon after William's birth a blaze started close to the Embassy. As the flames came nearer and nearer Mrs Meekins said, 'For God's sake close the window' as the curtains were floating out and sparks from the burning wood were beginning to settle on them. Years later, Martha described to William the sight of hundreds of burning houses and told him how, when a roof fell in 300 yards away and the sparks flew up, the eighteen-month-old Annie had clapped her hands and he had smiled in delight.

For all his promises of reform, the Sultan lost control as the revolt spread to Montenegro and soon to Serbia – an autonomous principality within the Empire – and Bulgaria. Abdülaziz had been on the throne for seventeen years. In 1867 he was the first Ottoman Sultan to visit Western Europe and his trip included a visit to the United Kingdom, where he was made a Knight of the Garter by Queen Victoria and shown a Royal Navy fleet review with Ismail of Egypt. Abdülaziz's greatest achievement was to modernise the Ottoman Navy. But now public demonstrations forced him to flee from palace to palace with his vast harem and finally to surrender power to his nephew, who for four weeks had been locked in a cellar to acclimatise him to his new role. The Sultan, after ceding power to his nephew, is alleged to have committed suicide with a four-inch pair of scissors.

Constantinople's Europeans now experienced the full blast of Mohammedan militancy against the Christian minority in Salonica. A Turkish Christian child was snatched from her village and forced to abjure her religion. Trying to secure her safety in a mosque, two of the most influential of the European diplomats – a French and a German consul – were brutally murdered, their bodies stamped on and their mouths stuffed with earth. Mercifully 1876 saw the completion of the Embassy project. The Simmondses were not going to extend their stay a minute longer than they had to. John packed up and was heading back to in Britain as soon as he could find a boat to take them.

It was not easy for John Simmonds to readjust to life in England. After a brief period with Martha's mother in Middlesex, he decided to try his luck in Scotland. He moved the family to Edinburgh, where his mentor Lessels had had a thriving practice. John would have an introduction there and, he thought, better prospects of work than in England.

We do not know what went wrong, but within five years, despite his connections in Edinburgh, John was back at Eton Wick, where he rented a small cottage and re-established himself as a master builder. The family remained there throughout William and Annie's early childhood. For William it was an idyll. To him it was the surrounding

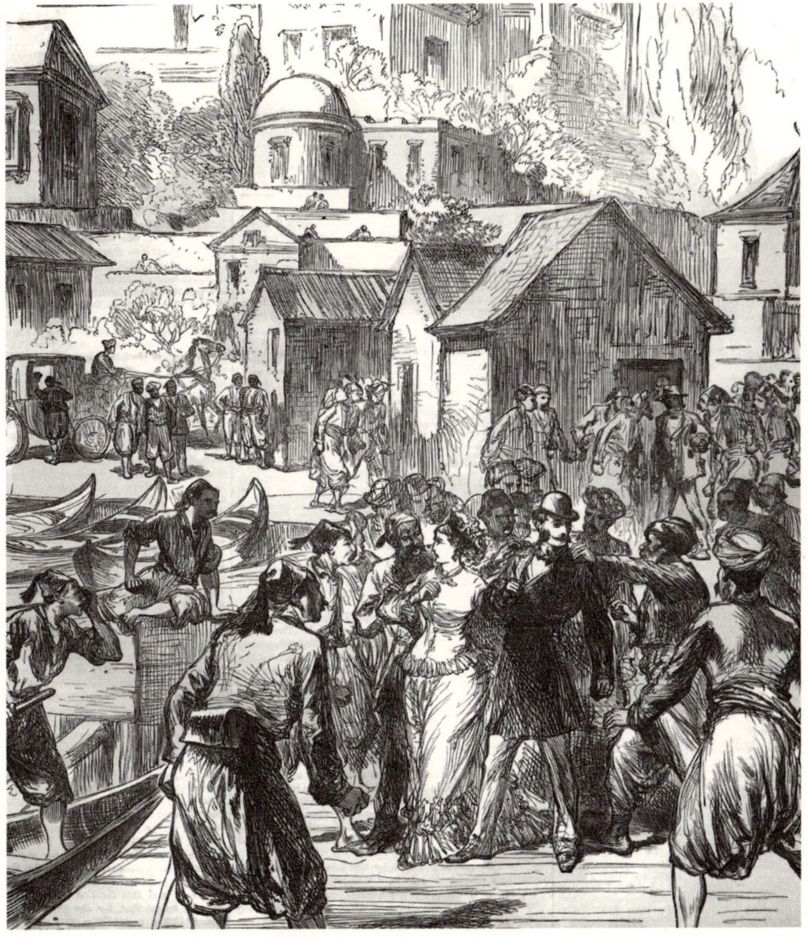

Europeans near the British Embassy in Constantinople insulted in the streets during the Simmondses' time in Turkey (1872–6)

farms, woods and fields that really mattered. On the flat, undrained farmland, he messed about in the deep ponds with their rich wildlife. He helped milk and plough and bring in the harvest. Soon he was tacking up the farmers' carthorses, feeding the pigs and milking the goats. He learnt the workmen's folk melodies and their mildly suggestive pub songs.

John was not slow to notice his son's affinity with the natural world. He gave him his old sketchbook and lent him pencils and crayons, and finally a paint box. By the time William was eight, he was out in the fields and meadows making detailed drawings: a sparrow's nest on the knoll near the church, a hedgehog or a frog in the reeds of a stream. By the age of nine, he was mixing his own paints.

William's first oil painting is a portrait of his pet guinea pig, painted with a skill and a humanity characteristic of the man to come. This much-loved creature, with its black, orange and white fur, snuffles within a bed of pristinely clean, sticklike straw. The straw was there for artistic effect only, for he lived indoors beside William day and night; William had house-trained him.

Ten years after returning from Turkey, having been promoted within the Urban District Council to Inspector of Factories, John moved from Eton Wick to Eton High Street, where he rented a house with a joiner's office on the ground floor. The ten-year-old William was taken away from his rural life, but the family was moving up in the world and John had ambitions to found a family partnership. When William was thirteen, John put him to work with him in the afternoons and a year later employed him full-time.

By good fortune a decade earlier the Great Western Railway had sold a plot of land in Windsor to a committee of local philanthropists to build the Windsor and Eton Royal Albert Institute. Their aim was to meet the growing demand for education for the working classes and 'to aid the pursuit of knowledge and art so loved by Prince Albert'.

Here William was allowed to attend evening drawing classes under the art teacher Charles Hollis, who recognised his talent. The institute gave William more than art classes. It had room for every kind of indoor recreation: a hall for music and for lectures, along with classrooms and a library. He lived in the library. The editor of the *Eton and Windsor Express*, Charles Knight, had been a local hero who had published plain, useful books without frills. William devoured the fine high-definition pictures in Knight's *Penny Magazine*, moving on to Knight's basic *Cyclopaedia* and his *Cyclopaedia of Arts and Science*. Later he discovered the historical novels by the local author, Margaret Oliphant. If his father could spare threepence, he would go to a Tuesday lecture – on parts of the world he had never heard of, or on Shakespeare or on 'Folk Lore, Legends and Superstitions'; and there were concerts – here he heard for the first time the comic operas of Gilbert and Sullivan.

By the late 1880s the trustees and the headmaster saw the institute as part of a wider plan, a training ground for promising art students who in turn could become teachers in the new art schools being set up all over England. Hollis forged a close relationship with the Department of Science and Art in Kensington and encouraged selected pupils to sit an exam for the National Art Training School, with a County Council scholarship attached. Even though William could attend only two evenings a week, Hollis watched over his progress with particular care. No one, he thought, was a more worthy candidate to be helped to the next rung of the educational ladder.

Over the next two years, William grew into a good-looking, self-contained young man with evenly proportioned features and a serene expression. He was quiet and shy but determined. When he was sixteen, he asked to see his father for a formal meeting to discuss his future. Could he please be released from his apprenticeship in the Simmonds business? He would be sorry to leave the family, especially his sister Annie, to whom he was close and with whom he shared his love of art. Although the Simmonds practice was winning more District Council work, it had no artistic content – just contracts in surveying and sanitary inspection. Could he not enrol at a prestigious London art school, like the National Art Training School, with whom the Royal Albert Institute had a special connection? His teacher was urging him on. If he did well enough in the exam, he would not cost his father a penny. Not yet sure of his vocation, he argued that he would be given the opportunity to learn many disciplines, from which he could later choose. Whatever happened, he would at least end up qualified to earn a living as a teacher.

The hour-and-a-half entrance test was surprisingly easy. William was given a card with the outline of two ornamental designs from which he had to make a pencil copy, freehand, on a slightly larger scale. Tracing paper, a ruler or any measuring instruments were forbidden. He had a brief pang of conscience when he found that he had automatically checked the design's width and height with his pencil. He was afraid it might disqualify him. Ought he to own up? He never did.

CHAPTER 2

National Art Training School

1893–1898

'Crane's appointment was like a sudden rush of fresh air.'

William found lodgings half a mile from the National Art Training School in a Dickensian bedsit in Merton Road, Kensington (now Kelso Place). Most of the original cottages and terrace had been demolished to make way for the Metropolitan and District line underground. Part derelict, part rebuilt with inferior buildings, Merton Road was no longer a true city street. To the east a filthy right of way forged a route to the Midland Railway coal yard. On the south corner, two builders, by chance named the Simmonds Brothers, owned premises. Facing Merton Road itself, blocking out the sun, stood a vast redbrick infirmary and workhouse, home to 400 mostly aged and infirm paupers, who looked out forlornly at William from the tree-covered courtyards and arcades in their 'airing grounds'.

Towards Exhibition Road the area changed radically into prosperity. The late-Victorian London of 1893 that greeted the seventeen-year-old William Simmonds was one of the most exciting places on earth, the first modern metropolis, with its underground railway, its busy streets, its gas and electric street lighting, its thick grey fogs and its vivid glimpses into an elegant fashionable world. Great things were afoot in the outside world – the Boer War, the Irish Independence movement and the foundation of the Labour Party – but William, innocently apolitical, was cocooned in his own aspirations. As he wove his way between the Hansom cabs to cross the main road and passed the South Kensington Museum (now the Victoria and Albert Museum) to the School courtyard, he felt exhilarated. Ahead of him lay entry to a new universe.

Amid the feverish change of the period, the School's heavily bearded Principal, John Sparkes, seemed a timeless fixture. A student at the School forty years earlier, he had emerged as a qualified teacher and a budding scholar. He travelled in Europe to inspect German and Belgian art schools and had established himself as one of the most eminent educators in the land, with several scholarly books to his name. Back as the School's Principal in 1875, he religiously kept to rules laid down by a previous headmaster, Richard Redgrave, a protégé of Prince Albert's favourite benefactor, Henry Cole. He had recently lost his wife, his eyesight was deteriorating and he had become prone to bouts of irritability. But retirement was never spoken of. Two damaging reports, commissioned by the School's board of trustees, had heavily criticised both him and the staff, but they gathered dust and no one pressed Sparkes to accept their conclusions.

William soon became familiar with the rigid teaching methods in the curriculum. The School's stated aim was to train teachers and craftsmen rather than painters of 'easel pictures', through a course of twenty-three steps, learning the 'grammar of design'. The deeper social purpose was to elevate the status of the designer-craftsman so as to engender respect from industrialists and manufacturers.

William's introductory class was the elementary course on Geometric Principles, some of which he had already covered in the Royal Albert Institute. From there he progressed to line drawing from plaster casts of classical sculpture and antique ornaments, then to shading in chalk and charcoal. Each task, worked on for weeks, sometimes months, had to be completed to the instructor's satisfaction before he could move on to the next. Typical was the teaching of Roman lettering. The class was given an alphabet of large Roman letters on separate cards. Each morning they had to do a letter, starting with 'A', by making a tracing of it. This they did every day until they knew by heart all the properties and proportions of the letter and could draw it freehand without tracing, at which point they moved on to the next letter. To the end of his life William considered these lettering classes to be an introduction to one of the high points of civilisation.

One teacher stood out from the mediocrity of the others. Edward Lanteri's lucid sculpture demonstrations were always packed. With his beguiling French accent and charismatic energy, he awakened an astonishing enthusiasm among students who, under the rest of the staff, seemed dead to their studies. The warmth of his personality left his pupils with a lasting affection for him.[1]

Lanteri thought the copying of idealised Greek classical casts too testing for beginners and gave them instead more striking and distinctive pieces such as Donatello's *Lawyer* and the head of the joint Roman Emperor Lucius Verus (AD 161–9). Like Sparkes, he believed that drawing practice was even more important for sculpture than for painting. 'Only by understanding the body's anatomical structure,' he wrote, 'will the sculptor avoid groping in the dark, gain confidence and find the necessary powers to express truthfully, in the simplest, fastest and surest means, his personal vision: and only then will he be ready to move to the living model.'

Lanteri never tried to restrict his pupils' creativity. In fact he thought individuality the essence of art, a 'supreme gift' granted to few, distinguishing it sharply from eccentricity or artificial striving after originality, both of which usually led to 'deplorable' results. His scholarship encompassed an understanding of every type of animal, not least the horse – the placing of the bridle, the importance of the mouth, the paces, ease and uniformity of movement in trot, walk and gallop. Following his own observation of the cart horses and trap ponies of Eton Wick, William became fascinated with the much greater possibilities of wild animals, listening intently to Lanteri on the horse, lion and bull.

William soon discovered another way of satisfying his thirst for wider knowledge. Close to the School the enormous South Kensington Museum bewitched him with its hotchpotch of rooms. He discovered 5,000 years of art in virtually every medium: metalwork, furniture, textiles, paintings, drawings, prints and sculpture. And among these remarkable collections sat some contemporary work, illuminated by the historic forerunners that had helped to shape it.

He would spend hours drawing in different halls. Unable to afford a meal in the green dining room, with its lavish William Morris tiles and beautiful stained-glass windows by Edward Burne-Jones and Philip Webb, or even tea in any of the museum's other refreshment rooms, he always ended up on the padded seats in the room with the Raphael Cartoons, the only place where he could sit and relax. Just once his savings allowed him a meal of buns and cheese in the grill room, where the cook varied the menu to suit the social standing of its customers.

Most important to William were the School's visiting lecturers who came several times a term to the astoundingly grand lecture theatre on the first floor. They descended like demigods into an auditorium lit by an enormous gaslight with some 700 fishtail burners, there to be worshipped by inferior mortals. Their 'performances' often included slides from the museum's collection, introducing students in this way to the vast range of its contents. A favourite, Professor Arthur Thomas, lectured on anatomy, which he expounded with magisterial brilliance, clarity and no little drama: he could draw parts of the body simultaneously with both hands on the blackboard. He would bring on to the stage a model to strike positions and demonstrate muscular attitudes; sometimes, with his long bamboo stick, he would point to the hanging bones on a gruesome skeleton that swung from a ring in its skull as if from the gallows.

But William found the permanent staff a disappointment. Their teaching practices worsened with each month. They would turn up intermittently and had little dedication, having received their Teacher's Certificate many years ago and, as time went by, they relapsed into resentful indifference. The cause of their dissatisfaction was the drop in the number of fee-paying students, from whom they derived the bulk of their income. With their pockets affected, they took it out on the scholarship students, whose work they randomly savaged. William's new grant increased his maintenance allowance but specified that he could only remain if he did well 'term by term'. As a scholarship boy, he felt the strain more than most as he awaited the result of his end of term report. Nevertheless he stuck at it: he was determined to show he could survive independently of his father.

After a year of frequent exams and dauntingly hard work, William obtained his Art Master's Certificate and entered the next four-year phase of the teachers' course as 'a student in training'. The same teachers were on hand.

He was now allowed into life drawing, where the standard was what was known as 'Sight-Size'. An object was to be drawn exactly as it appeared to the artist on a one-to-one scale, so that when viewed from a set vantage point the drawing and the subject had the same proportions. Students measured the subject using a variety of measuring tools such as string, sticks and a straight arm. The aim was accuracy and realism. Rejecting the romantic idea that the academic discipline of art schools stifled the imagination, he knuckled down to learn all there was to know about the theory and practice of drawing.

With little daytime supervision, William found he could go into any classroom and set up his materials. The students gathered in knots, chatting idly and occasionally breaking out into rowdy horseplay. If a lesson was more than ordinarily boring, he and his friend Charlie Pibworth, the son of a Bristol cobbler, passed the time sketching each other or the lecturer, under the guise of taking notes. Discipline had collapsed in mutual disrespect between staff and students. A lecturer who paused for a drink of water would be greeted with ironic applause; but William kept his head down, intent on obtaining his qualification at all costs.

He could attend as many lectures he wanted. Not so the female students. Separation of the sexes was complete. They were taught in different buildings, although at one point the two staircases touched. With less instruction than the men, the women had a strong feeling of being disadvantaged. Most of all they resented not being allowed into the life classes. The evening lectures at the museum were another bone of contention: the women were not allowed out after dark unless chaperoned.

The one place that the two sexes could meet on the School premises was in the art clubs, of which there were many: including Design, Figure Design and the Black and White Club. A tense moment came once a month when the students' work was placed on the walls for a master to criticise. The experience could be bruising. During one criticism-session, Sparkes himself was in charge and condemned the efforts of Janet Roberts, a rich student from a conventional Victorian family, as 'shoddy, commercial and Christmas cardy'. She kept a stiff upper lip until the end of the seminar, then fled to the ladies' room in the ABC tea shop beside South Kensington station. There William and Charlie Pibworth, who had witnessed her earlier humiliation, saw her in tears and invited her to the common area for a consoling cup of coffee. Pooling their sixpence daily food allowance (or 'remission of feeds' as it was called), they bought her an ABC special – a lunch cake. It was virtually unheard of in those days for the fee payers to mix with the poor scholars from working class backgrounds, but Sparkes's outburst was the start of an improbable friendship between Janet and William – albeit one that progressed no further than short conversations.

Despite her sheltered life, William noticed that Janet Roberts, separated in the Design Department, was no shrinking violet when it came to her own education. When she became interested in embroidery and then the Arts and Crafts movement, she was determined to hear a lecture by William Morris's daughter, May, the embroiderer. In the absence of a suitable maiden aunt, Janet persuaded her mother to send their cook as chaperone to escort her home after dark from the talk. To avoid confusion caused by the many entrances to the museum, Janet had arranged to meet her under a copy of Michelangelo's *David*, recently made decent, in case of a surprise royal visit, by a stone fig leaf retrieved from the museum basement. Confused by the size of the statue, the cook mistook it for Goliath and wandered off in search of David, leaving Janet waiting on her own for half an hour beside the statue. The hitch was typical of the minor obstacles faced by the female students. William bumped into her there and chatted away about May Morris until the cook reappeared.

The School's isolation from artistic currents outside its walls was total. Most students were largely unaware of the revolutionary movements turning Victorian preconceptions upside down. Not only was Impressionism never mentioned by the staff, but even the English Pre-Raphaelites and the Arts and Crafts movement were studiously ignored. Thus Janet's enthusiasm for William Morris's designs and the new shop Liberty, which promoted Arts and Crafts furniture, was of no interest whatsoever to her teachers. This was the more surprising because Morris's ideas and philosophy and his followers' efforts to make art accessible to the general public and to resist industrialisation coincided with the School's own aims.

It was not until the autumn of 1896, when the School suddenly found itself in the spotlight, that changes within the system began to take shape. Journalists had been shocked after an unexpected announcement that the Queen had given permission for the National Art Training School to change its name to the Royal College of Art. It would be granted the right to award diplomas. An article in *The Studio* magazine led the outcry: they queried the School's right to a royal title when its methods and practices, so recently lacerated in reports, showed no improvement.

The following year, as the Queen's Diamond Jubilee celebration in June drew near, crowds surged in from the provinces. Flagpoles swathed with garlands lined the streets, and drapes and more flags hung down from windows and balconies. A small town of

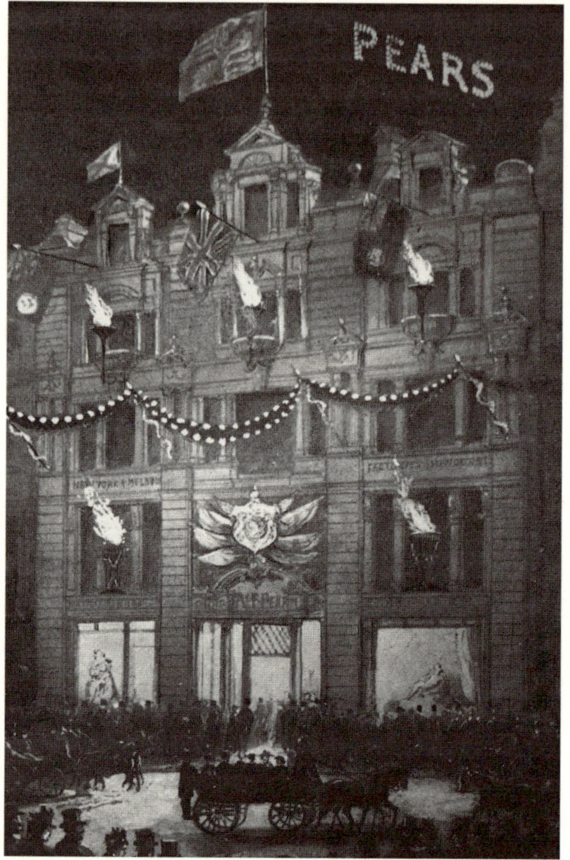

At the end of Queen Victoria's Diamond Jubilee celebration, William and friends mingled with dancing costa-girls outside the Pears store in Oxford Street

canvas tents was pitched in the park to receive troops from all parts of the Empire. The Queen's remoteness was felt and resented: her prolonged mourning of Prince Albert, dead now for over thirty years, had made the monarchy unpopular. But on this day, her sixty years on the throne revived the nation's affection and respect, even awe.

From an advertisement in a local paper, William had picked out a bakery south of the river as a vantage point from where to watch the procession. Detachments of soldiers lined the streets. Among the sandwich booths, picnic breakfasts and straw hats and boaters, the music of bands rose above the murmur of the crowd as it assembled in ever increasing numbers in the hot sun. It would be the hottest day of the year.

The Queen left Buckingham Palace at 11.15 am, followed by a glittering array of emperors, kings, princes and grand dukes and heads of state in uniforms of all colours, Indian princes in turbans displaying swords glittering with precious stones and, from Germany, in honour of Prince Albert, a magnificent old hussar and a grand cuirassier. Then came overseas troops: men in turbans, helmets and fezzes, all loudly cheering.

Slowly, majestically, the procession passed through Piccadilly Circus to St James's Street, the Strand and Fleet Street to reach St Paul's Cathedral. Here the Queen was greeted by the Archbishop of Canterbury. By now, because of her age and bulk, she had great difficulty moving, and she remained in her carriage for an open-air thanksgiving service and a *Te Deum* sung on the cathedral steps.

At last they crossed London Bridge and William's long wait was over. Craning his head out of the top floor window of the bakery, he saw carriages and horses, with rosettes on their harnesses and ribbons on their tails, slowly approaching to ripples of applause that grew to roars of cheering as the cavalcade turned the corner. A strange hush descended on the crowd. You could hear the clip-clip of hooves in the silence. Slowly and steadily eight cream-coloured horses covered in purple trappings came into view, drawing an open carriage set on springs. In it, for all the world to see, sat the tiny round Queen, rocked gently from side to side: a stately old lady with a bonnet and a white osprey feather on her head, and in her hand a black, white-laced parasol to protect her from the heat of the sun. As she drove by she bowed constantly to left and right. She was pale and almost overcome by the warmth of her reception; tears were streaming down her face.

Then over Westminster Bridge and back to Buckingham Palace, where the Queen appeared on the balcony in her wheelchair, waved to the cheering crowd and disappeared into the shadows of the palace.

If for the Queen the business was finished, for the Londoners it was not. They streamed into overcrowded buses and shouted excitedly from the open top decks. In the early evening William and his friends joined the crowds in Green Park. In Oxford Street, they watched coster-girls dance outside the Pears store, its massive shop window twinkling with coloured lights as if freshened with the famous garden-scented Pears soap, before leading their men on to revel throughout the hot night in Piccadilly, dancing to the music of the concertina and dipping hankies into the drinking fountains. In King Street fairy lights and gas signs were turned on. By ten o'clock the whole of Mansion House, swathed in flowers, was lit up. For the first time a royal pageant was illuminated by electric light. William, however, had left long ago. He was exhausted.

In William's last year (1898), just as the recommendations in the board of trustees' reports were finally to be adopted, Sparkes suddenly announced his retirement. The government appointed the Board of Education to run the School, by now renamed the Royal College of Art, and, in an act of daring, brought in Walter Crane as Principal and teacher.

Crane's appointment was like a sudden rush of fresh air. At the Manchester School of Art, he had established a reputation as an inspirational teacher. A brilliant illustrator of children's books, published and exhibited throughout Europe, he had been converted by William Morris to Socialism. Crane was also a protagonist of the Arts and Crafts movement and involved in the Art Workers' Guild, a union in which applied art, architecture and design were as highly valued as fine art and craftsmen of all sorts met as social equals. He also set up the Arts and Crafts Exhibition Society. If Morris was Socialism's universal artistic genius, its most original writer, poet, lecturer and polemicist, Crane was the movement's artist. His cartoons and drawings were blazoned on trades-union banners, published in Socialist newspapers accompanied by stirring poems, or sold separately to be pinned up in homes, factories and meeting places. The images he invented became the ultimate propaganda tool.

A shy man, short and fine-featured, he had immense drive and conviction as an artist, a craftsman and an adventurous – almost revolutionary – educator. He despaired at the way in which industrialisation had impoverished design; to him it was a terrible blight, an assault on the very soul of the nation. The highest standards of art must not only be saved from obliteration, they should, he insisted, be available to people of every walk of life.

Within a few days of his arrival Crane had planned a drastic reorganisation. He found the School 'in a chaotic state ... run as a sort of mill to prepare art teachers'. He would restructure the curriculum, expand the range of studies and rescue design from its role of decorative addition, irrelevant and unrelated to anything: he would return it to its proper status as the expression of an object's essence.

Drawing, he thought, should not be mere skill in copying but a creative process based on a close study of nature. The School should have a conservatory and an aviary. In learning to draw, students should make rapid sketches from life and then elaborate them. They should develop their powers freely. The copying of casts and historical ornaments should not be their sole reference and guide. He would bring in memory drawing and the study of figures in action with the help of the photographs of men and animals in motion by the pioneering English photographer Eadweard Muybridge. It was the antithesis of the stultifying methods of the old school.

On the principle that the best teachers were generally those who kept in touch with commercial realities and could help the students when they left, he acted quickly to bring in a new wave of practising potters, printmakers and bookbinders as evening lecturers, including the illustrator Joseph Pennell from the Slade, and May Morris, a rare business woman who managed her father's shop, Morris & Co.

All grades of student would be free to attend the life class, including women – to whose demands for equality he was sympathetic. He believed female students, just as much as the men, should gain technical knowledge of materials and the insight to adapt their designs to those materials for which they felt most sympathy.

William's first encounter with the work and approach of this prominent figure in the Arts and Crafts movement was a formative experience. Perhaps because of the shyness he had in common with Crane, a strong rapport developed between them. In explaining to William the symbolism in ancient design, Crane would reach for sheets of drawing paper, seize a crayon, deftly sketch a four-footed cross and explain how this image of 'the axial rotation of the heavens round the poles' had evolved into decorative designs familiar in archaic pottery, Roman altars and Scandinavian, Celtic, Saxon and Asiatic ornament. He would demonstrate a stream of designs of Syrian and Greek ornament and the frequent appearance of the owl in hieroglyphics. Sometimes he would switch, mid stream, to a tirade denouncing the Empire, which had 'crushed the arts in far away countries … the sole objective in our modern industrial system of society was to produce not "a thing of beauty and a joy for ever but something that would sell … "'. His advice to William personally was that 'Our English designers should throw into their art all they knew of their English life and surroundings, instead of going on copying Roman and Greek ideas. Was there no beauty or suggestiveness in our English fields and gardens in the fresh glory of springtime?'

Private tutorials were one thing, but William was astonished by Crane's inability to express himself coherently in public. He had to have a pencil in his hands or a blackboard in front of him to cope at all. At his first Club criticism in the Lecture Theatre in the spring of 1898, Crane stood with his back to the audience, gazing at the drawings around him. For what seemed an age, he fiddled with his hands and at last managed to get out: 'This … this … this … composition – this design … this painting needs, needs, needs … some of the quality which it lacks.' That was all. Nonetheless the students always asked for more.

But as Crane's year progressed the old guard closed ranks, obstructing whenever they could. The ancient life class master, infuriated by the students Crane had let into his class, set them a difficult anatomy test and failed all but one; the Director of Art gave unexpected notice, forcing on Crane new responsibilities including the Summer Course for Teachers. To William's pleasure, Crane awarded him first prize for a figure subject in the Summer Sketch Club. By the start of the autumn term Crane became ill. In October he wrote to William thanking him for his letter: 'glad to say I am better and pleased to offer the Black and White Club a criticism of the drawings each month.'

After several bouts of illness, the truth became clear. Crane's poor health and nervous stress were caused by the knowledge that he knew his reforms could never succeed: the old inflexible rules for obtaining the required Teachers' Certificate would continue to hold sway, and the other teachers – with the exception of Edward Lanteri, for whose teaching methods he had the greatest respect – would support them. His vision and idealism were not enough. He could take the departmental infighting no more. After his brief tenure of a mere eight months, Crane resigned.

Among the students rumour was rife: the resignation of their charismatic principal was due to the jealousy of the teachers; others whispered that Crane had been hauled over the coals for paying too much attention to the female students – particularly after he bought one of the girls a beautiful flame-coloured azalea. He had given the students confidence to face up to the more troublesome teachers. One of the many victims of the life class master was Janet Roberts. With Crane gone there was no principal to appeal to when she was thrown out of the life class. She went into action and entered her work for the life exam. To her astonishment she was awarded a star above first class honours. On hearing the news she marched back in to the life class room with head held high, ignoring the master as completely as he continued to ignore her.

Before Crane left, William confided to him that he did not want to devote his life to either design or teaching (something he had never let on to Sparkes) and asked for his help in applying for admission to the Royal Academy School to train as a professional artist. To Crane the Royal Academy stood for much of what he most disagreed with, but ultimately it was one of the most prestigious institutions in Europe. Ironically, his ambitious wife had tried for years to get him elected as an Academician, without success. He immediately wrote the letter of recommendation.

Even though William's four years at the National Art Training School had coincided with the School's low point and period of self-doubt, its legacy to him was entirely positive, and one he would never regret. Like Edwin Lutyens before him and Henry Moore and Barbara Hepworth after him, he always spoke with pride of what the National Art Training School and the South Kensington Museum had given him and of the freedom its students felt to follow whatever artistic path they might later choose. He left the school liberated, proud of his achievements. The grounding he had obtained was his for life.

CHAPTER 3

Royal Academy Schools

1899

*'Everything in nature is moving, nothing stands.
Weather is a capricious master whose whims must be met …
record nature's moods and study the work of great men,
Turner and Constable.'*

William's teacher George Clausen paraphrasing the
words of the Greek philosopher Heraclitus

One morning in early January 1899, William walked east through Kensington Gardens and Hyde Park, passing his old school on the right, then on to Green Park. He had kept his dingy lodgings in Merton Road. The evening meal was monotonous and unappetising but the room was cheap and he could afford nothing more. Not that he was seriously worried about money. The Royal Academy offered free tuition and grants for maintenance and materials.

A few yards short of the heavy wrought-iron gates of Burlington House in Piccadilly, feeling as awestruck as he had been on his first introduction to Kensington, he turned off through an arched stone doorway into a narrow wooden passage and slithered along its icy surface towards the almost hidden entrance to the Royal Academy Schools. In the hall he was met by *Laocoön*, the mythical priest, wrestling in agony with his two diminutive sons against giant serpents sent by the gods. And, stretching ahead down the long corridor, an avenue of more classical casts copied from the British Museum or donated to the Schools by the Academy's first royal patron George III, among them the famous statue of Hadrian's lover *Antinous*.

The most important figure in the running of the Schools was the Keeper, whose august standing was indicated by his occupation of a residence attached to Burlington House (the main building of the Academy itself) with a private studio and enough room for his family, a cook and two maids. Traditionally a practising artist, the Keeper, with two curators under him, looked after the smooth running of the Schools, the library and the casts and was in charge of discipline, which included monitoring the attendance of the students. He now gestured peremptorily to William to turn left into the lecture room, an imposing wooden-floored studio with north-facing windows flanked by velvet curtains.

It was here that Visitors' lectures and life classes were held. Sturdy anglepoise lamps jutted from the wall, their iron shades shaped like coned shells. On the shelves were more plaster casts and, near the stage, a large freestanding horse on a trolley, head down, neck arched and pawing the ground. Facing the entrance was a two-tiered semi-circle of leather-padded benches with attached wooden pencil trays. Already seated in the front row were two National Art Training School alumni, William's friend Charlie Pibworth and Walter Webster. Within minutes dozens more new students drifted in, half of them painters, the rest sculptors or architects.

The Academy was proudly independent of government control. Its members were all practising artists, elected by a self-perpetuating committee. Rather than employing permanent instructors, the committee selected from their membership nine 'Visitors' a year, to serve for a month each as teachers and mentors. Their duties were to examine and instruct the students and to set the live model's weekly pose, for which they earned a salary of a guinea a night, forfeited on failure to turn up. The models – four per term – were chosen by the Keeper and booked for three days a week. A life class curator would sit in on every session to ensure discipline and propriety.

For the first year William was on probation and could not touch a paintbrush. It took resolve on his part to prolong his drawing. He had to attend more lectures on anatomy and perspective, and submit daily exercises in drawing from antique casts. Later, to prepare for being allowed to paint in oils, he had to learn once more the art of drawing with charcoal, but this time with white chalk on toned paper to develop his understanding of grades of light and shade.

His uncomplaining acceptance of this regime was not unusual: it reflected the conventions of the time. Two centuries before, the Academy's first President, Joshua Reynolds, had modelled the Schools on the ateliers of Europe, in particular the French Academy of Louis

XIV. In a series of discourses, celebrated for their philosophical depth and historical range, Reynolds had lectured on the importance of copying the Old Masters and drawing from life and classical casts. Art was to be learned by training not just the hand and the eye but also the mind. Such a regime would form artists capable of creating works of high moral worth. Reynolds was suspicious of 'originality': 'Every opportunity should be taken to discountenance that false and vulgar opinion, that rules are the fetters of genius … rules are fetters only to men of no genius.' There was a hint of Plato's mistrust of undisciplined art in Reynolds's lectures, and the ethos had survived to William's day.

Over the decades artists and teachers had fought against the elite practices of the Academy and its Schools. Irritated by its monopoly of power, new generations had periodically set up breakaway movements, established less imposing galleries in which to display their work, or – particularly annoying for the Academy – departed for the continent to complete their education. But the committee was cunning. At crucial moments it had invited recalcitrant artists to 'join the club' and offered them the honour of membership: Edward Burne-Jones and John Singer Sargent were among its more recent successful seductions. At the turn of the century, the Academy's standing as the most prestigious art school in Britain was still unquestioned. William had no social standing and no pretensions to genius of the kind that would attract the attention of the artistic community. Membership of the Academy was his only hope of achieving recognition; only through the Academy could he meet and come to know the artists and critics of the day.

That first week of January, the week of William's arrival, four paintings by the brilliant neoclassical artist and founding member of the Royal Academy, Angelica Kauffman, had been discovered stacked away, deteriorating in the basement. These were being cleaned and relined to be inserted into circular mouldings in the entrance hall ceiling. William found the two imposing allegorical women depicting Colour and Design particularly beautiful. Kauffman's neglect seemed shocking.

Still more exhilarating, the Academy's annual 'New Year Exhibition' – opening just as the term began – displayed over eighty Rembrandt oils and 124 of his drawings. The school's morning classes ended at three o'clock and William could slip easily into the Rembrandt Galleries before the life class at six o'clock. Through intensive study of the Dutch master at close quarters, he hoped to transform his technical understanding of painting and draughtsmanship.

The Dutch School was not on the syllabus that first term; they focused instead on the Greeks, the Romans, the Middle Ages and the Renaissance, on sunset and sunrise and on individual painters – Titian, Burne-Jones and Tintoretto. Two of the Visitors taking life classes, George Boughton and the American Edwin Abbey, had travelled in Holland together in the 1870s. In their illustrated account of their journey, Boughton describes tracking down a Rembrandt in Middleburg Town Hall museum and how they had 'screamed with joy at the discovery'.

Abbey was the more approachable of the two. Regarded by his countrymen as their first great illustrator after the success of his pen and ink drawings for Dickens's novels and Shakespeare's comedies, he was a devoted Anglophile. As a young man he had revered the work of the Pre-Raphaelites. He was captivated by England's literature, its medieval architecture, its furniture and most importantly its museums and theatres. It was remarkably easy to find genuine historical costumes, armour and household objects that he needed for his paintings. At the age of thirty he had settled in London and turned to painting in oils.

The year before William's arrival, Abbey had been elected a member of the Royal Academy – an honour given to few Americans. Now he was serving on the Council and taking his duties very conscientiously. The students looked forward to his lectures with genuine excitement. He was a small but handsome man, full of wit and wise advice, who lectured in a relaxed and exotic combination of top hat and shirt sleeves. He was big-hearted and cosmopolitan. A committed advocate of hard, sustained application, he would say in his attractive American drawl, 'You should be sketching always, always, drawing anything. The dishes on the table while you are waiting for breakfast. People at the station while waiting for a train. Look at everything.' If a student was dedicated, he treated him as an equal.

It was some time before William could face Abbey without feeling self-conscious. His dark eyes searched you piercingly as he talked or demonstrated. 'Use the stump,' Abbey told him with a piece of charcoal, 'don't shade with the point, the stump lends itself much better to broad effects of tone.' But although authoritative in all matters of technique, Abbey was never dictatorial. He began his classes nervously, almost as if he himself were the pupil.

When handing back the piece after correcting William's drawing, he would apologise for 'making such a mess of it'. Towards the end of the year he took the transition to painting a step further by teaching William to paint *en grisaille* – using different shades of grey without the complexity of colour.

His interest in William's work was evident 'not in a patronising way', wrote William later. 'He recognised the advantage of exchanging ideas between the man of experience and the young man with new points of view. He always expected to learn something from us, while at the same time passing on to us his own great knowledge.'

William was diffident and remarkably unworldly for a twenty-three year old. His understanding of women was largely a product of the optimistic banter of his fellow students about the latest female intake. Women were not relegated to a separate building as in the Royal College of Art, but separate they certainly were, neither eating nor working with the male pupils, let alone attending life class with them. This had been a running sore for years. The older Academicians believed that young ladies should never be made to look upon the nude. The women students argued that since, according to the Academy itself, competence in drawing was essential to being a painter, and since such competence could only be achieved – again, according to the Academy itself – through the study of the naked figure, why should they be denied the opportunity? In the last few years some progress had been made: they were now allowed to draw from partially draped models.

A slow friendship began with the charming twenty-year-old George Swaish, the son of an ambitious Bristol pawnbroker on his way to a mayorship and a knighthood. George taught William all he needed to know about smoking – how to fill and tap down a pipe. But music was the icebreaker. William's rich baritone brought him popularity with E.H. Shepard and Frank Cadogan Cowper and their friends in the Upper School. Cowper, who stuttered terribly in ordinary conversation, would lead the bass in part singing with William as baritone, switching from ribaldry to a loud 'Holy, Holy, Holy', which echoed down the corridors as they came within earshot of the Keeper on their way home.

There were snatched moments of serious discussion as the young men cleaned off the paint and charcoal in the wash house after the day's work. The rebellious streak natural to students might have led them to push their teachers into discussing the new styles of painting

or, if the teachers were irrecoverably stuck in the past, to pursue independently the various movements that were bursting on the scene at
the turn of the century. But in practice it was from the recent past
– from the Pre-Raphaelite painters – that many of William's contemporaries derived their inspiration.

For William himself, who had come to the Schools through the
endorsement of William Morris's close friend Walter Crane, this was
not entirely a departure from the familiar. More surprising was the
admiration that the others, led by Cowper, had for the Pre-Raphaelites. Cowper, indeed, was becoming something of a fanatic. He
pressed William to go to Abbey's lecture on Burne-Jones and had
embarked on a painting of the Good Samaritan, designed to advance
by experiment his own understanding of Pre-Raphaelitism. Having
enlisted a family friend to pose for the wounded man (whom he proposed to rescue on a richly attired donkey), he was now searching for
a purple cushion with gold embroidery, to strap on as a saddle. For
the background he needed a skeleton: 'I'm going to try and borrow
from a surgeon I know the remains of a man who has been robbed
and murdered on the road.'

An annual spring Academy ritual of great importance was the
hanging for the 'Summer Exhibition'. Grandees such as Edwin Abbey,
Luke Fildes, John Singer Sargent, George Clausen and Lawrence
Alma-Tadema had the places of honour; Fildes was the leading
Social Realist artist and had become famous (or notorious to the
conventionally minded) for his shocking wood engraving *Houseless
and Hungry*, which had led Dickens to ask him to illustrate one of his
books. The Anglo-Jewish Solomon J. Solomon's growing popularity
as a portrait painter meant he now had his own hanging spot nick-
named 'Solomon's Corner'.

Although he could not yet submit his own work, William was
caught up in the tense atmosphere generated by the 'Summer Exhibition'. Varnishing Day and Press Day, the two days before the opening,
were crucial. Up-and-coming artists steeled themselves to see how
their paintings had been placed. 'On the line', close to the dado, neither too high nor too low, was the prime position for the lucky ones.
Here the public – or better, a collector or a critic – would see the
work to best advantage. The less fortunate could be seen on ladders
touching up their work, piling on brighter colours – William saw a
rather desperate fourth-year student splashing on scarlet in the hope
of drawing attention to his pictures. If a painting was noticed by *The*

Queen or the *Weekly Graphic*, the artist would be offered 3 guineas for an engraving, which had the added bonus of promoting the original for sale. If the reproduction covered a full page, the fee was a massive £10, and a sale was almost guaranteed.

When a student was considered sufficiently accomplished there were the winter competitions to enter. The spur to produce a major piece of work came in early spring when the titles for prize entries were put up in the Schools. William, being from the Lower School, was only allowed to submit drawings, but the biggest prizes were to be had in the painting section.

During the long summer break the more ambitious students tried to get away from London to complete a painting in time to submit it for a prize in the autumn selection. They would hitchhike with their oversize canvas to the depth of the West Country to a workman's cottage in Devon or Cornwall or set off to Sussex, where they were met at the station by a horse and cart and transported to a room in a pub.

Strapped for money, William confined himself to helping his father in Windsor, striking a deal to do his own work in the mornings. He set up his easel in the fields around Eton Wick among the shepherds' flocks and the sheepdogs, working until the advance of the midday sun had changed the light. Abbey's and Clausen's emphasis in their lectures on the value of natural surroundings had left their mark: 'The light and atmosphere must be the dominating motif,' Clausen maintained.

However much he felt he had improved, returning for the autumn term, William was envious of Frank Cadogan Cowper's summer, spent delving with missionary zeal into the Pre-Raphaelite Brotherhood. 'I now feel what I have never felt before and that is confidence in painting, because I have got a method – and understand it,' Cowper proclaimed, confident that he had mastered the theory of Pre-Raphaelitism and understood it better than anyone in the brotherhood – except John Everett Millais:

and Millais either painted in the proper way unconsciously because it came easiest without knowing why. Or else he understood it thoroughly having found it out from the Italians and was a beast and kept it to himself – unlikely because Millais must have looked upon Rossetti and Hunt as rivals although they were all upholding the same theory of art.[1]

Cowper's background gave him self-assurance. He had tracked down an old lady who had been friends with the original brotherhood and had known Holman Hunt, Dante Gabriel Rossetti and Ford Madox Brown intimately, and got himself invited to tea with her. He felt as if he had 'really dropped in to the PRB world and what there is left of it at last. Awful – all are dead or very old. Ruskin is 90 in his dotage – quite imbecile apparently. She gave an imitation of his mannerisms and affectations, only vanity left. The brain quite gone. Pitiable after what he has been.'

William observed the rise of Cowper with a wry awe. His ambition knew no limits. Nor did his style of dressing: he tried hard for a serious look, displaying none of the flamboyance of the eccentric artist in his clothing and keeping as far as was possible within his means to traditional dress (in later life he was reputed to wear the highest collar of any man in the country).

* * * * * *

Towards the end of October, politics crept into the washroom talk for the first time. The Boer War had broken out, a struggle for supremacy between the British and the Dutch settlers – the Afrikaaners, or Boers – in the eastern part of Southern Africa, where vast reserves of gold and diamonds had been discovered.

For all the Empire's famed military strength, the war was going badly. The British garrisons at Mafeking, Ladysmith and Kindersley were surrounded, with no relief in sight. Newspaper correspondents sent in ominous accounts of the sieges. Would the women and children be saved or would they be massacred or starved to death? William and his friends passionately debated the rights and wrongs of a colonial war fought against backward farmers.

Setback followed setback, culminating in the Black Week of 10–15 December and leaving the British people stunned. Even the reclusive and aged Queen was shaken into action. The illusion that trained troops would easily sweep aside the motley collection of Boer farmers that faced them had been dispelled. The army found itself out-manoeuvred by guerilla forces armed with smokeless modern Mauser rifles, at least their equals as sharpshooters and, being mobile, far more elusive as targets. They were also deadly at ambushes, since they knew every inch of their territory.

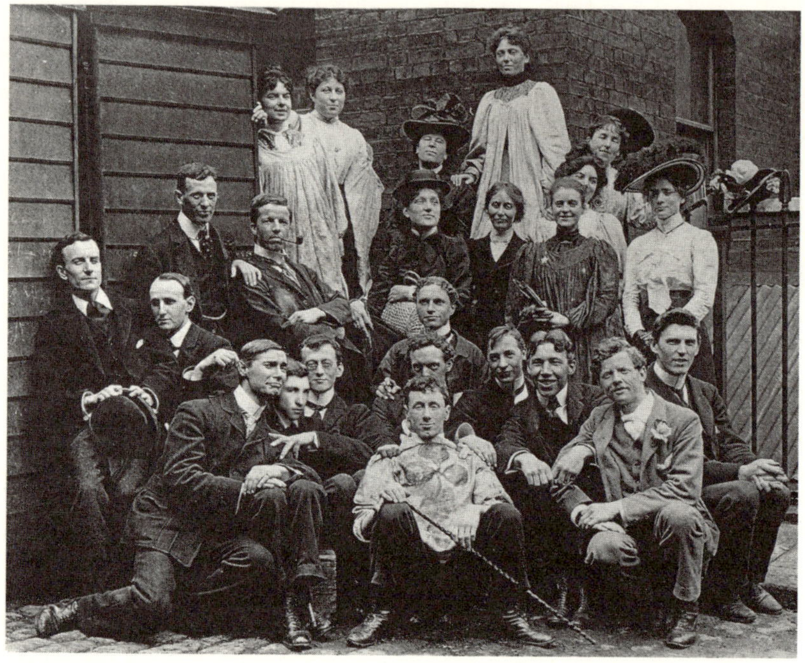

Royal Academy Painting School, 1900: William is third from the left

As the government poured more and more men into South Africa, the Prince of Wales found a new purpose: he inspected detachments of troops before they sailed; he visited barracks and hospitals; he chaired committees charged with coordinating the work of the agencies that were helping the war effort. Christmas at Osborne was cancelled and the Queen remained in Windsor, where she invited wives and children of soldiers to teas. To her anger her nephew, the Kaiser, was backing the Boers and was writing privately to the Prince of Wales, sneering gleefully at the British humiliation.

As the Royal Academy Schools packed up for Christmas, many of the students returned to their homes sharply divided in their attitudes towards the war.

CHAPTER 4

Upper Schools

1900–1904

'… once Sargent started, slowly and shyly, on a student's painting, his stuttering and hesitation gradually left him and he would grab the student's paintbrush with eyes aglow, his certainty intense, his movements confident, bursting with energy and dynamic enthusiasm.'

After the first year on probation, it was no certainty that William would be accepted into the Upper Schools. Attendance and 'attitude' were watched keenly by the Keeper. Any student guilty of absenteeism or indolence could be failed and William, sick and tired of nothing but drawing from antique casts for five long years, first at National Art Training School and then in this unnecessary induction course at the Royal Academy, did not have a particularly good track record on this point.

To his relief, however, he passed and was assigned a studio space. A new world beckoned. Visiting Academicians, reputedly the finest minds in the country, would shepherd him as tutors and guides. From now on it would be painting, painting all the way. His enthusiasm revived.

The Visitors were a formidable group of artists, names once glorious but now forgotten: John Lucas, Arthur Hacker, Walter William Ouless, Henry Stone, Solomon Joseph Solomon, Thomas Francis Dicksee and Edwin Austin Abbey, and others whose reputation has survived the years, like Lawrence Alma-Tadema, John Singer Sargent and Luke Fildes, all themselves trained at the Academy under legendary presidents: John Everett Millais and Lord Leighton.

Mostly in their early fifties, they were well read and highly cultured. They had travelled widely for study in Europe and had thought long and hard about every aspect of painting, its history and its meaning. Their learning and perspective epitomised Victorian values. They produced large canvases of exquisite technique depicting subjects set in theatrical poses with biblical, classical or mythological themes, each carrying some moral message. They had written books and articles or, like Reynolds, had given eminent lecture series. Once admitted into the Academy's 'Summer Exhibition', they had taken up the portraiture of the rich and grand. Large fortunes had followed.

George Clausen was different from the other Visitors. He was a brilliant but defiant artist with a strongly personal voice who, though finally inveigled into the fold, never accepted its monopoly on style or its insistence that Leighton and Millais were the only models to follow. Studying in Paris, where he had been influenced by Millet, Corot, Degas and Manet, he had evolved his own semi-Impressionist style and become a founding member of the New English Art Club, where the recent wave of talented artists began to flock. Elected an Associate Academician in his late forties, he began to work behind the scenes to press for Academy reform – succeeding at first with permission to display the 'Summer Exhibition' in Gallery IX, reserved for the less orthodox contributions.

It was some time, however, before William felt he was receiving the practical advice he needed. He had felt confident of Edwin Abbey. But at the last moment Abbey had called off his visiting duties, substituting his friend George Boughton, who specialised in paintings of fancy-costumed figures skating, or peasants at work with nice girls standing around doing not much. With unconscious parody, Boughton modelled his sentimental style on the cool landscapes of seventeenth-century Dutch art.

To William, Boughton was more of a hindrance than a help. He would seize William's favourite brush, grind it on the canvas so that it spread out fan shaped and tell him to 'carry on'. Marcus Stone, friend and illustrator of Dickens and Trollope, was little better. Vain and opinionated, and with an arrogance born from his considerable talent as a painter, he was fixated on the merits of elegance and style.

Nor was there any conceivable point of contact between William and Luke Fildes, another friend of Dickens's, who lived in intimidating grandeur on the edge of Holland Park in a house designed by Norman Shaw, a mile from William's room in Merton Road. Lectures or discussions with students on subjects that engaged his emotions were conducted with a fierce vehemence that unnerved the students. Hope arrived fleetingly with the appearance of the small and friendly extrovert Alma-Tadema, described by Cowper as 'a jolly little Dutchman'. He looked approachable and one of his lectures, 'England – loveable and paintable', left its mark, but he paid little attention to William.

Two teachers, John Singer Sargent and Solomon J. Solomon – or three if you include the painfully shy George Clausen – did make a real difference. Sargent, like Abbey, was American. For years his work had been despised by the Academy as unfinished, rough and without technique. But as his fame grew the Academy gave him the honour of inviting him to join its ranks.

A quiet man with a massive frame, Sargent had a powerful, charismatic aura. Talking to his students he was tongue-tied. In the lecture hall he was incoherent. But once he started, slowly and shyly, on a pupil's painting, his stuttering and hesitation gradually left him and he would grab their paintbrush with eyes aglow, his certainty intense, his movements confident, bursting with energy and dynamic enthusiasm. In a fever of conviction and concentration, he would stand at the easel, brush in hand, arm outstretched, head thrown back as his hand danced across the canvas. These performances, those of a man given over to the service of art, burnt themselves into William's mind. Sargent's lessons were chiefly about tone; the one thing he would not tolerate was trying for effect at the expense of truth.

Solomon was an equally brilliant teacher, in a diametrically opposite way. Practical and straightforward, he told William to start, as pupils had started over the centuries, with the traditional three-coloured palette of yellow ochre, English red and black. Many great painters, such as Titian, had used this to produce some of their finest work. Once William discovered the power of these basic colours, Solomon added a limited number of others that were needed for flesh painting and for many ordinary effects: three different whites, followed by three warm colours, then two cold colours – cobalt blue and emerald green – and finally raw, burnt umber and black. Only for special purposes would he add warm or lemon Naples yellow. He told William to remember to mix portions of the light, half-tone, shadow and background colours before each day began and to make sure to use a fully loaded brush.

*   *   *   *   *   *

The Boer War, still dominating the newspapers, continued to be a frequent subject of the students' discussions outside the classroom. Unwilling to consider defeat, the government had sent out two more divisions plus a number of colonial reinforcements. By January it had become the largest force Britain had ever deployed overseas. The Commander-in-Chief was replaced and calls went out for volunteers. The combination of larger-than-life magnates like Cecil Rhodes, undreamed of mineral riches and dangerous military reverses could have been shaped from the pages of a John Buchan novel.

In the Academy Schools the arguments between national loyalists and their liberal opponents became increasingly heated. But even those from soldiering families felt no inclination to volunteer: many of the students nursed a sneaking admiration for the plucky Boers, tempered by reservations about their oppression of the indigenous black population and anxiety about the diplomatic support they were receiving from the German Kaiser. The loyalists, too, had mixed feelings. It was hard to equate the lofty ideals of the Empire with remote English mining magnates.

By the end of February the balance of the war had swung. Lord Dundonald, the young war correspondent, with Winston Churchill by his side, entered Ladysmith and relieved the garrison on the afternoon of 3 March 1900. Dispatches from journalists trapped in the town, smuggled out by native Africans through the Boer lines, ensured the anxious British public were kept informed of the ordeal.

News of its relief reached London by telegram on the evening of 25 May. Theatre audiences broke out in patriotic singing; London finally had something to celebrate. With the help of their professor of sculpture, Edward Lanteri, the Royal College of Art students had built in anticipation an immense statue of the British Commander Colonel Robert Baden-Powell, which they sprayed with plaster and put on a sculptor's large trolley. At the last moment Alphonse Legros suggested adding a British lion.

Fifty or sixty students sallied forth in painting smocks, straining at the ropes of a trolley with a handful of girls, as the *London Illustrated News* wrote, 'marching behind, waving palms like some scene from the building of the pyramids'. Nodded through by the police and unhindered by traffic, the cavalcade moved down Bond Street to join forces with students from the Royal Academy. In a wave of elation after seven months of war, the growing procession, William among them, made a deafening chorus of song. Swept up in the crowds, amid red rosettes and waving white-and-blue windmills, tin trumpets blasting, they moved on to Piccadilly Circus to turn up Regent Street.

The students' celebrations continued in high spirits into the evening. To tease the life class curator Henry Bosdet, they formed a procession in the corridor, led by Shepard dressed as the Boer leader Paul Kruger in a black top hat and a billowing Newgate frill beard made of cotton wool. As they entered the classroom singing a funeral dirge, Bosdet waddled to the door to bar their entrance. After a short struggle he sank down on to his seat, mopping his neat little beard and brow and threatening to report them for 'an organised disturbance'. Edwin Abbey appeared in the doorway. Bosdet levered himself to his feet and whispered urgently in his ear, still fuming. Abbey looked at the bowed heads of the students now hard at work and with a broad grin started his life class.

High jinks of this type were frequent. A general lack of discipline among the students was reflected in the Keeper's annual report, adding to the pressure on the President, Sir Edward Poynter, an archetypal Victorian in every fibre of his being, now nearing the end of his illustrious sixty-year career. He had taken on both the directorship of the National Gallery and the presidency of the Royal Academy. Running two ships was taking its toll, and progressive elements in the art fraternity were challenging his authority. Reforms in the Academy Schools were long overdue. Aware that the students resented the schools' antiquated practices, now abandoned elsewhere, and acutely aware too of its falling pupil intake, the committee members determined to confront their intractable and ineffective President; if not by dismissing him or curtailing his powers, at least by wearing him down.

Indeed, at every meeting the schools' reform was on the agenda. Poynter's mood was darkened by the Queen's postponement of the annual signing of the students' diplomas. Nobody knew quite how ill she was. If she died under his watch the Academy's royal patronage would (for the first time in nearly seventy years) be under scrutiny. Could he ensure the same commitment from the future King? Reduced to biding his time, he wrote a fulsome letter congratulating the Queen on the 'miraculous escape' of the Prince of Wales from assassination in Brussels.

In early January 1901 more rumours spread about the 81-year-old Queen, cocooned in her palace, Osborne House, on the Isle of Wight and purportedly fast declining in health. At first news was guarded, but in the middle of January reports appeared that her illness was 'rapidly assuming a dangerous form'. She died on 22 January.

The old lady's death had a startling effect on the British people. They had come to believe she would go on forever. The whole country mourned, going about their work with bowed heads. On the day of the funeral the Academy sent a wreath of bay leaves and white flowers to Windsor Castle and closed the schools. The royal coffin left Osborne in the royal yacht, crossing the Solent with a procession of warships gliding behind and booming their salutes. As the cortège passed from Victoria Station and on to Paddington, the Queen's coffin was borne on a gun carriage with the new King, in plumed helmet and cloak, riding for the last time by his mother's side, with the Kaiser close by.

Crowds several rows thick, in deepest mourning with heads covered, lined the streets. William, edging his way to a vantage point in Sussex Place, found the quiet simplicity moving. The pageantry and cheering of the great Jubilee of three years ago were replaced by a hushed silence, broken only by the solemn thump of the drums of the funeral march.

The period of mourning having suitably passed, Edward Poynter, the President of the Academy, wrote unctuously to the new monarch: 'Royal Academy members cannot but feel emboldened to express hope that your Majesty will continue its protection and favour privileges which it has been in the proud position to enjoy under Your Majesty's predecessors.'

The King replied, assuring the Academy of the same support as that which had been granted by his mother and of his deep personal interest in the prosperity of the institution. Its royal patronage would remain intact: the King would recognise it as the foremost academy of arts in the world.

Few kings had come to the throne with lower expectations, but despite his age and raffish reputation, Edward VII rose to the occasion, taking on the role with indefatigable conscientiousness. In his eyes, his mother's reclusion since the death of her husband forty years ago and her complete withdrawal from society and public life had been a dereliction of duty. The sovereign must not just do the work, but be seen to do it. Believing in protocol and the importance of occasion, he revived the old ceremonial, reinventing and making it glamorous again, and combining all this with warmth and dignity. The royal palaces, shrouded for so long in an atmosphere of secrecy and decaying gloom, were restored to their former glory and their doors thrown open. Light flooded in. The King installed electricity and set about rehanging and repositioning the great art collections, and based the monarchy once more in Buckingham Palace.

William was infected by the optimism around him. The South African war was over, peace concluded. With its new King, the country had regained its zest. By projecting monarchy as tradition, King Edward was in fact modernising it. As if enriched by its Victorian inheritance and fully equipped to deal with the brave new century, England was alive with inventions – the wireless, submarines, flying machines and, of course, the motorcar.

This was the year William won his first Academy award – a second prize of £25 for six life drawings. He was pipped at the post by Walter Webster, but at least he beat George Swaish, who took third prize. In fact none of them expected a prize at all. There was a disturbing uniformity about the drawings on show. They had been told that 'originality of artistic expression' would count less than correctness of outline, elegance of form and the action and proportions of the figure, the position of the limbs and the setting of the head. Above all they would be judged on their ability to express the face and character of the model. An exact resemblance should be aimed at – though as William and his friend William Eden remarked, since the judges had not seen the models, they could not credibly evaluate the likeness.

The 1903 'Royal Academy Summer Exhibition' was a landmark for William. For the first time, one of his own oils would be shown. He was nervous, but at the same time felt exhilarated by the build up – the three Varnishing Days, the day set aside for the royal family, Press Day, and then the Private View, culminating in the doors being thrown open to the public on the first Monday of May.

The response to his work left him confident enough to give up his lodgings in Merton Road and take a lease on a studio on the ground floor of Pomona House in the New Kings Road, for £50 per annum. Part of a large red-brick mansion block purpose-built for artists, no. 6 consisted of a large enough studio, a tiny bedroom, washroom, larder and a coal hole. Already installed on other floors were three Academy friends. Down the road in Glebe Place, Ernest Shepard shared a studio with George Swaish (or 'Swish' as he called him). It was a combination of opposites with Swaish's quiet introvert character a foil to the wit and exuberance of Shepard. Swaish was hard to know but once his quiet front had been penetrated William found him a mine of practical information. He knew which junk shops had decent furniture for sale and why you should buy your odds and ends from Maples (whatever you bought, they gave you a free lunch).

Glebe Place was the hub of their social life. Shepard, as musical as William and equally impoverished, had been lent an old piano and there were evenings of song late into the night or, if the right friends had dropped in, chamber music with fiddle, cello or flute – and even an attempt at Handel's 'Largo'. Shepard's father was an actor and manager, and through him William became involved in the world of small theatrical productions – invaluable experience, as it would later turn out. He worked on a Burlesque at Sir Arthur Cope's Art School and on a revival of a W.W. Jacobs' ghost play at Queen's Gate Hall in Harrington Road. He was given crowd-scene parts and earned a few shillings to paint scenery for Shakespeare's *Measure for Measure* and sometimes on larger-scale shows in St George's Hall in Upper Regent Street.

During his last year at the Academy Schools, William turned up every morning at 9 o'clock and worked religiously late into the evening, often until 9 o'clock at night. The curator, Bosdet, watched the students like a hawk. After a two-year battle (towards the end of which Poynter fell ill) the schools' committee finally succeeded in bringing in their reforms. The Lower Schools' classes in painting, perspective and sculpture were abolished. First year students were no longer limited to plaster-cast drawing; no student over twenty-eight could compete for a prize; women would be allowed to attend life drawing classes; and a school of design was created. As a sweetener to Poynter, the General Assembly voted him to be the Academy's artist to paint a full-length portrait of Edward VII.

Although Poynter accepted the Academy's commission for the accession portrait, when he went to Buckingham Palace to offer his services to the Monarch, there was an awkward pause: 'Supposing, Sir Edward, it is not you who paints the portrait, whom would you advise me to choose?' Luke Fildes described Poynter arriving at his house in Melbury Road in a Brougham carriage post-haste from Buckingham Palace to let him know that he had recommended that Fildes do the portrait. The commission made a fortune for Fildes, who subsequently oversaw lesser artists as they completed a vast number of copies in his studio to be distributed to potentates and embassies throughout the British Empire.

None of these reforms affected William beyond evoking a sense of ironic regret that the improvements in both his art schools had arrived too late for him. But in fact it was a good thing that they had. He would be the last of the 'artists' – a product of the extinct traditions in art education that had formed the leading artists over the centuries.

Now was the time to refine his skills as a painter, to identify and tackle lingering weaknesses and to put his technical knowledge to the test. In his last year, it was the rebel Clausen, who had recently taken up a two-year position as Professor of Painting, who taught William how to achieve the depth he sought in landscape painting.

Clausen asked William to bring him his entire portfolio so that he could get a clear idea of his strengths and weaknesses and make suggestions on how to improve. He gave him the draft of his 'Six Lectures on Painting' – the notes developed from his recent lectures to the students. But if he had hopes of converting William from the conventions of the Academy, he would be disappointed. Few of William's oils from this pre-war period can be traced today, but fortunately we do have reproductions of some of his book illustrations. Methuen's publishing house was bombed during the war and many of their artists' illustrations were destroyed. These, as well as his canvases – *In Hiding* or *Spring Adventure*, painted on the slopes in the 'fishy meadow' around Boveney near Windsor – show the continuing hold on his work of Victorian realism and Pre-Raphaelite romantic storytelling.

In the 1904 'Summer Exhibition' William's painting of a scene from Shakespeare's *Henry IV* was praised by Edwin Abbey. In accordance with his usual habit of helping the brightest of the graduating students, he offered William a stint in his Gloucestershire studio. Cowper had long moved on and had been followed by Ernest Board. George Swaish was due to leave soon but could stay on to show William the ropes. Faced with the choice between Clausen and Abbey, William chose Abbey, sealing his artistic fate for a decade.

CHAPTER 5

The Genius of Edwin Abbey

1904–1905

*'But they had to earn a living – in the last age before
photography stole the illustrator's territory – and Abbey's
contacts were a passport to a publisher's pay cheque.'*

On the train from Oxford to Fairford, on his way to work for Edwin Abbey, William was captivated by the beauty of the Cotswold country. Through the window he watched the jumbled harmony of seventeenth-century grey stone houses slide by, with their high-pitched stone-slate roofs covered by stonecrop, moss and lichen, and the dry stone walls and the farm settlements, each with their due share of arable land and grass. The train meandered lazily in and out of seven villages and stations; past Lechlade, a mother and two children hopped off the front carriages to pick a few snowdrops in the flat Thames meadow, reboarding the rear carriage just as it was about to pass under the next bridge.

Originally intended as a through route to link up with Cirencester and Cheltenham, the railway line had never progressed further than Fairford; it came to a stop a good half mile outside the little town, remote from the place it was supposed to serve. Descending, William saw ahead of him a goods yard, with two buffer stops against an earth bank. He turned towards the marketplace to search out Abbey's house on the east edge of the town.

The chief claim to fame of the small market town of Fairford was its generously proportioned fifteenth-century church, with its twenty-eight windows described by Morris as 'the finest collection of medieval stained glass in Europe'. Equally important to William – and to fishermen as far afield as Oxford – was the fishing in its trout stream, the Coln, which snaked its way from Bibury, Coln St Aldwyns and Quenington under bridges and through breaks and ponds in and around the meadows, occasionally interrupted by ancient mill races which split off from the river, only to rejoin it a few hundred yards further on.

On the London Road (more a hoggin trackway with small farms on either side than the thoroughfare the name suggested), William found the gates of Morgan Hall and a drive leading to a serene eighteenth-century house with walled gardens facing on to acres of parkland and ancient trees.

He was looking forward to seeing Abbey again. Despite their difference in status and experience – William, now in his late twenties, was half Abbey's age – he considered him a friend to whom he could always go for advice. It was not so much aesthetic sympathy with Abbey's painting that had attracted him to work at Morgan Hall for what, in a sense, was the continuation of a long apprenticeship. It was more his admiration for Abbey's fastidious attention to historical detail and the astonishing scale of his knowledge, gleaned from his travels researching material from every corner of Europe. As for Abbey, he gained from William almost as much as he gave, imparting his own artistic experience and in exchange seeing his ideas refracted and sometimes, he admitted with characteristic charm, improved through the hand of his talented young protégé. Besides, he needed an accomplished assistant to complete his work. He had abandoned his previous practice of surrounding himself with students of varying ability, having adopted a more selective approach. As he wrote to a friend: 'I can't bother any more with more than one helper at a time – and take only those who have had as thorough training as schools can give them. Now that I have young men under me I do my best to keep 'em hard at science,' adding that 'slackers are treated with prompt severity.'

The formidable Anglo-American Mrs Abbey greeted William solicitously at the front door. Before her marriage late in life to Edwin, Gertrude, the only girl of nine siblings, had become an exceptional horsewoman and had studied and taught Latin and several other languages in America and Europe. Now she devoted herself to her husband. When his models failed to turn up from London for work on the Shakespeare tragedies, she would sit for him, posing as

Miranda in *Much Ado About Nothing*, with a model kneeling to her in the doorway of her cell. In all she posed for seven female figures in the plays. Now in her late forties, with a houseful of maidservants from Fairford and an army of sewing women under her guidance, she superintended the making of the costumes for Edwin's paintings and illustrations. Theatre in all its forms, William came to realise, lay at the heart of Abbey's work.

Mrs Abbey marched William off without delay to lodgings with a Mrs Wade in a cottage close by, where he found a good bedroom and a sitting room upstairs. Meals would be provided downstairs. Abbey would require him to assist six days a week, with Sunday off, for a small salary that would cover the 21s. (shillings) a week he would pay for board and lodging. In exchange, William could work in his free time on his own paintings with help and advice from the master. George Swaish would be there in the morning to show him around the studio.

In fact William had already compared notes with Swaish in London and thought he knew what to expect, but a period of overlap would be helpful; and despite the shared shyness that made communication difficult for both of them, William was pleased that Swaish's departure had been delayed longer than Abbey had led him to expect.

What he had not anticipated was the sheer scale of Abbey's operation. Swaish walked him into the vast barn-like structure to the right of Morgan Hall that Abbey had erected when he took a lease on the house a decade earlier. It was built of corrugated iron, was sixty-four feet long and twenty-five feet high and was reputed to be the largest artist's studio in the world. The meagre heating could do no more than take the edge off the cold in the winter months.

In one area, twenty or so partly finished paintings leaned against the wall within easy reach; another six or seven larger paintings in progress reposed on enormous easels. There was a writing table and shelves crowded with folios, art books and architectural reference works. Sketchbooks, albums and drawings were laid out on tables in preparation for Abbey's illustrations for the Shakespeare tragedies. Photographs of Elizabethan and Jacobean pictures were pinned around. Resting against the walls were props of every kind. Carved oak doors, panels and tapestries hung from heavy frames, not for decoration but for use as prototypes, and everywhere there were casts of curious architectural features, sculptures, arms and armour.

Dividing the middle of the room stood one of four huge circular lunette canvases, so large that a trench had been dug into the floor to

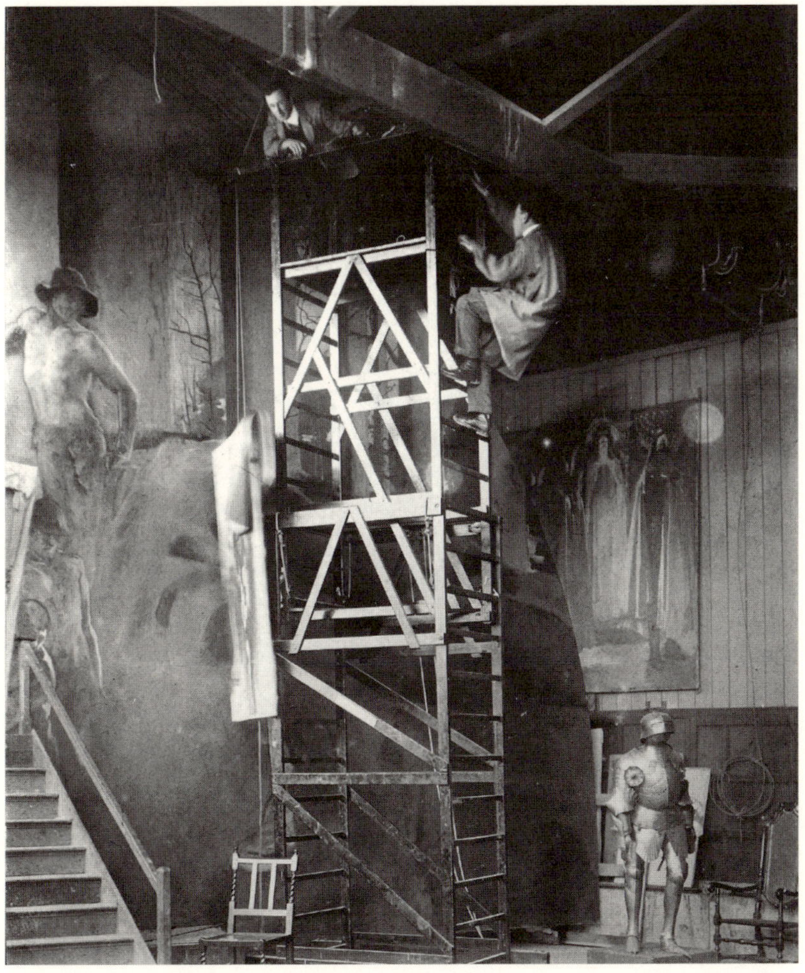

William completing huge canvases for Edwin Abbey in his barn in Fairford, reputed to be the largest artist's studio in the world, it was 64-feet long and 25-feet high

accommodate it. These were destined for the Harrisburg Capitol, a gigantic new complex to house the seat of government for the state of Pennsylvania, now being rebuilt on grander dimensions after fire had destroyed the original eight years previously. Other works were going to the House of Representatives, the Senate and the Chambers of the Supreme Court. The young architect Joseph Miller Huston was designing the whole with Beaux Art interiors, Italian Renaissance themes and a basilica inspired by Michelangelo's St Peter's in Rome, but Abbey insisted that in the rooms where his works of art were to be placed, he must have the final say on the colours and decoration.

His four lunettes, symbolising 'Pennsylvania's spiritual and industrial contributions to modern civilization', were thirty-eight by twenty-two feet and the four circular 'Medallion' canvases, each fourteen foot in diameter, were set in a gold-leaf background. All contained nine foot-high figures (often thinly clad near nudes), and were conceived on a scale he had never attempted before. His most ambitious paintings were three panels for the House of Representatives. The largest of these, *Apotheosis of Pennsylvania*, to be situated centrally behind the speaker's rostrum, contained seventy or so life-size figures representing the state's foremost statesmen, jurists and industrialists placed among shipyards and blast furnaces, symbols of Pennsylvania as home of the American Revolution and modern industrial capital of the United States of America. The two panels to the left and right would portray Pennsylvania's Treaty with the Indians and the reading of the Declaration of Independence.

At the eastern end of the studio, Abbey had constructed a wardrobe containing an Aladdin's cave of garments – dresses, hats, cloaks, boots and shoes – each one classified and hung in order (furs, guns and swords were stored elsewhere). Close by were chests of drawers crammed with samples of materials, velvets, brocades and silks. Abbey would study the architecture, costume and furniture, the arts and manners and customs of the period, and then ransack his stock of period clothes. While the drawing itself would take him only a few hours, it involved weeks of preparation.

Then, after talking it over with Gertrude, he would decide which new costumes to have made, which models to hire. 'Always look up three times as much as you will want to put in a picture,' he told Swaish and William. 'Economise everywhere except in the studio.'

Once William had recovered from the shock of his first exposure to the studio and the grandeur of the Pennsylvania commission, he found his collaboration with Abbey fascinating – not least because it was full of laughter, music and Abbey's huge personality. Abbey at work was a theatrical performance in itself. He was also an incredibly hard worker, with great energy and exceptional physical strength, both indispensable ingredients for a successful painter. He keenly felt the great weight of his responsibility for the Harrisburg project, which he had agonised over accepting when he realised that it could take fifteen years to complete. Now it had become his consuming preoccupation and he drove himself to the limit, keeping several pictures simultaneously on the boil and juggling others that awaited his attention in the background. Their day started at 9.30 and except for breaks when the model rested, they would keep at it until the light failed. Abbey possessed a capacity for concentration that enabled him to keep his whole being focused on his work. He would say, 'at this game you are using every faculty you have at once – mind, nerves and body ...'

His lighthearted enthusiasm, his encouragement for William and Swaish's efforts and his sense of humour swept them along. In an old soft felt hat, with a hole in the crown for ventilation, the brim well pulled down to shade his eyes, he would be making studies and sketches on one side of the canvas. On the other, Swaish and William would clamber up and down a ladder enlarging the sketches and painting them in. Abbey was not a silent worker. If a story came to mind, he had to impart it at once and – even though his words could easily have been heard from where Swaish and William worked – he would squeeze through to their side between the end of the canvas and the wall to deliver his anecdote, before going back to his work.

If dissatisfied with the sources to hand, Abbey would travel far afield at a moment's notice for authentic reference material. To get what he wanted for *The Spirit of Vulcan*, he journeyed to Northumberland to stay with the Northbournes, to make studies in the heavily industrialised sector of Tyneside, returning full of ideas for transposing iron smelting in Pennsylvania into an allegory of Vulcan, the Roman god of fire. On reviewing the painting, however, Abbey was still unhappy with its 'brown pasteboard landscape' and asked Northbourne's son, Walter James, to do 'a rough sketch of the kind of ground coal grows in – or iron? ... it must have cracks, or the capacity of having cracks by which seven nude men may descend into the bowels of the earth'.

Despite the difficulties, the Vulcan lunette, on which William had worked extensively, turned out to be one of Abbey's most successful works. The images of semi-naked miners climbing down into the earth and sweating ironworkers by a white-hot furnace gave the painting real power.

If a visit by Abbey to London coincided with market day in Fairford, William would hurry over to the Bull Inn in the main square to keep company with farmers and smallholders. In the bar, a low-ceilinged room resounding with noisy gossip, with a stone-flagged floor, a wide-open fireplace and a grate flanked on either side by hobs, he would have a pint of beer, a game of draughts or darts and a 'farmers' special', a huge mutton and potato pie, with root vegetables, cabbage and suet pudding. On the high mantle shelf stood a pair of candlesticks, some Toby jugs and a clock. Gazing serenely on them all hung a coloured lithograph of Queen Victoria, still in pride of place five years after her death, and next to it a prize bull painted by a travelling artist.

On Sundays William would set out on foot early in the morning to discover the country he had briefly glimpsed from the train on his way to Fairford. He walked across fields divided by grey dry-stone walls over land, which a few inches below the surface consisted of layers of cornbrash – Jurassic limestone made up of tiny shells, remnants of the time when the Cotswold district lay beneath the sea. After two-and-a-half miles, the track dropped down a steep, curving hill into Quenington, crossing the River Coln, to come immediately upon a paper mill and the village's ancient church. He sketched intricately sculpted Norman (some said Saxon) doorways, mercifully spared later alteration. On the far side of the church, he discovered an arch leading to the holy site of the Knights Hospitallers, a religious and military order prominent in the Crusades. Beside the church and through the medieval arch his diary noted a house and fine stables. These, too, he sketched. Since his Eton Wick childhood horses had been a constant source of fascination: 'among the horses a mare which had been through the South African wars and the Siege of Mafeking. Looked in v good condition.'

A mile on from Quenington, William saw, silhouetted against the skyline on the vast Williamstrip Estate, a ploughman driving two yoke of oxen, so primitive a sight, with their swaying stately movements, that he had the illusion of stepping back in time to some ancient pastoral scene. The farmer preferred oxen to horses, he said: the disadvantage was their slowness, but their small feet did less harm to the ploughland. He also kept old white-faced Cotswold sheep, the breed with extra heavy fleeces that had made the Cotswolds famous all over Europe in the Middle Ages.

When William had a full day off, he would travel past Quenington, Coln St Aldwyns and Hatherop, on the old Salt Road towards Bibury and Coln Rogers on tracks untouched for centuries, with an exasperatingly soft texture that in winter sucked his boots inches deep into cream-coloured mud. In summer the soil formed a dry dust, so white that when the partridges dusted themselves in it they emerged like a new species of pale creature scattering before him into the brown furrows. The route held firmly to the ancient path, forcing William up and down precipitous hills, scorning to follow the easy level of the Coln watercourses that wound slowly through the lowest part of the valley.

But it was worth it. He came into remote, self-contained, slumbering villages with proud smallholders, each farmhouse with a large barn and bordered by the meadows and woodland behind the villages, known since Norman times as 'the Gassons' from the French *gazon* (grass). Many of the farmers still spoke a form of Shakespeare's English with a broad, often unintelligible accent.

There were birds everywhere. William glimpsed a dipper bobbing to the reflection in the water of his white waistcoat and further along the river the fleeting blue and orange of a kingfisher.

Relying increasingly on William to complete the lunettes, Abbey forced his pace again. He felt he must produce an oil for the Royal Academy – it did not matter how famous you were, it was fatal for an artist's reputation to go too long without exhibiting there. He had begun research for a painting, which he called *Columbus in the New World* (see plate 6), an idea he had been toying with for at least a decade. The background would be a company of flamingoes streaming across the canvas, symbolising the departure of the untamed native on the arrival of the cultivated foreigner to implant civilisation. He settled on borrowing a flamingo skin from the Natural History Museum to study. The foreground figure of Columbus was trickier. He persuaded his eminent naval friend and fellow Academician, Charles Napier Hemy, that he would be 'a good typical Columbus' and asked him to get himself photographed in a pose meticulously dictated to him by Abbey. In his letter of request – or 'invitation' as he put it – he enclosed a velvet cap for his friend to wear that had been worn by the great Henry Irving in his role as Louis VI.

Researching his background ships, Abbey started looking for reliable Spanish vessels, built in 1492. After a long and fruitless search, he tasked William with making a fleet of models out of wood, cardboard, plasticine and string. Abbey dispatched a photograph of the finished article once again to Hemy, who knew even more about shipping and the sea than Joseph Conrad, and waited. 'I send them with some trepidation … the photograph is clear if you look at it with a magnifying glass. I am a little vague about the stern arrangements … are the sails tied up right?'

Within days Abbey received a blast: 'This queer lot of ramshackle freaks … this shabby fleet … given by you to your humble understudy are impossible! I protest! I could never have got over in them …' The letter ended: 'after this parting insult, I will shut up.' The criticism became a standing joke against William for the rest of his stay at Fairford, where everyone knew it was he who had built the model.

When he felt stale or especially exhausted by work, Abbey took exercise with the ardour of a fitness fanatic. He would engineer a break, give the model a rest and either go for a bicycle ride or take a brisk walk – or go to London on Academy business. Then William had the freedom of the studio and the props and would set up his easel in a corner. He was also allowed to hire Abbey's models. A diary entry to his first painting in Fairford, *Sweethearts and Wine*, records a Miss French and a Miss Lewes at 1*s*. 6*d*. each per session.

* * * * * *

The weeks passed into autumn and work in the studio intensified. The pressure on Abbey began to take its toll and Mrs Abbey watched her husband with growing concern (her affection for William was confirmed when early one morning she discovered him in the cold studio, entirely unsolicited, completing the medallion on law, destined for the base of the Capitol's dome). At the same time the lease of Morgan Hall was coming to an end. Maybe they should buy a house of their own, a more isolated property with a studio well away from the noise of farmyards and with room for the ever-increasing library? In the meantime, to William's astonishment, the Abbeys bought a Daimler. Unsuited to the muddy Cotswold tracks and rough stone roads it spent most of its time in the garage. But as the weather improved, house-hunting expeditions took them into Wiltshire, usually with the American author Henry James in tow, who produced piles of *Country Life* advertisements, but then, as his enthusiasm failed, advised Abbey to keep on quietly at Morgan Hall. He left him with a copy of the newly published Holman Hunt memoirs.

It was not only the Royal Academy painting or the figures and landscapes for Harrisburg that were proving so trying to Abbey. He had overspent, extending the studio for the extra large canvases, scaffolding and ladders, and letters were pursuing him on a backlog of uncompleted commissions. The most pressing demands were for an altar screen painting for the American Church in Paris, *A Measure for Measure* painting for New York and illustrations for the Shakespeare tragedies for *Harpers*. William calculated that these alone could take at least eight years. Abbey could not bear to think about them. He shunted them to the back of his mind, where they continued to nag away at his composure, although, loath to share personal anxieties with his assistants, he kept up his front of amusing chat. In any case, he felt at ease in William's calming company and their common dedication to work.

But in a letter to a friend eventually he does confide: 'I am working very hard – and wish I weren't. I can't leave my work and it would be better for us all if I could,' but then he boasts of the massive activity and prowess of his assistants: 'you can hear the bristles rasping the canvas for a mile or less.' Yet the letter ends with an uneasy sense of foreboding: 'They take up a lot of room … and involve a lot of exercise … full of people … I am inclined to think at times that a small back room all to myself would be desirable if only as a rest cure.'

CHAPTER 6

Signs of Expulsion and Emigration

1906–1907

'A demon I hope will be exorcised.'
Henry James, letter to Mrs Abbey, 1907

The year 1906 began with an intensely cold patch in January, followed by gales. Even in the coldest weather William was never without his sketchbook. A diary note mentions his constant search for Norman buildings and his obsession with fallen trees, their carcasses scattered around the countryside after the recent storms. He went west to Whelford and on to Poulton, walking the four miles each way in pouring rain. Here he found an ancient vicarage barn with high square holes in its walls for owls to fly through, and long medieval vertical slits to air the barn and prevent mould forming. Inside, choirboys were performing a production of *Aladdin*. Borrowing a horse he rode to Cirencester to buy an artists' Whatman board and to order a suit from R. Scott & Co. in the Market Place (it cost him £1 8s. 6d.).

Every now and then, to relieve his tension, Abbey would invite William to accompany him on one of his own walks. They were even longer than William's, but on these occasions what spurred Abbey on was not so much the hope of finding peace by observing nature but that by talking to William he could help him get ahead, encouraging him to discuss his work and giving counsel on the direction it was taking. He enjoyed cultivating each of his assistants' particular talents; in William he had immediately discovered a fine baritone. His own interest in folk music had begun twenty years earlier when he had illustrated a book of *Old English Songs*, and he had shared with William a repertoire drawn from Zoltán Kodály and Béla Bartók's *Hungarian Folk Song*. William in turn lent him Cecil Sharp's recent publication of anonymous seventeenth-century songs. While staying with a friend in Somerset, Sharp had heard his host's gardener sing *The Seeds of Love* and this had set him on a path that would become his life's work: to notate folk song throughout England.

William asked for advice on his new painting, which he sometimes called *The Seeds of Love*, from Sharp's book, and sometimes *The Sower*. Disappointingly, Abbey more or less ignored it, and instead lectured: 'When you reach a sticking place you must attack it with all your energies and turn it into the best part of the picture,' and firmly suggested that William should go and sketch the recently erected lambing pens over the wall beside Morgan Hall's drive.[1]

He had already noticed William's sensitivity in drawing animals. Forget the cold, he said; Sargent used to wear sabots stuffed with straw when working outside in winter. Knowing that William badly needed an income, he said that he would recommend him to Raphael Tuck & Sons, the graphic arts firm that dominated the new field of art postcards.

But their conversations would soon move on to larger subjects, and these walks were an eye-opening education for William. Abbey was both well informed and well connected; he knew personally many of the leading cultural and political characters of the day and some were intimate friends. The early part of 1906 was a tense time in politics. Both the major parties, the Conservatives and the Liberals, were split over Irish Independence or 'Home Rule', but the Conservatives were also tearing themselves apart over business, some wanting a protectionist Empire trade bloc, others wanting to stick to free trade. Even small Gloucestershire villages were caught up in the election fever. Walking along footpaths past Hatherop to Eastleach, Abbey and William came across a brass band serenading their rich Liberal landlord, Sir Thomas Bazley, playing on instruments he had given to the village. Factions had formed on the green and tempers were fraught. Bazley was a strong advocate of free trade to keep food prices down. Sir Thomas Hicks Beach, Abbey's cricketing friend from Hatherop and neighbour of Bazley, who had a Georgian mansion opposite his, was for Empire trade. Hicks Beach followers regarded the brass band as bribery and were furious that it had been hijacked by Liberal supporters. Abbey detested the 'unnecessary abuse' of the election, and completely misread the result: 'the Liberals would have had a better chance if the Home Rule bogey hadn't appeared.'

Nonetheless, elections had their uses. Friends with time on their hands could be plundered for ideas and help if one was stuck. Could Northbourne find a good quotation that he could use for his medallion on Art, a draped classical goddess to the fore, which required thirty-five words or so in white writing on a gold background? He had ransacked his books and found nothing, so could his friend help?

Henry James was the most obliging, spending hours on the chase and delivering Abbey lectures by letter: he should end up with something 'large and majestic, and not too philosophic and on all accounts avoid Ruskin who delivered well on Nature – splendidly often – but loathing Art'. Browning was 'fearfully unquotable' and Emerson – well – 'he had not a notion what [Art] is'. In the end Abbey found a perfect Plotinus quote in his own library: 'Art deals with things forever incapable of definition, and that belong to love, beauty, joy and worship, the shapes, powers and glory of which are forever building, unbuilding and rebuilding in each man's soul and in the soul of the whole world.'

* * * * * *

In an atmosphere of increasing anxiety, Abbey again delayed Swaish's departure and enlisted extra help. Early in February William was dispatched to the station to meet his old Academy friend Ernest Shepard, another of Abbey's protégés. Sargent's faith that most of his pupils had it in them to be great painters had left its mark to some extent on William but especially on Shepard. Abbey, however, had advised Shepard to concentrate on drawing. Even so, it was all hands to the pump now and Shepard would be useful for squaring up and enlarging his studies on to the canvas.

Besides helping with the grand project, Shepard also meant to ask his tutor for more contacts. Abbey had already introduced him to the editor of *Punch* at a Royal Academy Varnishing Day, and Shepard was being given his chance there as well as getting the occasional painting commission to illustrate books for publishers, but he had recently married without a penny.[2] Abbey might bring him fresh recommendations and solve what was turning into a serious financial problem.

His immediate need was to solicit advice from Swaish and William on his illustrations for a book about a volcanic eruption in Martinique in 1902, the most catastrophic eruption of the twentieth century, wiping out 30,000 people. As Shepard laid out his six watercolours on the table, he met at best a polite reaction. He had tried to catch the cloud of ash, the orange-red rush of lava into the burning town and the collapse of the mountainside, from which a boiling, black, pumice-filled wind had shot out at 400 miles an hour, but William was not impressed. He did not care to say so, but Shepard's effort suggested that Abbey had been right to advise him to concentrate on line drawing.

After a week, Abbey reported to Shepard that his contacts were responding favourably to his overtures on Shepard's behalf. First to reply had been Luke Fildes, no less. Now nearing seventy and about to be knighted, he had been far too grand to approach while at the Academy Schools, but a nod from Abbey instantly produced an offer of an interview with the *Graphic*, of which Fildes was a director.

Taking Swaish with him next morning, Shepard set off by the first train for the interview, leaving William somewhat ruefully behind to help Abbey on his new canvas that he was calling *Iconografía Espanola*, or *Queen Isabella of Castile*. He was put to work on drawing Gothic tracery for the staircase, cutting out in wood a small organ with a fretsaw, for Abbey to copy, and then asked to sketch in several figures. Meanwhile Abbey painted the Queen's head and dress, and used two local models to pose as nuns. The 84-year-old Mrs Jones's 'very fine old head' was perfect but the equally ancient Mrs Keble's was not. She had to be painted out after her departure.

With Shepard and Swaish back next day, Abbey set his assistants a fortnight of intense work, with Gertrude Abbey busy in the background making costumes. When Shepard was around, Swaish opened up and a most interesting character emerged, no longer reticent and shrouded in shyness. Whenever the three had a break, there were walks and long discussions. Truth in observation was the young men's mantra, the guiding star for their aspirations. Once at midnight they came across 'two swans over Keble's house making a weird, eerie noise at each stroke of their wings as they flew away into the moonlight', and once at dawn they tracked along the banks of the Coln with William's camera to take 'true photos by the river with frost and rhyme'.

But they had to earn a living – in the last age before photography stole the illustrator's territory – and Abbey's contacts were a passport to a publisher's pay cheque. To William's relief he had received an encouraging letter from Raphael Tuck & Sons, had negotiated terms with them and had begun illustrating *Aesop's Fables* and work on a series of art postcards called 'The Seasons'.

William's own work had become as intense as his work for Abbey. He, too, kept several drawings and paintings going simultaneously: *Sweethearts and Wine* chugged along, as did his sheepfold sketches, but *The Sower* needed more details and in Lovers Lane, east of Fairford, he searched for suitable ground for his young sower's pathway, for more trees, plants and hedgerows. It was freezing, sometimes with two inches of snow, and 'chilblains of importance and a moderate tree' were the result. For indoor work he booked Abbey's model, Miss Finch, out of hours, to pose for the maid's head in *The Sower*. He made a hood for her out of a flannel undervest, and dyed it with maypole grease: 'very successful and Mrs Wade sewed it into a painted cloak.' Working on more sketches, he persuaded the local police sergeant to lend him a beautiful brass shepherd's crook from the New Forest.

Shepard's first published cartoon for *Punch* arrived by post at Morgan Hall on Valentine's Day. Swaish and William stared mirthlessly at the clumsy drawing and the dire joke it illustrated on the studio table. At least Shepard had some work, though it would be precarious if he could not improve on the rough, overdrawn old woman and silly Apollo-winged husband they saw before them. Over time Shepard's pen lines became simpler and beautifully clear. By the end of the year he had been given a full-page spread. For the next forty years, through two world wars, he was to contribute without a break up to thirty *Punch* sketches a year.

Worried by Abbey's frame of mind, William started coming in early each morning and working longer in the evenings on the four medallions; he had finished Science's serpent and moved on to Art's red-clothed figure with a leafy wreath crowning the head, before painting in Law's dark drapes, sword and scales. Religion was more of a struggle and took the longest to complete: an embarrassingly thick-armed figure in white robes had a somewhat docile-looking dragon at her feet and at her side a stark-looking altar with a single, carved shell.

Desperate at the thought of failing to complete his multiple assignments, Abbey summoned William Wyllie, the marine artist, to help with the seafaring canvases. Working under two masters, William was delegated to paint rocks and sky and to draw in ships, complete with all their nautical details. He noted in his diary: 'sketched model by lamplight to get effect for large ships.' Diverting himself from the Harrisburg project, Abbey frenziedly brought out the altarpiece from the stacks and set William to work on that.

Work did not entirely dominate William's week. There were moments of pleasure to relieve the tension, when William was asked to dine with the two painters and join in the music. The Wyllies' taste was eclectic enough: on the first night they 'sang the old songs to Mrs Wyllie's accompaniment'. There followed soon after a more ambitious night of music – the Kreutzer Sonata, a Tchaikovsky waltz, and a 'new to us and very exciting' Spanish dance.

* * * * * *

Word of Abbey's stress was getting around. To cheer up his friend, Alma-Tadema appeared unexpectedly at Fairford Station. He was always a tonic. He had the gift of engaging fully in other artists' work, however much it differed from his own in style or intention. His brief visit left Abbey in much better spirits, and he deputed to William the execution of a new set of instructions.

The last fortnight in February, Shepard having departed, saw William and Swaish preoccupied with Holman Hunt's memoirs, which Abbey had passed on to them with an ambivalent recommendation: 'He reminds me of the little boy who wouldn't grow up – and has gone for years believing many things that are not. But it is v interesting reading.' As they sketched each other's portraits, they took turns to read the book aloud. For William it seemed to be a prolonged tirade against the 'lies and myths' relating to the Pre-Raphaelite inner circle. Holman Hunt seemed determined to correct the claim that Rossetti was the founding spirit of the 'brotherhood' and establish himself and Millais as its sole originators.

Holman Hunt's supreme article of faith – to which Abbey, too, had long subscribed – was that the artist must acquire a scrupulous understanding of the nature and mysteries of materials, the juices of plants and the substances derived from the earth: the crushed powder of natural rock, the mercury used in vermilions, the composition of true emerald green and, as important as any, the varnish to ensure permanence. Joshua Reynolds's mix of rich brown asphalt and bitumen had proved treacherous, dooming his surfaces to breaking up. For William this was a useful lesson from Holman Hunt's two-volume rant.

William's last two diary entries for 1907 are unlike his usual jottings. Strange words are used: 'Mr A. rather dull. Signs of expulsion and emigration but nothing said.' On Sunday 17 February he wrote: 'Mr A asked us to come to the studio at dusk. He would explain the work ahead … he had to go to London first thing.'

Abbey could no longer go on. He was headed for a total breakdown. He was taken to London where the doctor confined him to bed. When he was strong enough, he was moved by Mrs Abbey to the seaside town of Swanage. Henry James wrote to her that her husband's indisposition was a demon that he hoped would be exorcised.

The curtailment of a regular salary at short notice left William worried. But commissions from publishers were becoming more regular. He packed up, closed the studio with Swaish as best he could and took the train to London.

CHAPTER 7

All-Powerful 'Summer Exhibition'

1907–1911

*'The Academy has to jumble up all the vulgar
and popular rubbish with all the great work that
is in the huge crowded muddle.'*
Frank Cadogan Cowper, letter to his mother, 1907

Nothing serious was diagnosed at this stage. Abbey continued a long recuperation in Europe, closing down Morgan Hall for several months. William meanwhile earned a living by following E.H. Shepard's path of illustration. Abbey's connections had proved invaluable: the Raphael Tuck contract arrived and the terms were acceptable. The future was beginning to look good.

Other commissions came from Nelson & Sons, publishers who were concentrating on high-quality illustrated stories from the Bible, the classics and mythology. They had commissioned Arthur Rackham's illustrations for *Peter Pan* and Edmund Dulac's for the *Rubaiyat of Omar Khayyam*. Now they commissioned William to illustrate William Morris's poetic version of the legendary twelfth-century warrior Ogier the Dane and his relationship with the magical princess Morgan le Faye. William produced pen-and-ink drawings and two paintings in Part V of Nelson & Sons' 'Enchanted Garden' series and found himself sharing a platform with Burne-Jones, Alma-Tadema and Lord Leighton, and with writers such as Nathaniel Hawthorne, Hans Christian Anderson and Christina Rossetti.

Throughout 1907 William worked away, producing an illustration a month for colour plates: *The Parable of the Talents*, *Christ before Pilate*, *Ulysses and the Cyclops* and *The Encounter of the Queen of*

Sheba and Solomon. All the while he was waiting to see if two painfully conventional paintings – *The Seeds of Love*, the watercolour that he had started in Fairford, and *Fairies Frolic*, an oil painting – would be hung by the Academy.

Like his friend Frank Cadogan Cowper (who could afford to be cynical, having assured his reputation a few years earlier with the hanging of one of his paintings), William accepted that the Academy, despite the artistic revolution erupting across the Channel, remained all-powerful in British circles; admittance to or rejection from the 'Summer Exhibition' spelled success or failure in a young artist's career. William could try to show at the New English Art Club, where the members were hotly anti-Academy, but he was too orthodox to consider that. In any case, all roads led back to the Academy: whenever a genuine new talent appeared on the scene, the trustees would offer to elect him as an RA and the artist, however rebellious in principle, hardly ever refused; John Abbot McNeill Whistler was a rare exception.

A letter from Cowper put the situation frankly:

Every good artist who has confidence in himself does his best to become a regular exhibitor at the Academy because it is the recognised institution of the country and pictures sell better than anywhere else. But more important – if you can become a prominent exhibitor and eventually get elected to the body of Academicians you become a personage and can count on a decent income. Consequently the vast majority of the best art the country can produce goes to the Academy.

The trouble is that besides the good work, of which there is enough to make two or three lesser exhibitions, the Academicians very often admit, and hang well, very often a whole lot of pictures which they must know are not of the highest order but are popular and which most of the visitors really go to look at. The expenses of the Academy are so big that it cannot afford to ignore the shillings of the ordinary British public. If all the rubbish were weeded out and only four or five hundred real works of art were hung, which is what the critics are always crying for – it would be an ideal exhibition and here would be room to hang them all nicely. But it wouldn't interest the general public and only art connoisseurs would go to the show – so the Academy has to jumble up all the vulgar and popular rubbish with all the great work that is in the huge crowded muddle.

Discussion and analysis of the Pre-Raphaelites still linked William and Cowper. When Alma-Tadema's *Colosseum* went on show in 1907, many of their contemporaries ran him down. Not Cowper. Taking for granted he had a willing audience in William, Cowper told him: 'it is the most extraordinary and wonderful piece of work I have seen: it is also extremely beautiful. It is fine to see him at seventy years old working with the freshness and vigour he always had and producing work far and away better than any young painters of today.'

The Academy's letter accepting William's paintings finally arrived. He would now experience at first hand the annual ritual of Edwardian London's most important artistic event. After Opening Day a flood of congratulatory letters arrived from friends. To his surprise one of his teachers, Frank Dicksee, invited him as his guest to the Academy dinner. The culminating moment was an announcement in *The Times*: the Chantrey Bequest, a foundation that empowered the Royal Academy to buy 'Works of Fine Art of the highest merit in painting that can be obtained' had bought *The Seeds of Love* for the Tate Gallery, where it would be exhibited throughout August and September. A second wave of congratulations poured in. From Windsor, William's parents gloried in the success. Academy contemporaries sent cards; and one surprising telegram from Sylvan Boxsius, who had been two years below him. He wrote that he had read of William's 'great success'; and conveyed heartiest congratulations from himself and his family '… if you can spare the time to write to an old pal I should much like a card with your address. I am anxious to congratulate you in person.' He ended with: 'PS I am thinking of tapping you for a fiver when next we meet. I suppose all the old pals are turning up now.'

Nothing, however, could match Cowper's meteoric rise. After receiving an invitation at a ridiculously young age to become an Associate Academician, he changed his tune: 'Never could I have believed that an RA could have come so soon. I thought they would never elect a man unless he kept up some kind of show in his style of living. But of course they have done it and I can go on living as I like!' and with mounting vanity he added, 'It shows the Academy is getting really genuine and electing now on the merits of an artist's work alone.'

Cowper, almost lost in the narrow byways of late-Victorian scholarship and now virtually forgotten, is regarded as the last

Pre-Raphaelite painter. His work never evolved and remained stuck in a groove. After his early acclaim he sank slowly without trace. William, on the other hand, would within five years change course – so radically that in an interview for the *Observer* between the wars, he gives no more than a nod to his past life as a painter.

Commissions from Nelson & Sons for more classical and biblical illustrations continued and new ones arrived from the *Graphic* and private clients: in July the Watsons of Merevale Hall commissioned portraits of the whole family 'two full length and five Kitcat size' for £90 and then added an order for watercolours of their house and garden. The highlight of the year for William was a visit to Vienna where he exhibited paintings with three contemporaries, Walter Webster, Thomas Dugdale and Ernest Board. William now felt secure enough to survive without Abbey's regular income and at the same time could keep his obligation to Abbey to help him when needed.

* * * * * *

In September, Abbey, still suffering from exhaustion, reappeared in William's life. The lease on Morgan Hall was expiring, his wife was pulling down the studio to return it to a kitchen garden and Abbey was working in London before moving to Hampshire. He had been out of circulation for far too long; he had shown nothing at the RA, nor had he had time for other commissions. He had even turned down the unique privilege of painting a series of murals for the Palace of Westminster. Instead he recommended former students to work under his supervision – one being Cowper. His most pressing problem was the Pennsylvania State Capitol in Harrisburg. Would William give him a hand for a month to help him complete the paintings? The House of Representatives was to be executed in Italian Renaissance style and the Senate in French Renaissance style. With a massive amount of research still to be done at the Victoria and Albert Museum (V&A), planning was as arduous as ever – fifty-seven life-size figures would be needed for the William Penn scene alone.

Pushed by his ultra-efficient wife Gertrude, Abbey had found a place in London to show the first batch of Harrisburg canvases for ten days before their shipment to America. In the spring of 1908 his friends, including, of course, Ernest Board and William, were invited to a series of private viewings in the East Gallery of London University's Imperial Institute. The general reaction to the work, or at least the reaction of his admiring biographer E.V. Lucas, was that it was 'a new revelation of vigour and genius'. King Edward and Queen Alexandra made a royal visit, at which they expressed regret that such magnificent paintings were leaving England. Abbey's triumph ended in a dinner with the American Ambassador, where Alma-Tadema made a speech acclaiming him as the pre-eminent link between Britain and America.

In 1909 a new painting of William's was exhibited at the 'Summer Exhibition' and snapped up for a magazine colour reproduction. He then landed his first really big contract with a sumptuous edition of *Hamlet* for the publishers Hodder & Stoughton. These thirty full-page paintings must have taken him well over a year of intense work. The paintings are a mixed bag, the composition sometimes dull and the colours muddy; but at other times the royal interiors are perfectly constructed and the figures, in melodramatic poses and clad in costumes borrowed from Abbey's wardrobe, are often exceptionally well drawn. Many of the backdrops are lifted from the Gloucestershire countryside. Perhaps the best of the paintings, Ophelia drowning, finds her among the willows, reeds and meandering lines of the River Coln (see plate 8). In 1910 a green- and gold-embossed book appeared with William's name on the cover, while that of the illustrious Shakespeare critic Sir Arthur Quiller-Couch, author of the introduction, was relegated to the inside.

William's diary for 1910 has only one entry: '1910 – Nil,' and there is no record of his movements during that year. In 1911 he is back again full steam. In March he is designing two scenes – a castle courtyard and a banquet hall – for Sir Herbert Beerbohm Tree's *Macbeth*, for which he receives £18. In May Abbey re-appears, writing a sad and sympathetic letter to William:

I have not been in form until very recently (no varnishing days or other festivities) and deplore your exclusion from [a fellowship of] the RA. I should have liked to see your work, but have been so hurried and worried this past year that I've had no time to do what I should have liked to do: go about to some studios and see what is going on. We have been pulling up stakes at Fairford – an awful job to get the whole thing together.

Then Abbey comes to the point: the Harrisburg panels needed a much larger space for their completion. He had been lent the end part of the Machinery Hall in the White City in Shepherd's Bush, whose forty-foot ceiling was high enough for the canvases with something to spare. Could William lend a hand? 'Do you think you could help me get the whole thing together? I wish you could,' he pleaded, explaining that he had an area screened off but needed to get it straightened up: 'the place is awfully dirty, I must get it a shade cleaner … but it would be a good place to work in.' William agreed. Gertrude Abbey, in a high state of anxiety herself, was also pursuing their old friend Sargent and one of Abbey's earliest assistants, Ernest Board. She alone was aware that her husband's illness was an incurable cancer. She wrote begging Sargent to return from Europe immediately. Could he help supervise the work in the White City? Reluctantly, he arrived at Abbey's London home in Tite Street on 30 June 'to rescue the situation', as he put it to a friend.

After an operation in June, and now housebound, Abbey believed his poor recovery was due to the intense heat, which had begun early in May. He chased William with anxious letters: 'those two groups in the forge worry me and I must do some studies as soon as I am able … what about the sky around the stars. It should be neater in places I think … I don't think it will be ready – it is a parlous matter.'

Sargent looked in periodically to the Machinery Hall, complaining of the heat and the unsatisfactory task of looking after another man's work – however good a friend he was. He was more than pleased to leave William to execute most of the painting. One morning, feeling guilty about his own feeble efforts to help, he put a helmet on William's head and made a cardboard brim to check the effect of the shade for William Penn's forehead.

William visited Abbey in Tite Street in late July, where Abbey had a present of £50 waiting. On 1 August Abbey died aged fifty-nine.

* * * * * *

It is typical of William's modesty that it is Sargent and Board who are always named in the official texts as completing the Harrisburg paintings, whereas it was William who did the real work. After Abbey's

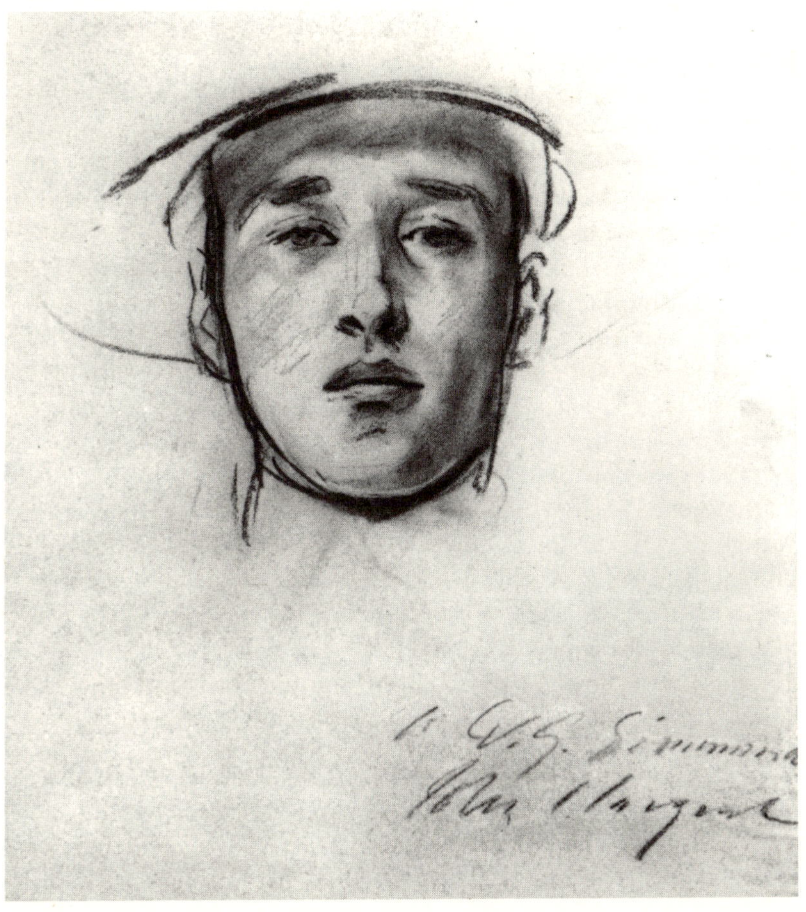

John Singer Sargent was annoyed at being summoned back from Europe to help his friend Edwin Abbey complete his Harrisburg paintings. In gratitude to William, who did most of the painting, he gave him this sketch

death, it was not Swaish, nor Board, nor Cowper whom Gertrude Abbey took with her to America, but William. Together they would supervise the instalment of Abbey's canvases. Would William come on a month's contract? The two set sail on 19 October 1911, arriving in New York on the 27th.

William's first sight of Pennsylvania's Capitol, with its five-story exterior faced with Vermont granite, its green, terracotta-tiled roof and its 272-foot dome inspired by Michelangelo's design for St Peter's

Basilica in Rome, left him astounded, just as its young Philadelphian architect, Joseph Miller Huston, had planned it should.

Before work started William toured the Palace of Art – room after room of paintings, stained glass, ornaments and furnishings by the best American artisans of the day. When President Theodore Roosevelt dedicated the building in 1906, he declared, 'This is the handsomest building I ever saw.'

William settled into the Rotunda and House Chamber for a month of painstaking work to fix to the walls the four medallion canvases, fourteen foot in circumference, and the four thirty-eight by twenty-two foot crescent-shaped murals. Then he touched up the blemishes. Two rooms from Abbey's commission were left undone, but the unfinished *Camp of the American Army at Valley Forge* was eventually relocated on to a north wall in the Senate Chamber, where it stands today. The remainder of the commission was given to the American painter Violet Oakley who completed the works using her own designs.

For all the fascination of the New World, William did not resent having to return with Mrs Abbey. He did not want to linger; a strong emotional attachment was impelling him to get home as soon as he could. He returned to England on 23 November in gales and high seas, arriving back home in Liverpool on the 30th.

CHAPTER 8

Eve Simmonds

1910–1912

*'Single-minded allegiance to painting was giving
way to other interests, the seeds of which had been
planted a decade ago by Walter Crane.'*

Before William left for America he had met an attractive art student, Eve Peart. The two had come across each other at dances at the School of Arms in Knightsbridge. Her father, who had been a successful dealer in fine mahoganies for furniture, had on his death left to his much younger wife enough money to afford an education for their seven children. Eve's two older brothers, both of whom were close to her, were also art students – Frederick, a sculptor, and Herbert, a painter.

Strong-featured, gentle and graceful, Eve had attended the Westminster School of Art. With its links to architecture, Westminster included in its curriculum courses in handicraft, stonework and design. For those who did not want to restrict themselves to painting, the School of Art was the place to be, a natural home for those drawn to the Arts and Crafts movement. But over the years, Westminster shared numerous pupils and teachers with the Slade which under its principal, the formidable Henry Tonks, an inspiring – and frightening – teacher, came to symbolise the British avant-garde. Long before most of his contemporaries, Tonks recognised the genius of Whistler, Sickert, Sargent and the French Impressionists, who had exploded on the artistic consciousness of Europe with an impact that could never be matched by the quieter, if scarcely less ground-breaking, evolution of design and craftsmanship.

Eve herself was tempted by painting, and when the Westminster School's premises moved to Vincent Square, where the charismatic Walter Sickert was to teach, her world brightened – his kindness was a consolation for the recent death of her mother, which had left her parentless. Through him she came under the sway of the Camden Town Group, which used to meet at his house.

This group, like the Salon des Indépendants in France, was in conscious rebellion against the conformity of the Royal Academy. More than half its members had studied at the Slade; others came from the Westminster School. Their unconventional use of paint and their intimate subject matter defined them: their interiors were small rooms – kitchens, attics, bathrooms – and their painting from nature no longer the romantic landscapes of the past but cityscapes, presenting the uglier, rougher side of city life. Eve started to shed the remnants of Edwardian and Victorian clutter, the biblical and classical dramatisations in painting and design.

For Eve, as for much of cultural London, 1910 had been a seminal moment. The exhibition of Monet and the French Post-Impressionists at the Grafton Gallery that November, organised by a Slade professor, the critic Roger Fry, was her first encounter with the works of Gaugin, Manet, Matisse and Van Gogh. Virginia Woolf later famously observed: 'On or about December 1910 human character changed', and no one in Eve's circle would have demurred. Her contemporaries included her fellow Westminster students Sylvia Gosse, Duncan Grant and Eric Gill (then taking a course in stone masonry) and Dorothy Larcher, who would eventually become her life-long friend. Ethel Partridge, who early on married Ananda Coomaraswamy, trained as a musician at the Royal College of Music and the slightly older Thérèse Lessore and Phyllis Barron were at the Slade.

As her studies came to an end, Eve concluded that she did not want to be a painter – not that the Camden Town Group would have accepted a woman anyway. It was not just the modernism of the Camden Town Group that had excited her. The Lessore sisters, Louise, later to marry Alfred Powell, and Thérèse, later to marry Walter Sickert, introduced Eve properly to the Arts and Crafts movement, which until then she had observed more as an interested outsider. Their hero, William Lethaby, the Principal of the recently founded Central School of Arts and Crafts provided the link between their generation and the early founders of the movement, John Ruskin and William Morris. Eve was affected by the social and moral code being discussed everywhere in the Arts and Crafts philosophy. Its resistance to the often-ruthless industrialisation and the factory-made ugliness of Victorian Britain was inspiring. The assumption that beauty and good design was the privilege of the upper classes, rather than a gift that should be available to ordinary people in every walk of life, irked her.

The shy, softly spoken Louise, a pupil of Lethaby, was the Lessore sister to whom Eve was closest, and through her encountered new territories of calligraphy, illumination and embroidery – and all forms of craft: furniture, textiles, printmaking and pottery from a range of countries, traditions, tribes, villages or periods. Louise's French grandfather, Emile Lessore, had been Wedgwood & Sons' most revered artist, whose painting on pottery and porcelain had received medals at exhibitions in nearly all the capitals of Europe, substantially enhancing the reputation of the firm. Louise's husband, Alfred Powell, ten years her senior, was collaborating with her at Wedgwood's where they, too, were making their name with a string of beautiful ceramic designs.

If William was aware of the conflicts between Eve's very different art school education and the tenets to which he and Edwin Abbey held, there was no tension between them. Far from it. He was eight years older and held in some awe for his friendship with Walter Crane; and he was respected for his family background as a builder, which underpinned his knowledge of architecture.

Besides Eve's artistic sensibility as a whole, two particular elements of it were to be crucial for William: her love of the natural world, especially wild flowers and every form of plant life, and her musical talents. She played the spinet and the clavichord and had begun lessons with the visionary Arnold Dolmetsch, whom she had met after a concert in the Hall of Cliffords Inn, where the Arts Workers' Guild held their meetings. Dolmetsch had come to England from France twenty years earlier to undertake research at the British Library and revive long-forgotten sixteenth- and seventeenth-century music and the instruments on which it was played. Now working for the clavichord- and harpsichord-maker Gaveau in Paris, he kept up with a handful of pupils and on his intermittent visits gave lessons to Eve. The lessons were occasionally enlivened by his furious denunciations of Wanda Landowska, Violet Gordon Woodhouse's rival for the reputation of the world's greatest player of early keyboard instruments. Landowska claimed, wrongly in Dolmetsch's view, that Bach owned

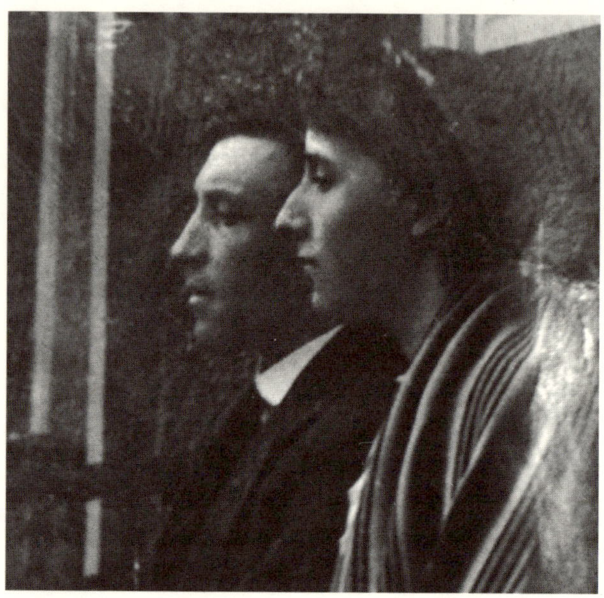

William and Eve just after they were married, photographed by the Indian
philosopher Ananda Coomaraswamy outside his Hampstead flat, 1912

only harpsichords. Dolmetsch would interrupt Eve's instruction to
rant about Landowska's 'wild articles and unfounded conclusions',
sometimes ramming home his point by grasping the small rectangular clavichord to give a practical demonstration of how Bach played
a similar instrument.

In March 1912 William married Eve. She was twenty-eight,
William thirty-six. The ceremony took place on her home ground
at Clapham registry office; neither were religious, in the sense of
being practising Anglicans, Catholics or followers of the Quakerism
common in the Arts and Crafts movement. Although William had
provided many religious illustrations for his publishers' children's
books, his own drawings and paintings were all on secular themes,
poetic, musical or literary.

With little money, other than a small income from shares Eve had
inherited from her father, William and Eve moved into a cottage,
Brookside, next to Eve's brother Herbert in the Wiltshire village of
Fovant. Herbert and Ada Peart and their two children had settled in
a farmhouse separated from Brookside by a stream and with a large

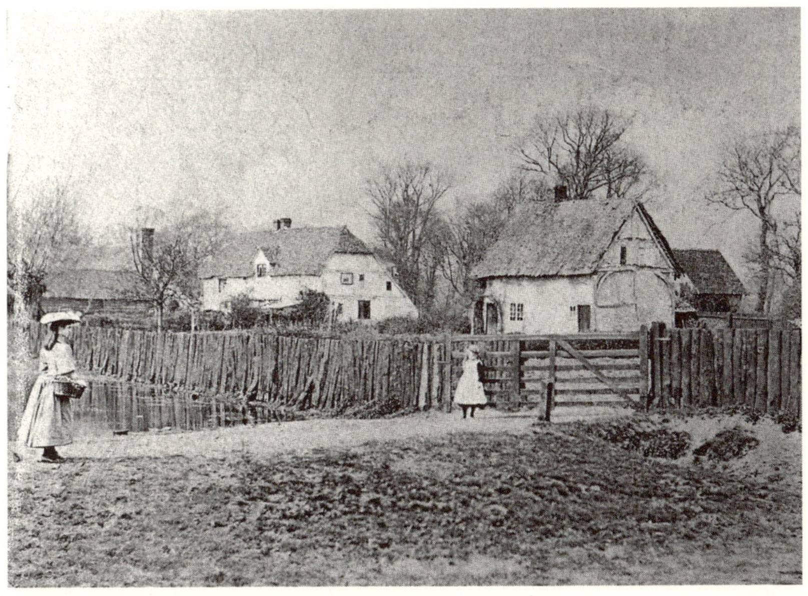

Early photograph of Fovant, Wiltshire where the Simmondses moved straight
after their marriage

barn on the border between the two properties. Here Herbert had
created a workshop, which he generously offered to share with his
new brother-in-law. For Eve, alive to the possibility of creating her
first garden, he and William employed a village boy called Alfred
Wyatt to dig her vegetable patch and help plant climbers against the
house. Along the water's edge, she chose yellow flags, marsh mari-
gold and water lilies to float and dance on the river surface.

The spring and summer of 1912 were among the coldest and
wettest on record, perhaps because of the massive volcanic eruption
several thousand miles away in Alaska. No clouded skies or down-
pours, however, affected the Simmondses' happiness. One is left with
an impression of a never-ending summer of expeditions, picnics with
children, pony and trap drives and long river walks, all preserved in a
series of remarkably sunny shots in William's first photograph album.
Nor did bad weather prevent a stream of visits from Eve's Arts and
Crafts friends.

The quiet, slim and dark Dorothy Larcher was Eve's closest
friend and the most mysteriously interesting. She had returned with

her erstwhile flatmate Alice Richardson from several months in India. She was full of her second visit to the Ajanta Caves north of Bombay as assistant to the Indian art scholar Christiana Herringham. The two had been copying and recording ancient Buddhist murals in the caves, helped by some art students from Calcutta Art School. The charismatic painter and cultural polymath William Rothenstein had accompanied them at first, but had moved on to other parts of India. Transcribing what was left of these glorious images in the dark, damp, tunnels with bats swooping around them, had been challenging but exhilarating work. From morning to night they had perched precariously on ladders to press sheets of tracing paper against the walls in the half light to outline sacred elephants, galloping horses and powerful goddesses in an abundant variety of dresses and with jewelled ornaments cascading down their bared breasts.

As for Alice, she had been combining cultural exploration with romance: having met the philosopher of Indian art Ananda Coomaraswamy, she ousted his wife, Ethel Mairet, and had been living with him on a houseboat in Kashmir while he was researching Rajput painting.

Alice's return to London, now married to Ananda, revealed a surprising metamorphosis into a sari-clad 'Ratan Devi'. She had mastered Indian music with Abdul Rahim of Kapurthala and taken to sitting on the ground performing Indian songs with a tambura. The Indian poet Rabindranath Tagore and Yeats rhapsodised about her performances, to which Ananda, before each stage appearance, supplied daunting intellectual introductions.

The Simmondses, however, having first known Alice as a pupil of Cecil Sharp, found it hard to take her new persona seriously and carried on as if little had changed. When Alice's infant son, Narada, appeared, they treated him as part of the family: Eve encouraged him to play with the Peart children and William made him toys – a boat, a chariot for careering around the village lanes and a large painted elephant on wheels.

In a glow of happiness, Eve scattered invitations to a wonderfully diverse group. The influx to London of a growing number of cognoscenti of Indian fine art, particularly of the ancient frescos in the Ajanta Caves – the 'jungle of masterpieces', as Rothenstein called them on his return – sparked a debate about India's centuries-old painting traditions. Inspired by Christiana Herringham's work in the Ajanta Caves, Rothenstein wrote a letter to *The Times*, co-signed by a range of artists and critics, including William's old National Art Training School teachers Edward Lanteri and Walter Crane, and several leading Arts and Crafts figures, in a coordinated attempt to educate public opinion and encourage people to join his new India Society.

William was being introduced to a new circle of friends – and through them was changing direction, though at first this was noticed only by Eve. His single-minded allegiance to painting was giving way to other interests, the seeds of which had been planted a decade ago by Walter Crane. It was around this time that Eve introduced William to Alfred and Louise Powell. It is no exaggeration to say that together they were to shape his career.

Older than William, Alfred had two decades behind him work-ing in every artistic discipline. He had studied at the Slade, then trained in the best of the Arts and Crafts offices in London under the church architect J.D. Sedding, one of William Morris's main intellectual heirs, and finally had set up on his own as an itinerant freelance architect. He made a point of overseeing his commissions scrupulously through to their completion. There was a fascinat-ing consistency to his vision, in which an architect should master all the crafts to understand the essence of good construction and design. He painted in watercolour everything around him: flow-ers, plants, people, animals, landscape, boats and buildings. He would talk with immense warmth and knowledge on a range of subjects close to William's thoughts. After the birth of their daugh-ter, Catherine, the Powells spent more time in the Cotswolds, in their cottage close to Ernest Gimson, and the Barnsley brothers' workshop. Alfred worked beside the village craftsmen and had taught himself woodcarving, metal and silver work, stone masonry and furniture making.

* * * * * *

In the late summer of 1912 William's father became seriously ill. He had continued working to the last of his strength but collapsed at home under Martha's care and was forced to retire. On his weekly visits to his father's bedside, William would sometimes go down to the carpentry workshop on the ground floor to sort out his father's tools and bring back pieces of wood to carve in his room. They reminisced about the past, about the Gilbert and Sullivan comic operas and the old Windsor Music Hall where as a four-year-old William had been taken to see the slapstick plays so popular in Victorian England.

Indelibly marked in William's memory from those days were some trick puppets, one of which had walked about with his head in his hand. Another, a fairy, had paved the way, in a magical transformation scene, for a strangely featured puppet whose head came off to make way for a cheese, then a second, then a third until the grotesque figure had ten cheeses in place of one head. To illustrate the puppet's movements and traction for his father, William carved him a small clown. His interest in puppetry sparked by these childhood images, and in part also by the atmosphere of excitement among Eve's friends as they rediscovered ancient folk traditions, William immersed himself in its history. He would carve out his own terrain, not as a historian or through reproduction, but as an artist. He found to his astonishment that puppets traced their origins back several thousand years and to many different civilisations, from India and China to Greece, and to Egypt where women processed with statues moved by hidden wires. Ancient classical comedy theatre, and in later centuries *Commedia dell'arte*, mime and pantomime – all these were in the same tradition, with stock characters, masks and improvised knockabout scenes. The opportunity for caricature, ritual and satire provided by figures manipulated by humans had evidently been of timeless appeal – and, it seemed to William, the possibilities remained inexhaustible. Even the avant-garde theatre designer Gordon Craig, Ellen Terry's visionary son, had recently translated a book on Javanese shadow theatre, where buffalo-hide puppets are mounted on bamboo sticks and held up behind a piece of white cloth to cast their shadows on to a screen. Meanwhile the genius behind the performance was the unseen puppet master who narrates the story in a voice modulated to increase the drama as good triumphs over evil, and a traditional orchestra in the background provides melody and rhythm.

William set about designing and sculpting two puppets, avoiding the aggressive, anarchic facial expressions of the clowning and cackling Punch and Judy in favour of the gentler, tragicomic characters and plots of *Harlequinade*.[1] Equally testing and interesting to William was the mechanical traction of his figures, their movement, their joints and their stringing. Maybe he would try them out on the Fovant children. Eve's garden boy Alfred Wyatt, full of initiative, extracted a promise for a show in the Village Hall.

In melancholic mood as his father's condition deteriorated, William took longer and longer walks along the lanes, meadows and streams in the wildest parts of Wiltshire, studying insects, animals, plants and trees. He never lost his acute sensitivity to nature and landscape or his love of architecture. Throughout his life he believed that an artist's depiction of nature and animals could only come through immersing oneself in nature, which must at the same time be examined with scientific rigour and minuteness as through a microscope. At this time he began the pencil studies he was to continue for the rest of his life of the farm wagons in Fovant and the cart horse and ox and pony carts in use in the Wiltshire villages. It was not only the external shape of the carts that he searched to understand, shapes that had evolved over centuries for transporting hay, logs, stones and manure, but also the mechanics of their moving interior sections and joints.[2]

On one of his walks to see the hill fort mounds near Whitsbury in Hampshire, he carried on towards Downton and came to a halt in front of a green horse-drawn caravan parked on a triangle of grass. Sitting in the sun on its platform, a red-bearded man with wild hair was jesting with a slightly older dark-haired woman, holding what seemed to be a puppet in black, witch-like costume. Below him lay a guitar and two young children were messing around and handing him tools. William asked him whether he would mind if he sketched the caravan, which was of a slightly unusual shape.

Arthur and Lily Wilkinson turned out to be artists, vegetarians and Socialists. They married after falling in love at a Labour Party meeting and were now out to reform the world, to travel and live the simple life of their dreams, surrounded by nature. They had set off in the spring from Letchworth Garden City (a town recently built on community Socialist principles) in the spring to tour the south-western counties in a caravan built by Arthur. With their horse 'Aunt Jane', they were now heading to Salisbury, accompanied by Arthur's much younger brother Walter, who helped with the household chores. To amuse their two children Arthur had made some puppets and had taken to giving the occasional show. They were hoping for a good crowd in Salisbury market place. Not that coppers in the hat mattered that much: Lily was the daughter of a rich Midlands businessman with her own private income.

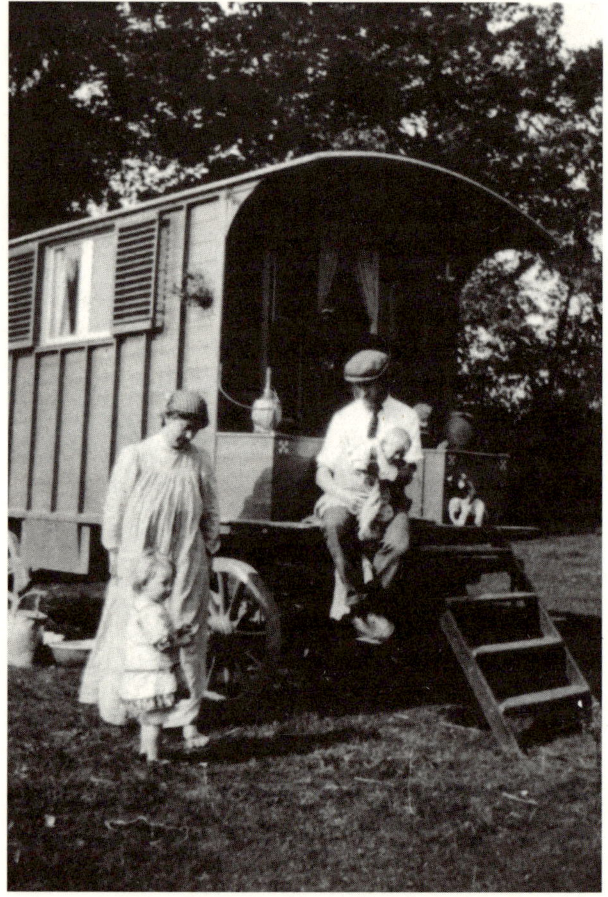

William came across Arthur and Lily Wilkinson in Wiltshire, travelling 'on the road' with their two children in 1913

The Wilkinsons were full of admiring tales of the romantic old showman Clunn Lewis who had bought the historic Middleton Show in the 1860s. This was a troupe that had performed on the road without a break since its first appearance in 1712. For over fifty years, with wife and extended family, Lewis wearing a top hat had pushed his theatre on a handbarrow through the roads and villages of England in the manner of an early Victorian showman. His music was the harp, the cornet and the dulcimer. At annual fairs a decade or so earlier he could clear £100[3] after expenses and present a repertoire of seventy plays, often improvising after reading up a new plot in the afternoon and trusting his native wit with the puppets in the evening. No longer. This was before the advent of the train and pictures palaces in every country town.

Now Lewis was receiving all the nostalgic publicity of a hero of a dying art. With testimonials from Cardinals Manning and Vaughan, and a host of supporting letters from churches, schools and orphanages, he had summoned the most eminent people in the theatrical world, Gordon Craig, Bernard Shaw and G.K. Chesterton among them, to help save his marionettes from oblivion. The playwright Harley Granville-Barker wrote: 'May you and your puppets flourish, for if we cannot see in and through them all the poetry and wonder of the drama, we shall never see.' Most famous of his puppets from the Middleton Show was the eigthteenth-century Old Mother Shipton, a hideously ugly hag modelled on a Yorkshire soothsayer who had predicted Henry VIII's victory over the French. With beetle eyebrows, jutting chin and warty nose, the puppet had a mechanism that allowed her to smoke a pipe on stage.

The Wilkinsons' puppets were amusing, in a rough-and-ready way, quite close to the Clunn Lewis tradition but very different from William's nascent ideas for making his own troupe. He had, however, a fellow feeling for the Wilkinsons' romantic nomadic way of life, so dismissive of its hardships and so enthusiastic for its pleasures. It was the beginning of a long, though sometimes rocky, friendship.

* * * * * *

John Simmonds died on the last day of November 1912. On the face of it, William's life remained as it had been. Colour-plate illustration work from publishers was still providing him with some income. But as he carried on carving, imperceptibly his inner world was changing.

During the quiet weeks beside his father, he had pressed, stroked and etched into the wood's surfaces. He was fascinated by the differing degrees of malleability, the colour and texture of different species of tree. Late in 1912 came William's first piece of real sculpture, *Spring*, a strong-faced girl with fine chiseled nose and curled hair, carved in seasoned meadow oak. Originally intended for a wagon wheel spoke, like a rustic caryatid, she stood erect and serene, clutching intricate sheaves of corn in her beautifully sculpted hands. This piece was fol-lowed by *Shepherd Singing*, a carving in ash of a youth singing in a sheep pen beside a ewe with her new-born lamb.

The promised Christmas puppet show for the villagers was loom-ing. With little time to complete the four figures he was planning, William rushed through a Magic Lantern Show instead, using old Victorian storylines. In a series of exquisitely drawn cut-outs, which he pushed and pulled in a dark box stage, he created a sense of wonder among the children in the village hall as they watched his cameo scenes.

But it was not long before his *Harlequinade* puppets were ready to perform. This time the experiment – a silent mime, with music and dance – was for family only. He placed his box stage, with a back-drop of a village fair, on the Pearts' kitchen table. Beneath it, hidden by a tablecloth, Alfred, who was musical, and now far more than a garden boy, accompanied the puppets' antics on a mouth organ, supported by a knee drum or sometimes a trumpet. He played in the village band and had become fascinated by William's carving, assist-ing him whenever he could.

Eve was impressed – and inspired. She fell to discussing possible characters for new puppets with William, with ritualised scenes of jeal-ousy, love and old age embroidered with real music and stylised dance. They settled on a dialogue and a full-length story revolving around an incident in the lives of the five main Harlequin characters. Harlequin loves Columbine; Columbine's greedy father Pantaloon, in league with the mischievous Clown, tries to separate the lovers; and the servant, Pierrot, is involved in chaotic chase scenes with a policeman. Eve would choose the composers and the instruments – which she, of course, would play. And that is how, in the Wiltshire farmhouse kitchen, the seeds of a parallel career for William were planted – culminating in performances that for thirty years would entrance literary London and artists all over England and Europe.

CHAPTER 9

Secret War Work

1914–1915

'William finished a tiny ivory carving, wrapped it in a matchbox and posted it home to Eve for safekeeping. His sculpture collection was growing.'

In June 1914, without a care in the world, Eve and William took a fortnight's holiday in Holland, returning to Fovant in early July. The assassination of Archduke Ferdinand in Serbia on 28 June barely registered with William. Certainly nothing suggested that Britain might go to war. There were confusing rumblings in Europe throughout the next month – of threats, alliances and complex diplomatic manoeuvring – but they did not seem to involve Britain apart from for its puzzling guarantee of Belgium's neutrality, which William presumed to be somehow connected to the defence of France.

As the situation deteriorated, France and Russia declared war on Germany, but the newspapers still played down the risk that Britain would be drawn in. David Lloyd George, Chancellor of the Exchequer, told a journalist: 'the clouds are clearing, European problems will soon be solved.' Prime Minister Herbert Asquith wrote to his friend Venetia Stanley that in the event of war Britain would just be a 'spectator'. Civil unrest and troubles in Ireland dominated the English press. *The Times* did not acknowledge the gravity of the situation in Europe until 25 July 1914.

But in the first days of August events moved fast. The Cabinet's ultimatum to Berlin not to violate Belgium's neutrality expired at eleven o'clock on the night of 4 August as the German army rolled across the Belgian border en route to Paris. The Prime Minister addressed the nation through Parliament: 'With infinite regret His Majesty's Government have been compelled to put this country in a state of war with what for many years, and indeed generations past, has been a friendly Power.'

The news reached William and Eve next day, utterly taking them aback. But without radio, cinema or front-line war correspondents, tales of the war, passed through word of mouth, made the distant conflict seem almost unreal. It was not until accounts appeared in the press of German atrocities in the Belgian invasion – civilians hanged from lamp posts, used as human shields or burned alive in their homes – that the brutal facts produced a sudden hatred of 'the Hun' (the Kaiser's boastful description of his own countrymen at war).

When the Simmondses visited London in September, London had been transformed. There was much less traffic than before. Within days of the declaration of war the motor-bus service had been drastically cut back as 1,200 bus drivers were enlisted to drive lorries on the front. In the streets there was a sense of mingled unease and patriotism in the ebb and flow of people trudging on foot to their destinations. Allied flags were displayed by shops over their doors and by motor cars on their bonnets. Taxi cabs attached placards calling men to do their duty. Recruiting posters were pasted on street walls with Kitchener's eyes and his accusing finger pointing straight at you beneath four words in blue letters: 'Your Country Needs You.' To keep people's spirits up, the weeklies reported life at the front as if it were an everyday affair, with touches of romantic fantasy. The *Illustrated London News* depicted a group of reserve officers temporarily prevented from active combat by appalling weather, organising a hare hunt with a pack of beagles to break the monotony. The French army was portrayed as an amiable crew of eccentrics, pictured setting up stages for Guignol puppet shows – the gruesome local variant of Punch and Judy.

The Powells were carrying on much as before. Alfred believed that the war would not last long. He and Louise had taken a lease on elegant eighteenth-century Volta House, near Hampstead Heath, and the two were dividing their time between there and the Wedgwood factory in Staffordshire. For William, the idea of enlisting simply did not arise. Initially it had been widely believed that the war would be over by Christmas – and in the very unlikely event that it dragged on long enough for conscription to be introduced, as a married man not far off forty, he would presumably be among the last to be called up. Not many of his friends and contemporaries were quick to volunteer, either, though some were caught up in the patriotic fever that was sweeping the country. Of his former colleagues from the Academy Schools, Thomas Dugdale had signed up in a yeomanry regiment and Shepard, initially prevented from enlisting as a married man, before long managed to obtain a commission.

Among Eve's Slade friends and contemporaries, Dora Carrington's two brothers had enlisted immediately, Paul Nash had signed up for Home Service as a private in the Artists' Rifles, and Richard Nevinson, rejected from the army as unfit, had seen early action in Belgium as a Red Cross orderly in a Medical Corps ambulance unit (at the end of January 1915 he was back in Highgate, unwell and too shocked to return to France). Some, like Mark Gertler, loathed war on principle – as did the Wilkinsons, who had disappeared to France before the invasion of Belgium and had reached Florence, where they were involved with Gordon Craig's theatre school. Rumour had it that they were running out of money there and that the theatre had been requisitioned by the military. Phyllis Barron had gone to work in a hospital in Belgium, but was soon back in London, having found herself a job painting luminous compass dials for the Royal Flying Corps, which of course had no lights on its planes.

The Slade was still accepting students but the Royal Academy's Burlington House was no longer its old self. In the back courtyard, drills were carried out every morning. Classes for male students were closing, though the 'Summer' and 'Winter Exhibitions' would continue as before. The most valuable works of art were stored away in the basement, freeing some of the galleries for the army, and rifles were stored in the refreshment rooms. In securing safety from air raids for London's national treasures in other museums, however, there was a somewhat foolhardy delay. It would not be until December 1915 that all the great works were distributed to provincial art galleries around the country.

With Christmas approaching, William and Eve's visits to London became more frequent. They were increasingly shocked by what they encountered there. In December, after the destruction at Ypres of Britain's expeditionary force, they found themselves beside a hospital train being met by a silent, fearful crowd. The platform was littered with stretchers, from which ashen faces stared with unseeing eyes. The road outside had been cleared for a stream of ambulances. Growing numbers of women dressed or veiled in black were to be seen on the streets, unmistakable reminders of sudden bereavement. Near Volta House, pushing the Powells' baby daughter in her pram, Eve found shops with '*Ici on parle français*' signs in the window. London had turned into a cosmopolitan city – a vast hostel for Belgian and French refugees, with the more well-off families taking furnished houses in central Hampstead.

* * * * * *

As the prospect of an early end to the war faded, the Simmondses' circle entered a miserable period of brooding on what was to come and how they should respond. They were plagued by doubts and distressing feelings of inconsistency born from conflicting principles of patriotism and pacifism, sympathy for the wounded, horror of Germany's cruel militarism and a seldom-confessed fear of death or maiming. There were hard decisions to be made, ones they would have to face on their own terms and then live with forever. News of fellow artists continued to trickle through. After wrestling with his conscience, Stanley Spencer joined the Royal Army Medical Corps and later followed his brother's example by transferring to an infantry regiment. The redoubtable Slade principal Henry Tonks resumed his medical career, first at home, then at a French Red Cross hospital and then in Italy, producing harrowing drawings of the faces of wounded soldiers.

William was struggling to reconcile his longing to distance himself from the war with the growing conviction that he must make some contribution – but in a way that would employ one of his skills, preferably as a draughtsman. With each month he was more affected by the news. The declaration by Germany of unrestricted submarine warfare against neutrals, the first use of poison gas, the appalling casualties in Flanders and the loss of several battleships of the supposedly invincible British fleet in the Dardanelles, close to William's place of birth, all shook him to the core. He could no longer stand aside. He must somehow find a way to help the war effort.

A lesser motive for seeking new work was financial. He could not be certain how much longer he could guarantee an income from his publishers, Nelson & Sons. For the moment, the firm seemed in robust health and had signed him up for more colour plates for its biblical series, but elsewhere magazines were closing. Writers who relied on book reviews and articles saw their incomes dwindling to nothing – unless the subject was the war.

William soon found what he had been seeking. In March 1915 he took a position as a draughtsman in a Kensington laboratory run by an industrialist, Colonel R.E.B. Crompton, the inventor of electric lighting. In the interview, William's art school background did not impress the practical seventy-year-old Crompton. But when William produced a folder of his drawings of boats and the moving parts and joints of horse-drawn carts, Crompton found their precision extraordinary and engaged him for a trial period.

Two weeks later Crompton called William into his office a second time for a very different sort of interview. Swearing him to secrecy, he explained that as an expert on traction, he had been asked by a committee of naval architects, politicians and engineers established by Winston Churchill, the First Lord of the Admiralty, to submit designs for a machine that could cross enemy trenches while protecting its occupants from rifle and machine-gun fire. There was an urgent need for such a weapon, provisionally code-named the 'Landship', on the Western front. Several companies and naval engineers were working in parallel on competing designs, but Crompton, a military man from his youth with a successful career behind him as an inventor and engineer, was confident of his ability to come up with the best design or at least to improve on the ideas of others.

Absolute discretion was essential: the Landship Committee's project was to be concealed not just from German spies but from the Admiralty Board, the Treasury and even Kitchener at the War Office – all of whom were expected to resist it as a distraction from the serious business of making traditional weapons of war. Crompton was taking a calculated gamble in telling William this, but there was no time to spare and he had experienced enough to feel that he could trust his instinct for judging character.

In Crompton's secret mission William had stumbled across everything he could have wanted in the way of a war effort. His first military assignment came shortly after his arrival, when he accompanied a small team of experts on a reconnaissance to northern France to analyse captured German fortifications in Neuve Chapelle. In the event they were unable to study the trenches, let alone measure them accurately, as the village was not secure: it had been much fought over and was now partially retaken by the enemy. Crompton had, however, seen enough to grasp the magnitude of the problem. What was needed was a machine that could repel bullets; crawl over craters, parapets, barbed wire and sodden ground; fire from different angles and do all this while being nimble enough to navigate narrow French country roads. Two basic design concepts were the front-runners – a large wheel with adjustable feet instead of a rim and a continuous caterpillar track. Crompton was asked by the Landship Committee to explore the possibilities of the wheel, but although he built a working model he concluded in the summer that the continuous track was the more promising direction.

To his friends William presented his work as low paid and inconsequential. So far as the Powells knew, his heart remained entirely in his carving and his puppets, while his drafting work for a successful electrical engineer was just a day job. Whenever he travelled to factories or to experimental grounds to watch tests on site, he carried a piece of ivory or wood and a whittling knife in his pocket. On a visit to Lincoln to sketch an early model of the Landship for Crompton, he finished a tiny ivory carving, wrapped it in a matchbox and posted it home to Eve for safekeeping. His sculpture collection was growing.

Yet as the purpose of William's work became clearer to him, the task ahead became increasingly absorbing: its goal being no less than to break the stalemate of the trenches. Throughout 1915 testing and research at Crompton's laboratory continued its feverish analysis of the ideas and inventions competing to be the prototypes for large-scale manufacture of the Landship. Having already extended two floors beneath Thriplands House to take on extra draughtsmen, when the moment came to accommodate a full-scale mock up model of a Landship, Crompton was forced to hire extra space in a nearby building in Kensington Church Street. The technical problems of combining armour, firepower, reliability and speed in a very heavy machine using a novel method of traction seemed at times insurmountable. Gears, steering, weaponry, tracks and engine power all required complex decisions about whether to buy them in and adapt them or to design them from scratch. Crompton considered every question from first principles; a true scientist, he embraced failure as an important part of discovery.

William worked all hours, swept on by his boss's indomitable drive, attention to detail and analytical acuity. Often he only just managed to catch the last bus home, which left Eve nervous and

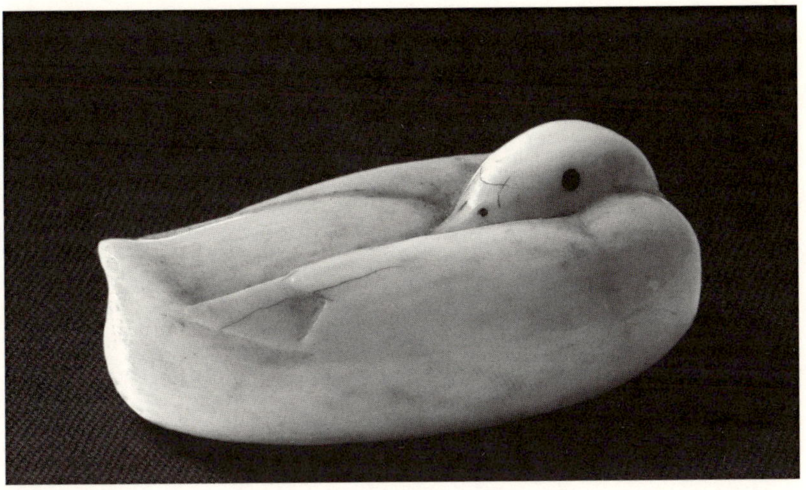

The ivory duck that William carved during his lunch breaks while working on the development of the Tank invention with Colonel Crompton during the First World War

worried. Secrecy was hard to maintain as the circle of insiders grew. Crompton's team was fortunate that Sir Henry d'Eyncourt, Chairman of the Landship Committee, was able to cut through interdepartmental disputes. Nevertheless, a multitude of design adjustments thrown up by testing the Landship model revealed there was still much to solve. When it came to d'Eyncourt's ears that some wives had been loose-tongued, Eve was paid a private visit and told under threat of internment that it could cost many thousands of lives if the secret of the weapon ever reached the enemy.

William's work in the Kensington laboratory had a surprisingly strong link with his art. The mechanical precision required was of a very similar kind to the piecing together of his marionettes. His designs for the Landship's joints (in these early days Crompton was experimenting with hinging the body and the wheel perimeter in sections) were related in William's mind to the way in which he thought about the anatomy of his marionettes. To the puppet's torso he affixed legs, loosely jointed at the knee and ankle; the arms, too, had to be jointed at the elbows. Most important was the material with which to fix them all in position – hinges of metal or leather, wooden pins, screw-eyes or stiff wire looped at each end. The figures were always operated from overhead by strong threads and attached to a wooden T-piece, which included a detachable section to which the knee strings were tied. Of all the types of puppets, William had chosen the most complicated and hardest of all to manipulate.

In the spring of 1915, the Powells offered the Simmondses a lease on their top flat in Volta House 'with its beautiful view of the Crystal Palace'. For William it was not too much of a wrench having to leave Wiltshire. Hampstead, traditionally a home to artists, was relatively cut off from the teeming city and close to deep country, with fields, streams, ponds and hills reminiscent of the landscapes of Turner and Constable. They would keep the Fovant cottage for when either of them could get away. Eve consoled herself that her garden might be kept from going wild if Alfred Wyatt, who had joined the 3rd Dorsetshire Regiment, could spend an hour or two mowing and weeding on his intermittent visits home.

Besides, her deepening, close-knit friendship with Louise – a friendship in which they worked closely together and developed each other's ideas – was something on which she had come to rely. She was considerably more skilled at sewing than Louise, and Louise in turn helped her master the advanced techniques of embroidery. It was 'something everyone used to do in those days', Eve later modestly said. Her exquisite little garments, starting with the smocks she made for her nephew in 1910, have now become collectors' pieces.

Another consolation for leaving Wiltshire was the news that Eve's clavichord teacher Dolmetsch, now nearing sixty, had returned to London to set up a workshop in Hampstead. He was revising the final proofs of his masterpiece *The Interpretation of Music of the 17th and 18th Centuries* and was as full of enthusiasm, energy and obsessional persuasion as ever. When Eve renewed her lesson he told her, 'forget the piano … The touch and sensitivity of the Spinet and Virginals are ideal for the nimbleness of fingers you must acquire.'

He proudly showed her a small clavichord with only four octaves, quite adequate, he believed, for the full range of the early compositions. But he had also created a new, larger virginal with a five-octave compass. Its simple form, without highly priced, lavish decoration, would cost only 25 guineas. One would be ready for her by 15 July, 'before the summer holidays'. As a special concession, Eve could pay in three instalments as long as he had other orders – he wanted twelve in all. Roger Fry was already looking for more than one for the Omega Workshop.

Eve fell in love with her new instrument. And in Dolmetsch's manuscripts she uncovered a repertoire of seventeenth-century composers she thought ideal to accompany William's puppets. Her first choice, written out in her beautiful handwriting, was four songs by Giles Farnaby, a Baroque composer. When Alfred Powell was not away at the Wedgwood factory, he would try out pieces with Eve on his piano, singing the songs she chose in his magnificent baritone as William listened, observing intently and trying to imagine the whole from a spectator's viewpoint. These were his characters, and he alone held the thread connecting song, movement, voice and narrative to the sketches. He did not want Dolmetsch's influence to dominate. For him Cecil Sharp's early folk and country-dance discoveries – gloriously English and humorous – were equally important for what he wanted, if not more so.

There was an instinctive understanding between Eve and William about the puppets. Whatever imaginative source had inspired her husband in bringing his drawings to life, what he was creating was not representations in these miniature men, women and animals but depictions of their essence through suggestion and subtle intimation. Eve paid particular attention to their adornment. As each new puppet came along, she would clothe it in materials begged off Louise or given her by Phyllis Barron from her studio a few streets away. Working hard for the Flying Corps (for the princely sum of 5s. for completing a small dial and 7s. 6d. for a large one), Phyllis managed three hours a day of intensive painting to earn enough to live on to continue her researches in museum libraries. Her real passion now lay in the extinct art of wood blocks and hand-blocked design. In her studio she was experimenting with Indigo-vat dyeing.[1]

Alfred's enthusiasm for the marionettes was contagious. He helped William set up a small proscenium on the ground floor for puppet practice while Louise and Eve cooked the evening meal. Friends began to drop in to watch progress, sometimes staying long into the night, as if trying to shut off the horrors that seeped out from the front. Meals at the Powells' kitchen table downstairs in Volta House turned into a hotbed of debate. Conflicting feelings about the war were never far from the surface. If anyone succumbed to depression, Alfred produced positive anecdotes of young officers back from the front on leave. A favourite was a message thrown from a German trench into an English trench – 'We are firing into the air.' But it was from his visits to the Wedgwoods' family home, Barlaston Hall, spending evenings with Cecil Wedgwood (the company's Senior Partner) on his leaves from the front, that Alfred gained particularly illuminating insight into the contradictory aspects of the war. Although fifty-two and well over age, Cecil had insisted on volunteering for active service, as well as raising three local battalions. Having opened the hall to refugees, he now took in conscientious objectors – an act of extraordinary magnanimity for a man who abhorred 'shirkers'. In this gesture he reflected the strong liberal and pacifist strain that ran through his family.

Two controversies to which they kept returning but never resolved were the women's vote and art's place in society. The Suffragettes imprisoned for their militancy had been released at the outbreak of war to enable them to help refugees; and Emmeline Pankhurst had closed the movement's newspaper, reopening it under the title *Britannia, For King, For Country*. With Alfred Powell and Eve committed supporters of women's suffrage and Dolmetsch an equally committed opponent, William was restricted to the occasional wry comment in his attempts (not always successful) to cool the atmosphere and dissuade Phyllis Barron from stomping off to her studio in a rage.

Nothing stirred them up so much as argument about the ultimate purpose of art. England's then arbiter of taste, Roger Fry, the Bloomsbury critic, saw the artist as a superior being, observing humankind from above. Alfred Powell utterly disagreed. For him – as for all the Arts and Crafts crowd who gathered round him in Hampstead – art was about the absorption into a life in which the ordinary and the creative were completely integrated. Their Morris-inspired philosophy was not exactly pacifist, but the war to them was a hideous intrusion of all that was morally most bankrupt. For as long as they could, they simply averted their eyes from its ugly reality. They looked back to an idealised medieval Gothic era and the early Renaissance and forward to a healed world in which art and utility, craft and manufacture would join with enlightened education to produce a perfected new generation. William had recently discovered a Croatian sculptor, a newcomer to the London scene who had been given the rare honour of a one-man exhibition at the V&A. The strength and love of freedom and humanity expressed in Meštrović's figures, many in wooden bas-relief, gave William an almost prophetic hope in the outcome of the war. From a technical point of view, Meštrović's brilliant carving in an unfashionable medium gave William confidence about his own ambitions.

Dolmetsch's return was symbolically important to them. The excited public reaction to his rediscovery of early music and restoration of authenticity to its performance seemed to justify the Arts and Crafts movement's own backward-looking philosophy. He had acquired a new admirer in W.B. Yeats, who was in search of music to revive the lost oral tradition of Irish verse and had been learning to chant verse, accompanied by a psaltery. Dolmetsch, who had made the psaltery, encouraged Yeats to chant poems in friends' houses all around Hampstead. To the ear of a musician like Alfred Powell, these excruciating performances resembled nothing more than tuneless droning. Soon enough Dolmetsch himself admitted defeat and brought them to a stop.

As William developed his marionette sketches into miniature plays, Alfred and Louise Powell recognised in them an original art form, which they were determined to launch into the world. Moving the box stage into the panelled drawing room, they sent out invitations to a wider circle of acquaintances. Word of mouth proved a highly effective method of promotion and William's performances at Volta House were full to the brim. It was no longer possible just to 'drop in'. Only by cadging an invitation from Alfred or Louise could a newcomer gain access to what was becoming something of a cult occasion. Of the many poets, sculptors, biographers and architects who came to the Powells, William later said that it was the co-founder of Dove's Press Emery Walker, poet and playwright John Drinkwater and writer Henry Festing Jones who were to give him the most valuable practical start. But from 1917 until the Second World War, the Director of the Cambridge Fitzwilliam Museum, Sydney Cockerell, was the most committed to what William was hoping to achieve. At first he tentatively suggested bringing his scholarly musician cousin, Walter Cobbitt, to tea:

> to discuss the difficulties in getting complete co-operation between musician and the puppet … [Cobbitt] would I think regard the puppets subsidiary to the music and you as an artist in puppets would naturally take the opposite view and I think quite rightly. Also, he is probably unaware of the immense art needed for the manipulation of puppets such as yours.

William's reply to Cockerell makes it clear under what conditions such a visit would make sense:

Of course we would be very pleased for you to bring him, but don't you think perhaps we might get a better idea of the possibilities and limitations of the thing if he first came to see a show? ... I feel I could talk the matter over with him better if he had seen the complete show and he would then see at once the kind of unity there must be between the music and the puppets, and that the puppets govern both the musician and the manipulation. To get the best out of them you must let them have entirely their own way and do what they can. I have always found that a puppet has some certain obvious movement which you may or may not have designed it for, and you must choose the music to suit that particular action. This might be a difficulty in a Hall. Anyway it will be an interesting discussion. If you think it a good plan, I will let you know the first opportunity we have for a show. Yours sincerely W.G. Simmonds.

* * * * * *

The threat of a Zeppelin attack, hanging over Londoners since the beginning of 1915, made Eve increasingly anxious about William's travel back and forth to work in Kensington. Initially, as if testing their vulnerability to ground fire and their performance in different weather conditions, the Zeppelins had been used to attack Yarmouth in the Isle of Wight and King's Lynn in Norfolk. Now in the summer, with the authorisation of the Kaiser, they were being used to bomb London, hovering too high over the city to be in range for fighter planes or anti-aircraft fire. Then a bomb was dropped during the day in Tottenham Court Road, exploding to a shriek and boom of anti-aircraft guns and filling the streets with shrapnel. A terrified crowd rushed down the spiral staircase into the underground.

Eve and William's first sighting of Zeppelins came in September, when a siren sounded the arrival over Hampstead of two dark 500-foot cylindrical airships, with rounded points at both ends, floating in to bomb Golders Green on their way to Bloomsbury and the City. In the absence of any purpose-built shelter, the Simmondses followed official advice by closing the windows against a possible poison gas attack and joining their neighbours in their basement.

Although the damage inflicted proved in the event relatively small, the Zeppelins' sinister appearance and their initial impunity caused disproportionate fear, and the fact that their attacks were suspected of being aimed at civilians gave rise to a sense of outrage. The charge of barbaric German intentions had already been inflamed in May by the torpedoing of the Cunard liner *Lusitania* by a U-boat off the coast of Ireland, with the loss of 1,200 passengers.

The final Zeppelin raid of 1915, on 13 October, saw the pilot over-shoot his target. His load fell on the theatre district along the Strand, creating panic in the packed auditoriums. The days when civilians could feel safe away from the front had come to an end.

CHAPTER 10

Sculpting Becomes the Consuming Passion

1915–1916

*'They say we must prepare our minds for a furious air raid
as soon as the spring comes. Pray heaven the beastly business
might be over then.'*

Alfred Powell, letter to his brother Edgar, January 1916

The first full year of the war had brought despondency. Morale had been sapped by a series of disastrous engagements: the second Battle of Ypres, the Battle of Loos in Flanders and the amphibious Gallipoli Campaign, where Commonwealth and British troops were suffering terrible losses. Already Britain had suffered nearly 300,000 casualties and the prospect of more pointless massacres loomed. It was scarcely imaginable that 1916 could bring horrors that would dwarf those of the year just endured.

In the meantime, however, the Landship Committee's existence had at last registered with the War Office, and responsibility for the project was transferred to joint army and navy control. The squabbling Defence Chiefs, bogged down in bureaucracy and suspicious of the freelance inventors secretly marshalled by Winston Churchill, determined to put the next stage of its development in the hands of William Foster of Lincoln, a tried and trusted maker of agricultural machinery. Crompton, as the committee's engineering consultant, had concluded that Foster's caterpillar tracks would prove superior to the alternative system he had been asked to develop. Gradually, as difficulty after difficulty was overcome, fresh adherents joined the cause, which was now given a new code name – the Water Tank, shortened to the Tank. By December 1915 it was ready for testing.

The experimental grounds at Wembley were too exposed for the demonstration of the Tank. Arthur Balfour, who had succeeded Winston Churchill as First Lord of the Admiralty, came to the rescue, offering the army his cousin Lord Salisbury's estate at Hatfield, just north of London. Trenches were dug and craters and parapets constructed in a secluded area of the park. The Tank was sent by train and unloaded before dawn. On 2 February 1916, the Chancellor of the Exchequer, Lloyd George, and the Secretary of State for War, Lord Kitchener, were among those invited by Balfour as observers. The specification was the ability to cross a five-foot wide trench and climb a four-and-a-half-foot parapet, but Lord Kitchener insisted on taking a drive himself across a nine-foot wide trench. The tests were met without difficulty and orders were placed for fifty tanks to be put into immediate production.

In January Neville Chamberlain, in his new role as Director General of National Service, had announced the Military Service Act. After sixteen months of war, fear of a French defeat on the Western front had convinced the general staff of the need for national conscription – a move Kitchener had long been advocating. No longer would an able-bodied young man be allowed to guard the railways, join the St John Ambulance, work the land or sign up to the local branch of the Civic Guard. From March onwards it would be compulsory for fit, single men aged eighteen to forty-one to enlist in the armed forces unless they were engaged in vital war work or otherwise exempted. In May the call-up was extended to married men.

The Wilkinsons, back at their house in Letchworth Garden City, got in touch with William and invited themselves to tea. Arthur had no intention of volunteering for any form of duty, let alone joining the army, and considered it his right to disregard patriotic exhortations. If accosted in the street in his civilian clothes, assailed with white feathers and accused of cowardice, as he sometimes was, he robustly argued the case for pacifism, quoting Bertrand Russell. And Lily, oblivious of Eve's attempts to show off about the Volta House launch of Simmonds's puppets, was full of her own recent artistic success. She and Arthur had carved a new puppet family in Florence and returned with them, as their daughter later wrote, 'to cheer up the war lunatics'.

Almost immediately they had discovered Margaret Morris's theatre in Chelsea. Margaret Morris, London's answer to Isadora Duncan, was teaching and performing her new system of natural, expressive modern dance technique reconstructed from ancient Greek vases. She had also started a club, attached to her theatre, for a beleaguered circle of anti-war artists and writers. Here, the Wilkinsons had staged a puppet show with success and joined in open discussions and debates on conscientious objection and pacifism. It was the ideal meeting place for the determinedly optimistic Arthur and Lily, blithely detached as they were from the grim realities of war. As Margaret Morris put it in her memoirs: 'The first year of the war passed quickly, and did not affect us much … An occasional Zeppelin passed over, but we just carried on.'

If William's double life – working secretly for the military and openly as an artist – was a strain to him, it did not show. But his usually serene outlook on life temporarily deserted him. Chamberlain's announcement had come as a shock, awakening his conscience and forcing him to reassess what he was doing. Of course he was exempt by virtue of his war work; if necessary he could always produce his official Certificate of Exemption, and Crompton would confirm his value to the war effort. But to the outside world, which knew nothing of his secret work, his apparently peaceful office employment might raise eyebrows. Should he consider enlisting? Or should he, too, go abroad to help refugees or prisoners, as Alfred Powell was planning to do?

Out of the blue, Alfred had announced that he had signed up with the Quakers. He would leave for Holland to help teach Belgian refugees new means of earning a living. If he could not mirror the Wedgwoods' combination of patriotic military service and Liberal politics, at least he could follow their charitable lead. Besides, the ceramics business – now in the hands of Cecil Wedgwood's sister, Doris – was less active in the absence of the male family members, and now that William and Eve were ensconced in Volta House he felt less anxious at leaving Louise and his much-loved daughter Catherine. Having talked the future over with Eve, William decided to carry on. He knew that what they were achieving at Crompton's laboratory was more than enough justification to stay there.

* * * * * *

In February the German army launched a fearful assault on the French forts at Verdun in north-east France, and the resulting battle was to last for ten months and turned out to be the longest and most devastating of the First World War. In the spring there was a scare of invasion and trenches were dug to the east and south of London, but still London's musical and artistic life carried on. Eve went with Phyllis Barron to exhibitions in small rented galleries where many ex-Slade friends from the London Group, recently amalgamated with the Camden Town circle (of which Phyllis was a part), were showing their work. No longer able to portray battle as a noble patriotic sacrifice, these painters were striving to find new forms of expression. Paul Nash and Mark Gertler took on the subjugation of humanity to the new brutal instruments of modern warfare, tackling the ugliness of the front head on and imbuing it with its own kind of beauty.

The icon of the London Group was Richard Nevinson. He had taken what he needed from his pre-war obsession with Futurism and Vorticism to portray the transformation of man in battle. In his first war painting, *La Mitrailleuse* (The Machine-Gun), his images of French soldiers were of cold-blooded automatons engaged in blind, mechanised slaughter. At the private view of his one-man show at the Leicester Galleries in 1916, the paintings struck Eve with the same bleak force later felt by readers of Wilfred Owen's war poems.

To some of the traditional artists, the hallowed depictions of the glory of battle remained acceptable; the Academy exhibitions continued to reflect the orthodox themes of masculine courage and quiet domestic acceptance of grief. But not all Academicians felt able to follow the line. In private, George Clausen was painting his extraordinary *Youth Mourning* (inspired by the death of his daughter's fiancé in 1915), in which a luminous female nude crouches in foetal position in a muddy, bleak landscape. It was at once a lament for all the war dead, an intense evocation of mental agony and a powerful expression of the finality of death.

Another Academician, William Orpen, an Irishman of unusual sensitivity and the most established portraitist of the day, continued to produce conventional images of serving officers and heroines such as the nurse Edith Cavell, but his true interest lay in the faces of ordinary soldiers, compassionate and honest pictures in which the pain of the trenches was etched on their features. Of William's Academy friends, Shepard, no longer painting in oil, sketched soldiers in moments of rest amid the daily horrors of life at the front. He was to fight through the Battle of the Somme and was awarded a Military

Cross. At the end of the war he reflected that his troop duties had allowed him to send back only six cartoons for *Punch*.

Thanks to the extraordinary William Rothenstein, a Hampstead friend of the Powells, many of these artists would go to the front not as soldiers but as official war artists. Rothenstein had settled his family for the duration of the war in Iles Farm, close to the Powells' house in Gloucestershire. His German Jewish parents had instilled in him a respect for the culture of their forefathers (he himself had a perceptible accent) but he was an English patriot of the most romantic kind. He had refused to follow his brothers in anglicising his name to Rutherston.

In 1915 Rothenstein had gone on a brief, unofficial visit to the Belgian headquarters, four miles from the German lines at De Panne, to draw the Belgian King. Determined to get nearer the front, he had manoeuvered his way into the British war zone, passing through the town of Bailleul, close to Ypres. It was for him a seminal, almost mystical experience: 'Like a city of the dead … houses mere empty shells … livid, scarred with white wounds against a lowering sky … as though the great buildings felt the agony of approaching death … like witnessing the anguish of a stricken lion.' He was among the first to find visual poetry in a ruined building, a blasted tree and a desecrated landscape. Intensely moved by the courage of the soldiers and the impact of life near the trenches on the men and women waiting, preparing, suffering and celebrating, he vowed to tackle anyone in power who would listen and persuade them to send artists to the front to record the British role in the Great War.

He succeeded in his mission by bringing round the War Propaganda Bureau. Thanks to him a number of eminent writers became involved in promoting Britain's cause and a series of distinguished artists went to France, including Orpen, Tonks, Nash, Nevinson and, in 1917, Rothenstein himself.

Alfred Powell wrote from Holland that he had found the Quakers' war relief camp in Uden overflowing with Flemish refugees. His role was to build more huts from the quantities of equipment that had arrived from the London headquarters; he was also expected to teach carpentry and a taxing range of other crafts, such as boot-repairing, clog-making, woodcarving, raffia weaving for shoes, basketry, Gobelin tapestry needlework and language classes.

Louise put on a brave face about her husband's absence but Eve, not deceived, noticed that she was feeling bereft and increasingly exhausted, having to look after the three-year-old Catherine while fitting in her work, keeping open house for friends and acting as William's impresario.

Just before Alfred left, he had given the puppets a particularly big party and, as a farewell to William, scattered invitations far afield. Neither he nor Louise had noticed Bernard Shaw slipping in. The brusque letter that arrived four days later is evidence of the Powells' generosity, and perhaps also of Shaw's annoyance that no one had made a fuss of him.

> 5th April 1916.
> Dear Sir, I went to see the puppets, and missed the most important thing in a theatre: the pay box. I walked in; took the front seat; saw the show through; and no man took round the hat to me nor challenged me … The puppets were very dainty; but why all this humbug of illiteracy and vagabondism? … It is silly to waste so much labour on a joke. Take it seriously and try to make every bit of it pretty or witty; and something may come of it … The real puppet showmen [such as Clunn Lewis] are the most respectable vagabonds in the world, always striving for distinction … Unless educated people start from their highest level with the same strenuousness, the result can be nothing more than a lark … You cannot keep the thing up on such lines … Yours faithfully G. Bernard Shaw.

Alfred passed Shaw's letter on to William, who was ready for a critical analysis but not for this rather muddled rant. It was easy to see that Shaw was irritated, but hard to see what he was driving at. The implication that William's show was slapstick and falsely peasant-like was nonsense. William shared Shaw's admiration for Clunn Lewis, but he was also highly cultivated, as was Eve, and their creations bore no resemblance to Victorian farce. Nonetheless, he made subtle improvements to the dialogue. He felt no need to readjust the music: of that he was confident. The various versions of their repertoire had a number of fixed musical elements. 'Greensleeves' was always the overture. The sad and stiff old Pantaloon, who sat down with difficulty, always began with the mournful Elizabethan love song, 'Sweet Kate'. *The Harlequinade* opened with the first characters, Harlequin and Columbine, dancing in to 'Oranges and Lemons' accompanied by violin and spinet. William's *Pastorale*, with its gentle characters of Faun, Stag, Lamb and Shepherdess, opened with the dance-like

'Summer Icumen In' with its famous Cuckoo song, lifted by Eve from the earliest known medieval manuscript in rota, in which both religious and secular words were written to the same piece of music. The folk song 'Little Turtle Dove', discovered by Cecil Sharp, was another highlight of the piece.

Emery Walker, Chairman of the Art Workers' Guild, followed up a visit to a Volta House puppet show with a letter to Louise, offering William a marionette slot to perform in the Guild's new premises in Queen Square in June. He wanted to invite not only the usual contingent but also potential patrons 'because all of us who have seen the extraordinary beauty of [William's] figures are eager to let our friends share', adding in deference to Louise that it would be 'a rare occasion when ladies [will be] admitted to invade our tobacco smoke'.

Louise and Eve were determined to look their best – especially Eve. She would be invisible when accompanying William behind the scenes, but would be on show for the party afterwards, at which she would be meeting some of London's elegant cultural elite – including possible new cognoscenti, not only for the puppets but for William's sculpture. Moving as always with the times in her own subtle style, she had discarded her constricting full-length Edwardian dresses for a simpler line bearing the hallmarks of the 1920s. Her hemline now began to expose the calves and she had saved up for a pair of black silk stockings.

But how many people would come? After dusk the city disappeared into darkness. A blackout had been imposed earlier in the year and such few street lights as were lit were painted dark blue. The best prospect of finding one's way without mishap was when the moon broke through. And despite the improvement in London's defences, the Zeppelins had returned, navigating uncertainly to central London by the flickering reflections of the Thames.

If the Simmondses were nervous about the reception of their first professional performance, however, they need not have been. The hall of the Art Workers' Guild was packed and the audience, several of whom went backstage to examine the little creatures, were entranced. Even before they had life imparted to them by the puppet strings, the exquisite marionettes were seen as delicate works of art in their own right. The horrors of Verdun were held at bay, if only for an evening.

For William, a perfectionist, the contrast between practising with his friends and giving a public show on stage revealed how much he

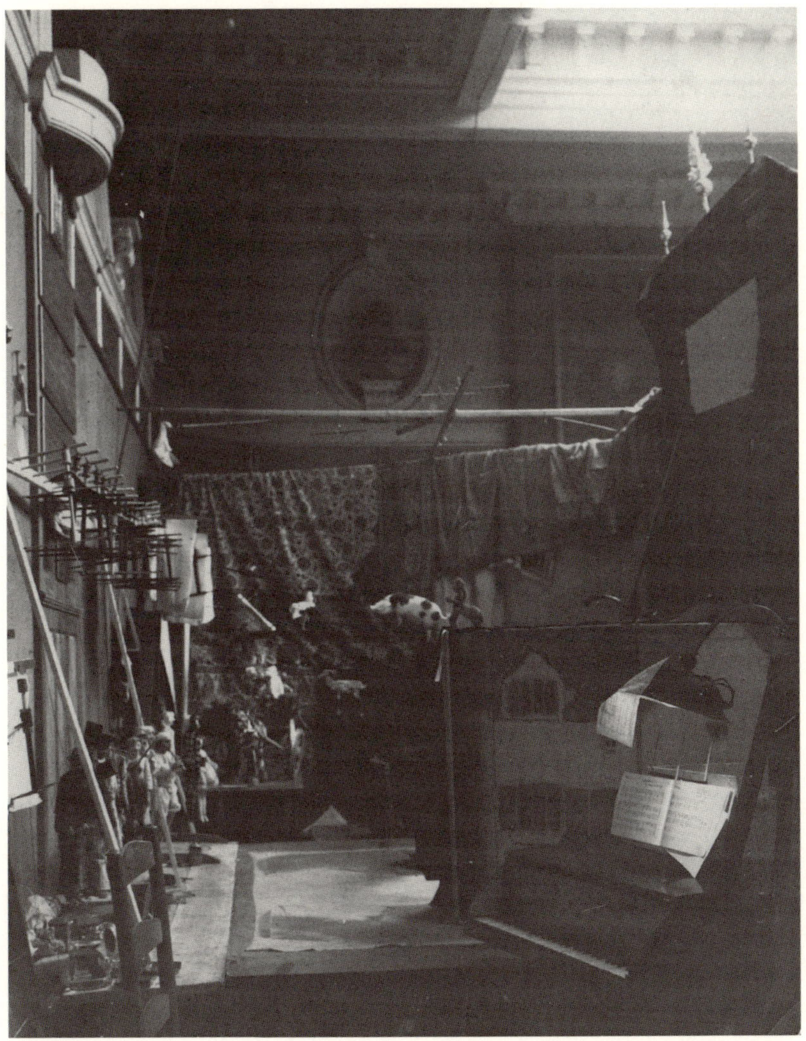

William's puppets performed at the Art Workers' Guild during the height of the First World War and again in 1922. Both performances were a sell out and had to be extended

still had to learn. Even with Eve performing by his side and an assistant at hand to pass each marionette, he was almost overwhelmed by the sheer complexity of the many-layered art to which he had set his hand. The characters had developed a life of their own, and it was not easy to make them submit to his will. In the effort to hold together simultaneously sculpture, strings, song, dance and words, while ignoring off-stage noise, tapping, coughing, sighing, roars, ringing bells and shifting painted backdrops, there was one aim only: to engage and work on the emotional imagination of the audience. Above all he must both adapt and improvise to suit what he found in the spectators on any given night.

Unaware of the effort and soul-searching involved, the audience was captivated. And Emery Walker's plan to invite potential patrons had worked. Charles St John Hornby, heir to the W.H. Smith chain, promptly booked William for a Christmas soireé in Shelley House, his palatial London home on the Embankment. Hornby had established a private press here, which the wartime paper shortage and rising production costs forced him to close, though not before he had produced enough fine print work to be accepted into the Arts and Crafts set. Other invitations began to pour through the Powells' letterbox for William. Would Mr Simmonds consider performing publicly at a London theatre? Would he care to give a private show in Cirencester for Lady Apsley? It was an unexpected way to arrive in the Guild's inner circle, but arrived he had.

In June Londoners' morale was further dented by Lord Kitchener's sudden death by drowning. His ship had gone down as he was on his way to shore up Russia's crumbling will to continue fighting. A month later, the British attack on the Somme was launched without his reassuring presence. Designed to draw off pressure from Verdun, the Battle of the Somme proved equally catastrophic. The casualties on both sides were horrific: over one-and-a-half million men, many of them blown to shreds and impossible to identify. These appalling losses and the complete lack of progress against the German lines convinced General Haig that any hope of victory must rely on the tank. If successful, a tank attack could revive confidence in the ranks and turn the tables on the Germans. He doubled the original order, demanding that the machines be ready by 1 September. Frantically working at the laboratory on modifications, William was astonished to meet his old teacher Solomon J. Solomon again; Haig, with characteristic attention to detail, had him appointed as a special adviser on camouflage.

Foster's industrial workforce worked on the tank in secret night and day, struggling to meet Haig's deadline, incurring suspicions that they were not doing their bit for the country. (Haig would later pay handsome tribute to them and award them war service medals.) The French, who were building a smaller and lighter tank, were less advanced and as 1 September drew near, they asked for a delay, on the grounds that the impact of a massive combined Anglo-French surprise onslaught would be decisive. Haig, however, stuck to his decision. Winter was approaching without any appreciable success and his tanks could make the difference between defeat and victory in the final stages of the Battle of the Somme. On the night of 1 September, with enormous difficulty owing to their weight and size, fifty vast tanks were loaded on to trains at Thetford Station, their hulls marked deceptively in cyrillic script 'Petrograd – With Care'. Five times they were unloaded and reloaded during transit as they crossed from Avonmouth to Le Havre to reach Abbeville behind the line.

On 15 September, thirty-nine of the tanks went into battle at Flers-Courcelette on the Somme. Only nine of them made it across the craters of no man's land. Out of nowhere, these huge monsters slowly lurched forward, smashing through barbed wire, careering up, over and through the trenches, mowing down troops and scattering cavalry, the horses bolting and falling. Secrecy had been watertight. The enemy was astonished and terrified. Three days later Haig told d'Eyncourt: 'We have made the greatest victory since the Battle of the Marne. We have taken more prisoners and more territory with comparatively fewer casualties. This is due to the tanks.' Despite their frequent breakdowns, he immediately ordered another 1,000.

In Crompton's Kensington office, the sense of relief at a mission accomplished was tinged with regret: the French were probably right and that Haig's tanks had been deployed on too small a scale and before their reliability under battlefield conditions had been properly honed. The final modifications for the next generation of tanks were under way.

William had been working out of hours on several small pieces of sculpture. Now that he was a fully recognised member of the Arts and Crafts crowd, he had been invited to submit his work for an exhibition at Burlington House in the autumn of 1916. This ambitious venture was engineered by the new President of the Arts and Crafts Exhibition Society, Henry Wilson, who had taken over after Walter Crane's death the previous year. To put on an event of this scale in wartime was demanding enough, but to overcome the Royal

Academy's antipathy to all that the society stood for, as well as find-ing independent backing for it (Hornby on the finance committee must have helped), called for someone of rare determination and imagination. Wilson was the very man for the challenge; he was a true visionary and had boundless enthusiasm and an immense range of artistic interests. Apprenticed in his youth to Alfred Powell's old boss, the architect J.D. Sedding, he moved on to metal work, jew-ellery, sculpture and church plate – all of which and more would be reflected in the twenty large and small galleries at Burlington House. His own pieces, of course, were included throughout but spe-cial prominence was given to the Cotswold artists – the Powells and Barnsleys, Charles Gere, William Rothenstein and Ernest Gimson – several of whom assumed responsibility for the exhibition's layout and construction. To keep the peace with the 83-year-old Poynter as guardian of the Academy's traditional values, Wilson included two RA artists, Clausen and Sargent.

William was to submit woodcarvings, drawings and watercolours to be distributed in three separate rooms alongside the work of the most respected artists. Louise was asked to take on the design for one of the rooms. How she would manage with Catherine constantly with her was a problem but, leaving aside the prestige of being given space for her own work, she needed the money. She persuaded Alfred to take leave from Uden for a fortnight in July and they managed between them to prepare eleven of her eight-foot six-inch by three-foot six-inch panels. On returning to the camp he wrote to his brother Edgar of having had 'a strenuous time slaving away'. He was proud of Louise but worried for her and pleaded for help:

> to make it easier for Lalla to pull along. She has had a hard time of it to make all of it go and keep above water and keep Catherine flourishing and happy ...
>
> If only you could tell her how well she has done and does all she has to do. It would startle most and to be with her and watch her teaching Catherine day by day is a liberal education for anyone. It is all so true and perfectly connected. A chain of progressing which lives in the little creature's mind and does not fade or get lost. But it takes a lot out of Lalla – write her a happy letter and think of her, she so likes to to be remembered and thought of by others – and herself thinks of everyone – helping where she can.

Edgar duly wrote the letter and a month later Louise replied:

> It is to be a very big and important show. I have done a lot of
> work. It is a national effort to stimulate our trade and encourage
> our industries – and I only hope it will do so. Alfred and I have
> decorated a room which has been rather an undertaking but hope
> will be a success. Alfred might have short leave to come over and
> help finish up but I may have to manage myself.

William could only get off to help on Sundays, but Eve began to
share Louise's burden. The staging of the show flirted with disaster;
Wilson had not taken into account the constraints after two years of
a war that showed no signs of ending. Burlington House's high glass
ceilings were a perfect target for Zeppelin attacks as their size and
height made them impossible to black out. In the early hours of 3
September, at 2.15 in the morning, Eve was awakened by a giant fire
storm in the sky. She got out of bed and watched in shocked silence
as a massive burning airship fell slowly over Hertfordshire, north
of Hampstead. A British plane, armed with a deadly new mixture
of explosive and incendiary ammunition, had shot it down. Amid
scenes of jubilation, 10,000 Londoners would visit the site to see the
mangled metal carcass. But for Eve, pity for the hideous slow death
of the helpless crew outweighed any feelings of joy at the victory over
an enemy.

Setting up the galleries had to stop at dusk, and with autumn
approaching the hours of productive work diminished each day. With
barely any professional workmen to help, Louise, fighting against
time, began to feel, even with Eve's help, that she was losing the battle.
In the end, however, they managed to get the job done by conscripting
a batch of enthusiastic but inexperienced female art students.

Press Day was postponed by a week, but that was not enough to
prevent scenes of frantic disorder, with few of the exhibits properly
assembled. William saw to his dismay that in one of the three rooms
with his woodcarvings, it was so dark that people could barely see
the tiny objects on display. There was nothing he could do about it.
Regulations prevented the galleries being lit by artificial light and any
glimmer of natural light had been dimmed by a hideous white fabric
screening, dingy and soot-stained from London's winter pollution.

When, after yet another week of delay, the general public was
finally allowed in, there was no catalogue. The printers had failed

to complete the layout on time. This, however, had its advantages. Wilson was able to insert into his introduction a *cri de coeur* from a soldier who had already visited the exhibition: 'Thank God there are people in England who care for these things. After the War it will be too late. It Must be Done Now.' His last five words caught the head-lines and became the slogan of the cause.

In the end the exhibition was a huge success. The early chaos was forgiven and forgotten by sympathetic newspaper editors and journalists, who were highly complimentary about the retrospective gallery displaying the movement's father figures: William Morris, Edward Burne-Jones and Walter Crane, and the small room contain-ing Arnold Dolmetsch's reconstructions of ancient instruments. All the murals were praised except for William Rothenstein's *Academic Procession to Confer a Degree on an Unknown Soldier*, a forty-foot by ten-foot memorial to those from British universities who had lost their lives. This was coolly demolished, as was Roger Fry's Omega Workshop display.

Gimson, who had a long-standing following and had been exhib-iting in the Arts and Crafts Exhibitions since the 1890s, was singled out from the rest of the Gloucestershire crowd as the presiding genius who 'lived in a house situated at the bottom of a valley of almost unbelievable beauty … in the village of Sapperton by a windy cor-ner of the Thames and Severn canal … One of Gimson's dreams for the future is that it would be re-populated and our waterways used for the carriage of village-made wares to the towns.' Louise Powell's room was beatified: 'executed in panels of egg tempera, conveyed … a magical evocation of spring', as was her furniture: 'exquisite painted ebony and walnut cabinet was perhaps in retrospect the star exhibit, built with the help of the Guild's revered Sidney Barnsley.'

With good reviews virtually everywhere, the public flocked to the exhibition. There was a visit from the Queen and Princess Mary. The first wave of excitement seemed over in late October, when out of the blue Louise showed William an article she had discovered in the *Observer* in which the critic identified William's pieces as 'far and away the best on display … Many of the exhibits are remarkable but nothing quite reaches the standard of W.G. Simmonds …'

Alfred had not come back to help finish the Powell Room, nor did it look likely he would return for Christmas. Anxiously he tried once more to enlist help from his brother:

These days are rather disturbing the pros and cons of the war and the peace proposals. No one seems to know whether Holland is coming into the war – and all seem to think it not unlikely. We have 200–300 Belgians to entertain for xmas including children. I wonder if you have been to see Lalla [Louise] at all lately. I find it difficult to know exactly how she is situated for money. I send her cheques but they don't always get to her. – please put £20 in bank for me for her. I will pay you when back. Do you mind? Just sort of find out when you go …

William, too, was about to be precariously short of money. He had not quite taken in that his Crompton job would soon come to an end, but now it had. His only other source of income, Nelson & Sons, had lost much manpower to the front and its foreign markets were now closed. But when in December he handed in his last colour plate to his editor, he felt a sense of relief. The constricted manner in which he was painting had become stultifying to him. Indeed painting at all, however much Eve encouraged him, was something he now wanted to abandon. Sculpting was his consuming passion; but he would have to see the war out before he could make it his career. In the meantime he must look for new war work. His earlier doubts had passed, and he knew where his obligation lay. With the pace of developments in mechanical engineering, firms were crying out for highly skilled technical draughtsmen, so he felt reasonably confident that he would find an interesting position. Meanwhile, wherever he went he would always carry with him a piece of ivory or carefully selected wood to work on.

CHAPTER 11

War Work for De Havilland

1917–1918

*'Lethaby tells me what we have to aim at now is
"Strength to exist, with generosity" in which lies much
help … oh Edgar what a complicated coil it all is.'*
Alfred Powell, letter to his brother, London, October 1917

The pervasive sense of gloom in the new year of 1917 was intensified by the icy weather. The thermometer never rose above freezing, it snowed constantly and the relentless thick black February fog surpassed anything Londoners could remember. William was sad to part company with Colonel Crompton and Legros but, as he had expected, he soon found new work. An old friend from the National Art Training School days, Reginald Wells, was looking for an engineering draughtsman. William had known him there as a dedicated sculptor, a year below him, though his last bulletin on Wells was that he was working creatively in a multitude of disciplines: making bronze figures, studying architecture and setting up his own independent pottery studio. It now turned out that he had also become an entrepreneur and inventor, having recently turned his hand to aircraft design. Behind the scenes, somewhat to the mockery of friends and family, he had spent solitary hours in peacetime designing and building models of flying machines. When war broke out, he had realised his ambition to construct a full-size operational plane, converting his pottery company into a factory – Wells Aviation Co. – on an acre-and-a-half of wasteland he had developed in Chelsea.

On arriving for his interview, William found an assortment of buildings housing 1,600 employees, with workshops, saw pits and a timber yard holding stacks of seasoned ash wood. There was an inescapable hum from the woodturning machines that produced fuselages and wing struts – all wooden in the planes of the time. The War Department breathed down their necks with insistent requests for better performing aircraft and increased output, and the work was under strain. William's skill as an expert draughtsman was especially needed on the DH-4, named after the initials of its designer Geoffrey de Havilland. Planes were still in their infancy, having been flown a mere six years before the beginning of the war, but as early as 1914 the military had already been pressing for improved reconnaissance aircraft to direct artillery fire and pinpoint the position of the enemy's reserves. By the time William joined Wells in early March 1917 several prototypes of machines, much faster and safer than their predecessors and now carrying guns, had been developed and were in production. Here, too, the company would issue William with a Scheduled Occupation Certificate to exempt him from being called up.

To reach Chelsea from Hampstead on public transport was a long haul and increasingly difficult. Petrol was banned for private cars, which disappeared from the streets. The poorly serviced motor buses broke down frequently, causing delays while the engine was cranked up with a large, stiff handle, and the overcrowded daily ordeal of rush hour brought out the worst in people. Hats were knocked off, umbrellas broken and feet trodden on, people shoved, punched and kicked in the crush. Little respect was shown even to the disabled.

Conscription was now taking a heavy toll on munitions production, and yet another national appeal went out. With a desperate need for shells, Howitzers, machine guns and anti-aircraft guns, the government had no choice but to call on women to swell the industrial workforce. A quarter of a million women a year were recruited to the arms factories, which advertised crèches for babies, peaceful gardens, hospitals, canteens – and better pay than many soldiers received, though working men earned more. Headlines cheered them on: 'The Lady of the Lamp Will Fuel the Power of British Artillery' and 'Shells Made by a Wife to Save a Husband's Life'.

Finally Eve responded in her own way. She volunteered as a nurse at the Kensington War Hospital surgical supply depot, which was described in *Punch* as 'a power for good' with 'ingenious adaptability' shown and 'quiet efficiency' in the production and distribution of vital materials, such as bandages, swabs, crutches and splints.

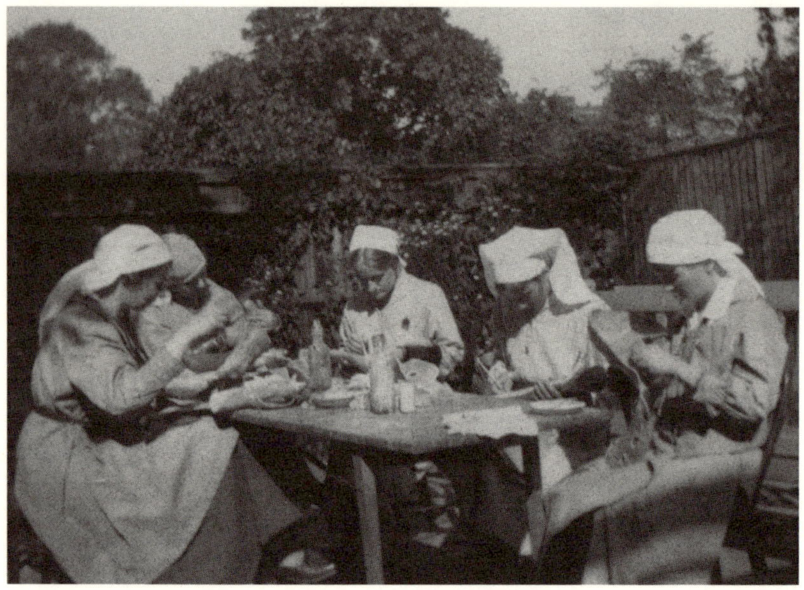

Eve (second right) took on war work at the Kensington War Hospital, 1917

Adding to the misery of travel, the cold continued into spring, which saw a late fall of snow. There was an acute shortage of coal, with the miners periodically on strike and London's supplies requisitioned by every department of war. Chilled to the bone, William would return to the Volta House panelled sitting room to warm himself by the fire, which Eve only lit in the evenings. When the coalshed's meagre stock finally ran out, no more could be had for love nor money.

Eve had long ago allotted herself the role of housekeeper-in-chief, making it her priority to produce enough food for William's evening meal, and of course for Louise and Catherine when they were at home. Prices had doubled since 1914; there were shortages in the basic essentials and queues formed for the first time in butchers and green grocers. Potatoes disappeared altogether and the bread on sale was a strange grey-brown colour – though Eve characteristically saw its flour's high grain content as healthy and made something of a name for herself with her homemade recipe. Sugar was so hard to find that she had to cut down her annual batch of preserves to a few jars. There was no question of fruit and vegetables from their Fovant cottage, where the garden was a lost cause. But Alfred Powell had rented an allotment up the road on the heath and Eve kept it up – never digging – but planting as many vegetables as the space allowed.

In March the news of fearful casualty lists and the overthrow of Britain's ally Tsar Nicholas of Russia was mitigated by two acts of extraordinary German folly. Kaiser Wilhelm decided to allow his submarines to attack all shipping, including neutral American vessels; and British codebreakers decrypted a secret message from Berlin offering Mexico aid to recapture Texas after the war if it joined the Central Powers now as an ally against France and Britain.

As a result, the United States, which until then had been neutral, declared war on Germany in April. This unexpected event caused a sudden surge of optimism and London seized its chance to celebrate. The Union Jack and the Stars and Stripes were hoisted together on Mansion House. At every corner American flags went on sale for buttonholes and a thanksgiving service was held in St Paul's Cathedral. Within weeks the city seemed to fill with Americans. American troops paraded through London, marching past the King and taking the salute at Buckingham Palace. It was common knowledge that America was militarily unprepared, but the sight brought renewed hope that victory might be only just over the horizon.

Meanwhile, Alfred had not returned from Belgium. In April he had taken fright at a warning of 'very considerable risk' of being torpedoed or captured, but in the end he had stayed on. His work was still somewhat mundane; he had progressed to teaching woodcarving, weaving and chair-making, and there were compensations such as being taken to Amsterdam to hear Bach's *St Matthew's Passion*. He wrote desultorily that each day he wished he could see Louise. His letters to Catherine were filled with drawings of birds and beasts but he wondered whether the censors might be suspicious.

William had had no idea when he started work at Wells Aviation Co. how precarious its financial condition was. The cost of holding stocks of raw materials, parts and half-finished airframes – let alone the expense of developing the Chelsea site – had strained the company's balance sheet. The creditors were pressing and the Treasury had better priorities than to keep Wells going by extending its loan. Within two months William sensed bankruptcy in the air and started looking elsewhere.

Colonel Crompton and Lucien Legros stepped in, recommending him to the aircraft designer de Havilland personally. The first

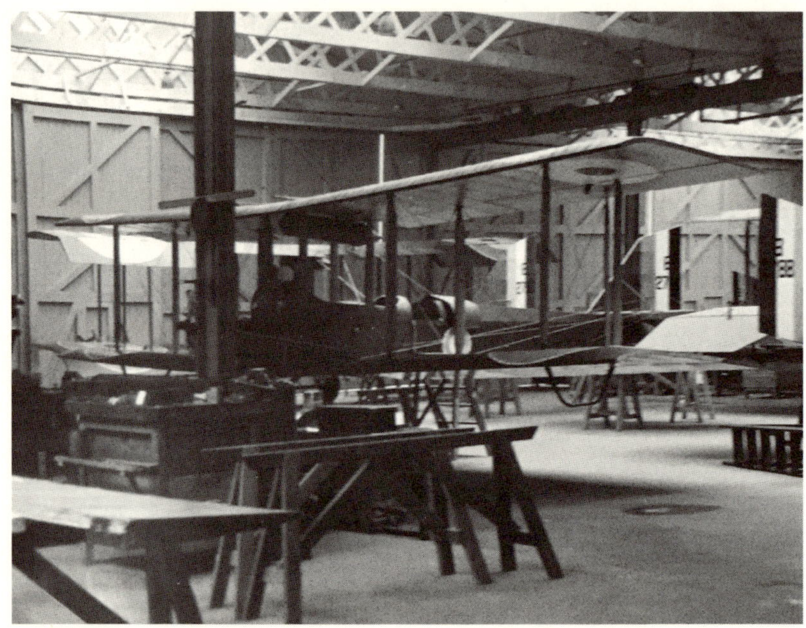

The De Havilland factory in Hampstead where William worked, 1917

Englishman to build and test-pilot a plane, de Havilland was already a legend. His FE-1 had been purchased by the War Office in 1912 as soon as it proved airworthy, and in 1914 he had been snapped up as Chief Designer by the newly founded manufacturer Airco. Success followed success, first with the BE-2, the Royal Flying Corp's principal aircraft at the start of the war, and later with the DH series, on which William had worked at Wells. William was taken on initially on a trial basis and assigned to Farman Airplanes and Seaplanes, an Anglo-French firm with a licensed production facility beside the de Havilland factory at Hendon. In the first week of June, after only a few days in the job, he was called in to the main office by de Havilland himself, who explained that his staff of designers, stress mathematicians, draughtsmen, test pilots and managers consisted of a mere seventy-two men and that the work would be strenuous. Long hours of effort would be involved in the race against his rival Anton Fokker, the young Dutch designer leading the German fight for supremacy in the air. If William could handle the pressure, a position was available in the Technical Department's experimental office at £3 a week.

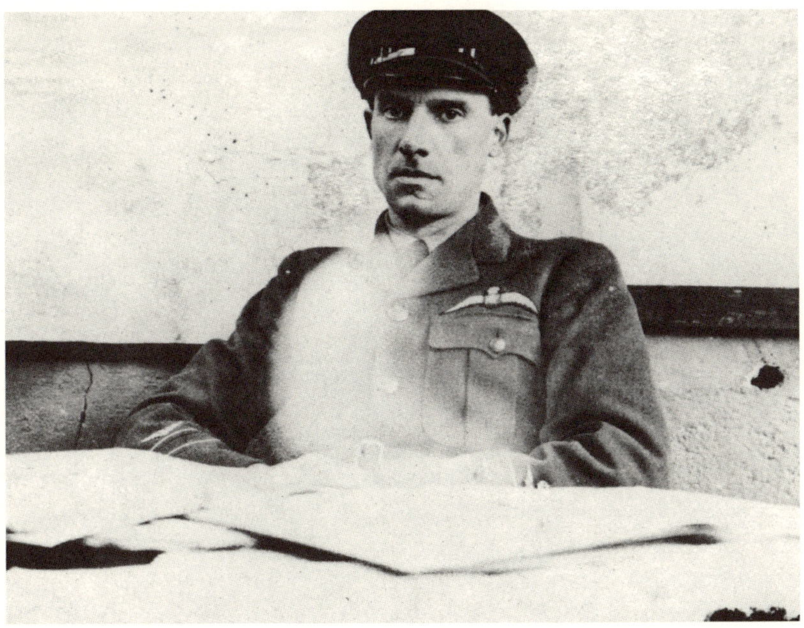

William's personal Kodak photograph of his boss, Sir Geoffrey de Havilland, 1918

Plunged immediately into a hectic schedule, William nevertheless found time to write thanking Colonel Crompton, who replied somewhat condescendingly with his congratulations:

Crompton Laboratory,
Thriplands, Kensington Court,
London W8
June 16 1917

My Dear Simmonds,
… I think on the whole you are to be congratulated … not the least point being that the works of the aircraft manufacturing company at which you are now engaged cannot be very far from your house in Hampstead.

I am very glad you think your time at Thriplands laboratory and drawing office has taught you something. I think the benefit was mutual. You did valuable work for me and have had the good fortune to get in confidence with Legros which no doubt has been the cause of his being able to procure a suitable post for you. When I think of the large number of men of considerable parts and skill who are engaged on quite unsuitable work I think you are to be congratulated.

Yours sincerely, R.E. Crompton

William charitably ascribed Crompton's tone to the fact that he was no longer at the epicentre of affairs; responsibility for developing the tank had been transferred to the manufacturers. De Havilland was now the rising star. The DH series was now focused on the DH-4, a single engine fighter-bomber and reconnaissance aircraft that proved Britain's – and later the United States' – most versatile and effective military plane. It had been delivered in March. By the end of the war de Havilland's Airco had produced thirty per cent of all Britain's and America's planes, the great majority of them versions of the DH-4, many built in the United States.

Getting to work was now infinitely less disagreeable. There was as yet no underground that far, but in spite of occasional cancellations because of petrol shortage, William was usually able to take the no. 2 omnibus at a stop outside Hampstead Heath Railway Station. On a fine day he would walk the forty-five minutes to Hendon across open country, reflecting with some pride that his work was contributing to London's defences. Since the spring, as the weather eased, upgraded Zeppelins had renewed their attacks, now supported by a new heavy bombing plane, the Gotha. On 13 June, William narrowly missed the bombing of Highbury that obliterated one of his regular omnibuses.

The puppets were still in demand from private patrons – up to a point. After several postponements, the Powells' country neighbour, Lady Apsley, determined she would not be put off by the blackouts and the fear of air raids and would go ahead with a performance for her London house, 'in a fairly small room'. William was becoming more professional. He had worked on more scenes and offered a two-hour performance for a fee of £60, to include himself, an assistant (to pass the puppets), a musician and the set up of the stage. If a shorter performance of an hour was wanted, he had another show with glove puppets. The music was of course an important part of the show. As his scripts evolved he inserted more compositions into the marionettes' songs – jigs, lullabies and soldiers' ballads from Cecil Sharp's collection of folk songs – supplanting some of his original Dolmetsch portfolio.

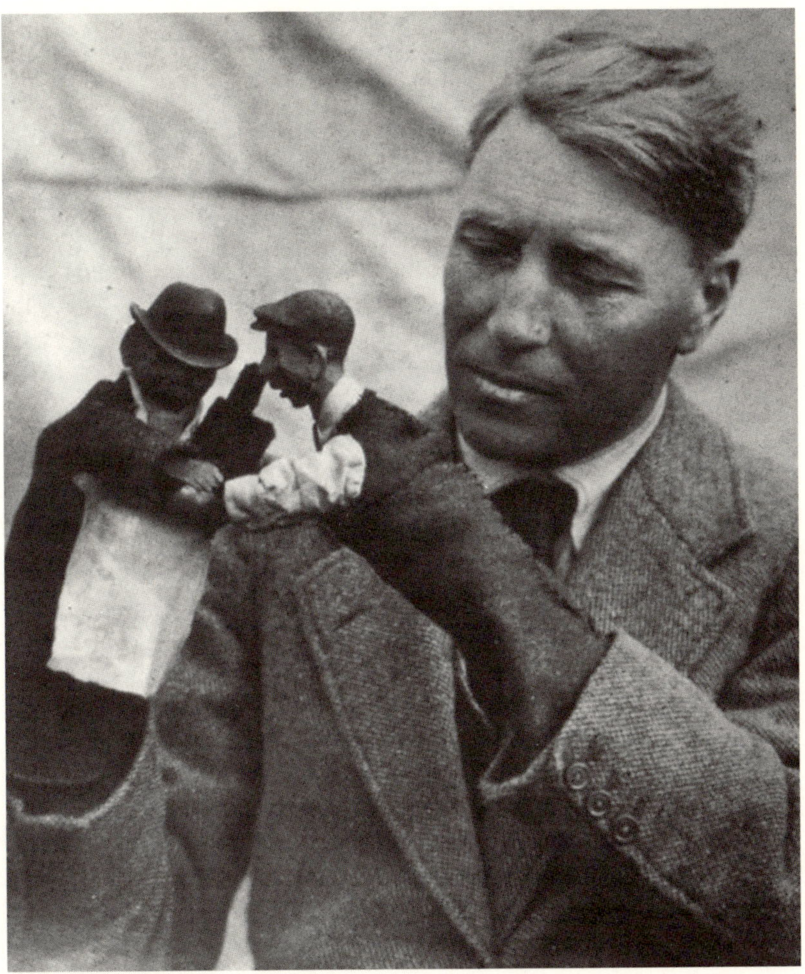

William with glove puppets 'on the road' in Somerset

That people found solace in the magic of William's marionettes – in these painted creatures expressing themselves in gesture, song and word – was not as strange as it might seem. Men and women indeed sought out light-hearted musicals like *Chu Chin Chow*, but were thirsting too for the catharsis that classical music brings. In the intimacy of the drawing room, they came to hear chamber music by the cream of the Belgian violinists, cellists and pianists who had flooded London to seek refuge, or by the harpsichordist Violet

Gordon Woodhouse's interpretation of Scarlatti, Bach and the early music discovered by Dolmetsch. People came on a scale unknown before the war to hear the Hallé Orchestra, the London Symphony, the Royal Philharmonic or the Beecham Opera Company, led by the people's favourite conductor Sir Thomas Beecham.

At the front, the grimmest struggle yet was unfolding. The German army, reinforced by troops released from the collapsing Russian front, planned to break the British army before the half-trained Americans were ready to come into the line. The French army was dissolving into mutiny and Britain was close to strangulation by U-boats operating from Belgian ports. Haig determined on a pre-emptive strike at Ypres. The rupture by shellfire of all the drainage systems, combined with unprecedented heavy rain, produced a massive quicksand of mud, in which soldiers and horses drowned and tanks sank. The British casualties in what became known as Passchendaele have never been established, but are thought to have totalled more than 250,000. Haig gained five miles and recorded the battle, which lasted three months, as a victory.

William felt uneasily conscious that his own contribution to the war effort was devoid of danger. Even if he had not lost any of his friends at the front, anxiety and a sense of guilt unsettled him. Galleries drew the suffering into their orbit, offering spiritual comfort and reflection – especially now that some of the exhibiting artists were at the front in an official role. Nevinson's work was no longer in the limelight. After obtaining Official War Artist status he spent a month in the summer of 1917 sketching, but this time well behind the lines, or as a passenger on a plane flying on reconnaissance missions. His artist's vision had softened, as if detached from the war zone.

It was Nevinson's friend, Paul Nash, who would take centre stage. He had fought in the trenches in Flanders and was now on his way to Ypres as a war artist, determined to get as close to the action as he could. His images of suffering were closely connected to his love for England's countryside and the natural world. For him, as for Rothenstein, the experience of nature was something almost mystical; in his paintings he portrayed nature despoiled and devoured in a landscape of bleeding, devastated trees and disembowelled hills. To William, as to others, his paintings supplied a perverse nourishment, a response too deep for words to the tragedy through which a once civilised continent was living.

When the Powells were away, Saturdays at the Wilkinsons could be an antidote to depression. Arthur and Lily's conversation was self-centred and fiercely cheery, and their attitude to day-to-day life ebullient. Surrounded by non-judgmental neighbours, they lived in the Garden Suburb as in a world apart. Founded on cooperative community principles, the new town was a haven for their brand of social idealism; along with nearby Letchworth Garden City, it had the highest proportion of conscientious objectors in the country.

There were other intervals of relative calm and moments of light relief between periods of intense work at de Havilland's. Mostly they were provided, in lunch or tea breaks, by William's friend Adrian Comper, like him a recent arrival. Adrian Comper was the son of Sir Ninian Comper, one of the last of the great Gothic Revival architects. Part of Comper's role was to assist the test pilots by recording the performance of planes under various loads. His task was to lean over the side of the gunner's cockpit with stopwatch in hand, noting on a small clipboard the time it took from shooting and revving the engine to the wheels leaving the grass – and then the time to climb each multiple of 1,000 feet. Comper himself was a qualified pilot and laughed off his work as simple. To William it seemed extremely dangerous.

One day Comper took to the air with the ace stunt pilot, B.C. Hucks, to test the ability of the latest version of the DH-4 to with-stand the stress of a new type of high-speed combat manoeuvre. It was William's job to check whether the output of his department was being compromised under the strain of coping with the flood of new design concepts. No sooner were they airborne than Hucks began a violent display of aerobatics, testing the plane's structural strength to the limit. Centrifugal forces alone kept Comper's stopwatch in hand in the gunner's seat. He saw the earth flashing around in every direc-tion and felt himself floating in mid air. As the plane neared stalling speed, to William's intense relief, Comper was able to grab the sides and prevent himself from falling out.

Watching the drama in the air, William became horrified as splin-ters of varnished wood exploded in all directions until it seemed that the plane would disintegrate. He never quite shrugged off the memory of the debacle. But Hucks managed a brilliant landing from which, as usual, he emerged smiling and unscathed, undisturbed by the flight. The episode had been far more alarming for the ground staff and the top-hatted spectators than for Comper and Hucks.

On 9 July Alfred at last returned to London, transported in a flotilla of '10 boats and a naval escort from the Hook to Harwich', to find 'all well at Volta House'. In truth all was not so well. From early spring Gothas and Zeppelins had continued dropping their bombs whenever the wind was favourable. Two days before his return, family and friends had undergone 'the Great Battle for London'. In broad daylight, twenty Gothas had appeared in the morning sky over London, surrounded by irregular British fighters above and below them breaking up the attackers' formation just over Marble Arch. Liverpool Street was hit hard and falling British shrapnel was also responsible for a good deal of damage. Over the months crowds had settled into the tunnels whether there was a raid or not. The sanitary conditions consisted of buckets of sand and a 'canvas decency screen' erected where possible. Only now were decisions taken to coordinate public warnings and organise more systematic defences; when two weeks later rumours (for once correct) came that the Germans planned to set London ablaze with night-time raids, police and fire brigade stations were ready. They fired their own guns, blew whistles and attached 'Take Cover' notices on bicycles and cars. For the 'All Clear', police rang hand bells and boy scouts sounded bugle calls.

Alfred, having been away for over a year living under relatively easy conditions, was shocked by the London life Louise and his friends had endured. There were shortages of what seemed like everything – meat, bacon, tea, margarine, butter and cheese. His ebullient optimism drained away and gave place to something like anger. He threw himself into finding work, rising each morning at 5.30. His first commission was helping Lutyens with his plans for New Delhi. At the same time he joined a committee to establish a village settlement for wounded soldiers, where he could advise on training disabled men for work and building their homes. He foresaw the bombing of historic village buildings and set his heart on making a register of early English and Welsh cottages 'to save them from unnecessary destruction by rabid re-housers wanting "jobs"'.

September saw nine Gotha raids, which killed fourteen people. Morale succumbed to the relentless destruction of London's buildings; shops were looted. One evening William and Eve heard guns in the distance; the sound of firing came nearer and nearer, followed by the crash of bombs, shrieking shells and the roar of airplanes. Then an eerie echoing sound and more guns blazing from Regent's Park. It did not stop. 'We had such a night of it,' wrote Alfred:

with the guns on the Heath crashing away at some unseen humming Hun and making all our midnight windows rattle and
walls to tremble. Lalla [Louise] woke me to say there is a raid
on and don't be frightened – so we looked out o' windows and
heard machine guns high overhead, (like popguns in the chimney), bombs falling far off – guns going all around, and every now
and then the deafening crash of the one at the Stone Pond, 200
yards or so away. Then it stopped and in an hour began again to
the same infernal (or supernal!) humming that seemed it would
never pass. Then in 10 minutes we were all asleep again. Catherine asked what we said it so loud for – half awakened and soon
asleep again … she is beginning to talk French to herself now.

After the war was over, Eve related how the returning tenants of the
other semi-detached part of Volta House had found a bomb. It had
fallen through the roof 'and it had only failed to explode because
it had lodged in the wire mattress of the bed. William and I were
alongside!'

The Dolmetsches had had enough. Terrified, they left London
to take sanctuary in a friend's empty house in Surrey. Their valuable instruments were safe, and within months Dolmetsch bought a
house in Haslemere where he established the workshop from where
he would teach, hold concerts and make instruments for the rest of
his life.

But William's morale did not crack, even when Bloomsbury was hit
on 1 October, provoking the evacuation of hundreds of Londoners.

CHAPTER 12

When the Fighting Stops

1918

*'I came to the conclusion that no country with a
large population of Quakers would be able to hold
its own against other countries, but that a small number
to hold up good, though almost impossible, ideals before
us are a strength to a country.'*
Christiana Herringham, letter to Alice Rothenstein, 1907

As 1918 opened, the unthinkable, unutterable possibility loomed that the country was indeed on the brink of defeat. The German High Command had launched a violent spring offensive, reinforced by more troops released from the East after the surrender of Russia. A million shells rained down on the British lines and the trench line was broken. Berlin's propaganda machine began to celebrate victory.

For those reading the news aghast in London, the crisis was revealed when the press printed a communique from the Commander-in-Chief of the British Army in the West, Sir Douglas Haig:

Every position must be held to the last man: there must be no retirement. With our backs to the wall and believing in the justice of our cause each one of us must fight on to the end. The safety of our homes and the freedom of mankind alike depend upon the conduct of each one of us at this critical moment.

People walked the streets in a daze. How could it be that after three-and-a-half years of Allied 'victories' and terrible enemy losses, Germany could still manage to mount this devastating, and perhaps conclusive, attack? All the sacrifice endured would count for nothing. Once more the guns were close enough to be heard clearly from France. Disaster suddenly seemed a real possibility.

The government's response was to recruit yet more men for the army and to keep munitions at maximum output. The workers at de Havilland's agreed to forgo their Easter bank holiday, giving up their traditional Monday on Hampstead Heath (see plate 4). Conscription now would include all men up to the age of fifty-one; every available horse was requisitioned for the front.

To fund Britain's huge military expenditure and ever-growing debt, the government capitalised on the tanks' recent success to issue national war bonds. William discovered a battle-scarred tank squatting in Trafalgar Square serving as the office for the 'Tank Bank' campaign. The sight of the extraordinary object caught everyone's imagination; a month later more battered objects, romanticised with their frontline nicknames such as Crusty, Egbert and Perfect Lady, went on display all over London. Soldiers brought military pigeons to the houses of those who wanted to invest. Their applications were placed in a metal holder and fastened to the bird's leg, whereupon the pigeon took off on its 'postal service' back to Trafalgar Square. Unable to resist the charming sales pitch, William bought a £5 bond. He kept it for over twenty years before cashing it in.

* * * * * *

Meanwhile Alfred was busy with his commission for New Delhi as well as preparing for his and Louise's ceramics exhibition to be held in early spring at the Alpine Gallery. But work was not enough to calm him; he moaned to his brother:

> if we don't end the war it will end us – I hear that 'we' think that if we can hold the Germans for a few more weeks they will come to terms. I don't believe it but that's a report from those who are supposed to know something. I am still digging up an allotment on Hampstead Heath – 3/4hrs each week-end. I have put some shallots and some potatoes in and rhubarb and artichokes.

William believed his friend Rothenstein much more than he did the papers. Rothenstein had been sent to the front as a war artist and suddenly found himself in the hottest place of the conflict; any thought of his recording the war as an artist had vanished. The spiritual experience he had three years earlier at Péronne near the Somme had been replaced by a sense of desperation.

During the horrendous bombardment in March he wrote to Alice:

> I am hard at it day and night helping nurses as well as I can … looking after the crowded wards. Never as long as I live shall I forget these days … can't think of drawing now, while I can be of the least service, and people keep pouring in … from the bombardment … you will know much more of these things than me [from press reports] … keep from the beloved children any such sights as I have to look on while they live.

Soon afterwards all war artists were ordered home. In May Alfred took William to Rothenstein's exhibition of gouaches 'On the Péronne Front' at the Goupil Gallery. It was a sell out. The work, conceived in 1915, laid bare his vision of the austere beauty and desolation of war: 'Truth to tell', he was to tell William later,

> [at that time] I never valued life more highly than during the weeks spent in making those records … I wanted to draw … with the care of a van Eyck. Every hour spent in drawing was an hour given to a sacred task. My soldier friends could not understand what appeared to them unnatural industry, and that I dreaded recall.

* * * * * *

Phyllis Barron continued to work harder than ever. She had mastered the techniques and chemistry of natural dyeing. Her breakthrough had come in 1917 when Ethel Mairet promoted her work in the Hampstead drawing room of the Russian emigré artist Boris Anrep. This was one of the favoured gathering places of the Bloomsbury crowd and thus ideal for finding a discerning following. Eve, the first to arrive at the opening, had immediately set the ball rolling by buying a length of cloth from an early experiment with French blocks, a design Barron called 'Lizard'. Sales followed swiftly to Roger Fry,

Virginia Woolf and a long line of friends, who bought yards and yards for upholstery and curtains.

A far greater gift from Eve to Barron that night would have been an introduction to Dorothy Larcher. But she was still in India, and even when she returned Eve held back from organising a meeting between them, perhaps reluctant to share her dearest friend with the forceful Barron. The meeting, when it finally came, changed Barron's life, but it would be another six years before Eve introduced them.

Eve, less stalwart than William, began to show signs of mild ill health, retiring to bed at the slightest sign of a sore throat, terrified of the 'flu epidemic that was reaching its peak. With Louise no longer in Volta House, her friends rallied round. But she missed her adored Dorothy. Her ties with the Ajanta Caves project were over, her patron, Christiana Herringham, being now permanently confined to a nursing home having had a nervous breakdown. Gossip had it that Mrs Moore's experience in the caves in E.M. Forster's *Passage to India* was based on a similar trauma Christiana had experienced alone with a man in one of the caves. Dorothy had adopted – like Alice Richardson – an Indian name, Sunni, and wrote Eve long emotional letters, one of which in 1918 included a light but enigmatic poem. On the surface it is playful and teasing, with references to the comfort of Eve's bosom and to William's love for his wife expressed in exquisite ivory. But it is hard not to see in it a veiled love poem to her close friend:

To a brooch in Carved Ivory
On Eve's warm chest
You've come to rest
So closely pressed
In little nest
Oh mother kind
With babies blind
Your tails entwined
great comfort find!
But – tiny mice
Take my advice
Keep habits nice
In Paradise!!
For William made you for his dove.
All out of Ivory and Love.

*　*　*　*　*　*

In Hampstead Garden Suburb the Wilkinsons still seemed blissfully unconcerned with the unfolding war catastrophe. Their diaries, written daily by one or the other in a similar tone of voice, record watching a Zeppelin in the sky, meeting William and Eve in a hayfield in June 1918, and soon after for an afternoon in their garden: 'William and Eve came to tea, stayed on to a risotto supper … made lots of fun on our spinning wheel – what a centre of attraction – they too made a firm resolve to spin and weave.' In two entries in early July, Lily wrote:

> After supper we played Eve's Virginal. Eve plays with much more certainty after lessons with Dolmetsch … the old Elizabethan music is all he tolerates. He does not praise her, he scolds her and goes into frenzies when she plays … she said to him by way of excuse that her hands were stiff – 'it is not ze hands he cried, ze hands are alright, it is ze brain' – and William sang …

Competitive as ever, the entry ends 'we want a virginal of our own'. Four days later, on 9 July, 'Two tables together in the garden. Mrs Powell brought Catherine – who played in the garden – and Eve to tea … Catherine very shy.'

But on 19 July 1918 the police came to the Wilkinsons' house and Arthur was arrested, along with his brother Walter. How he had managed to escape conscription for so long was never explained. William had no inkling of the situation until he returned one evening, exhausted by a long day's work, to find a letter from Arthur. Their claim was still under investigation and now they were awaiting a court martial. It was vital to prove that they had held genuine long-standing beliefs as pacifists. Separately they were appealing urgently to William. Would he write endorsing their characters for their lawyer?

His testimony was never more needed: the recruiting officers, desperate to find new bodies to throw into the struggle, were cynically dismissive of all 'Conchies' as shirkers. But the irony of switching from work on one of the war's most advanced forms of weaponry to be a character witness for a pair of conscientious objectors was not lost on William. As he sat down to write the letters that night, he had no compunction in defending the Wilkinsons' honesty and sincerity. His friends encompassed the whole range of attitudes to the war – from angry pacifist to ardent patriot – and whether their actions sprang from instinct or obedience to a personal code of conduct, William knew that each one had searched his soul how to respond to the catastrophe that had befallen their country. Whatever path they chose, he would respect their decision. Sometimes they would confide more to William than to their closest family, for he was entirely devoid of the need to indulge in moral condemnation. For that, and for his loyalty, he was loved by his friends.

The brothers had been kept in Hounslow Barracks pending their court martial and Lily was at home with the children. In some districts she was the object of anger and resentment when people discovered her husband sat safely cocooned in prison, but the Garden Suburb neighbours could not have been more sympathetic. She wrote to William:

This is to let you know that Arthur and Walter are ALL RIGHT. Just as well and cheerful as ever. Still singing 'It's good to be alive'. I have seen them several times – three glimpses and short talks on Saturday. They have very comfortable quarters and are treated with friendliness and respect by everybody ... Don't tell the public, but they say 'everybody is happy in prison'!

Unaware of William's work pressures, Lily wanted him to visit Hounslow with her on his one day off: 'Sunday next? Visiting hours are 2 pm on Sunday and 4 pm other days – it would take 1 and half hrs to get there from Hampstead. It is awfully remote – after the Court Martial I go back to the caravan.'

A true friend, William went. He waited two hours outside during the visit, then took them back to Hampstead. In spite of their exhaustion, the Simmondses continued to keep up Lily's spirits; they took the children, Pino and Bimbo, on expeditions, invited them to tea and tried out more of William's new puppets. Above all William kept in touch with the brothers through letters.

In early summer, sudden salvation arrived. The German High Command under General Erich Ludendorff had overstretched itself and could not supply its troops over the desolate, pitted ground so vividly portrayed by the war artists. The offensive ground to a halt and the tide turned. In the face of an Allied counter-attack the German army went into headlong retreat. In August Bulgaria became the first of the Central Powers to seek an armistice.

The Wilkinsons were unaware of anything but their own plight, and they kept William up to date on their case. The pre-trial proceedings went smoothly and no one tried to dispute the authenticity of their beliefs. 'Indeed,' Walter wrote, 'everyone is polite and friendly to an almost embarrassing degree.' On 5 September they were moved to the Duke of York Military Barracks in Dover. Their trial and sentencing would follow soon after:

The Guard Room, Duke of York's School Dover
September 5th 1918

Dear Brother,
I was very glad to get your letter, we are very much among philistines here and under these circumstances letters have special value.

I have heard all about the expedition to the Natural History Museum. You could not make me more happy by paying attention to my two babies & taking them on such a spree ...

We have both been awarded the DCM, that is to say District Court Martial, and will be tried after a bit and religiously persecuted all in order. We work in the open most of the day and we're both very well and cheerful as ever. On my arrival they've done you a great service and stripped me of my whiskers. They cut my hair as short as they could and I'm like a plucked chicken. The effect is astounding you'd never recognise me in Khaki.

Things really do look a bit blue – but brother and I were determined that personality should triumph and kept calm and now we have the whole camp – the Colonel included most respectful. We have many acts of kindness shown every day and the Colonel himself has arranged a vegetarian diet. The Army idea of Veg. Diet is rather a joke. In Pentonville on the other hand the food was very good indeed ...

But I am not grumbling – we keep one another cheerful and it has been a great thing that we kept together all through this adventure.
The very best wishes to Eve and to yourself,
Arthur Stanley Wilkinson

Walter wrote equally optimistically:

You would have a job to recognise us with our scrubby heads and chins and our sunburnt faces – we are new puppets altogether – why my weight increased 3lbs in Pentonville and I believe is still increasing!! There's luck for you – but you understand this is the first holiday we've had for four years. A cheerful guard has just unlocked my cell door and said 'hello – you a bloody conscientious objector?' I reply 'yes that's me'. He replies 'all right mate. I've got a brother-in-law a C.O. Cheer-oh'. And away he goes whistling. We get a good deal of rough (very rough) sympathy and what little opposition there is very polite. The chaplain has paid us a visit – the first time he has ever been known to visit the cells. We felt highly honoured!! Specially as he admitted that war is quite incompatible with the teaching of Jesus Christ. On our part we admitted that war was equally incompatible with our teachings – so with such an interchange of confidences we had a most friendly interview.

To keep them occupied, William encouraged Arthur and Walter to produce more puppets and somehow found a way of getting carving tools into the barracks. Arthur wrote with gratitude and a tinge of sadness from the guardroom, anticipating many years in prison:

The Guard Room,
Duke of York's School Dover

Dear Brother,
We are both delighted with the ivory and set of tools & if we don't come to an end of our carving before we leave here – we're half inclined to get them into our next new home – but it's a different matter getting things in to getting them out and sharp edged tools are awful wickedness in the eyes of a gaoler and might ruin our character, for ever. Sempre Correggio.

We are going along calmly and well. We have been tried and I have to thank you for standing by and I've reason to thank you – for they accepted us as genuine C.Os on our own written statements and the letters from our friends …

We have to wait some days before we hear our sentence – but we are more or less indifferent – that's their business not ours – all we wait for really is the day they say we can go home – then we will wake up and be off like lightning.

Now you won't be hearing from us for many a long day perhaps – but we shan't forget you and we'll have some happy days
together yet!

Please give our love and best wishes to Mr and Mrs Powell.
Love and best wishes to Eve & yourself from yours as ever
Arthur Stanley Wilkinson

Walter was determined to keep up his courage, but the tone of his
last letter was wistful:

Now that we have been duly Court Martialled and will soon be
stowed away, here is a last note to wish you all good luck and to
thank you for the helpful letter to the President.

But now after all is the time to be serious when we are con-
fronted with I don't know how many awful years of imprisonment
… we are going to look forward to those brave days in the future
when we shall all be free to really see something of one another: in
the meantime, I for one, shall frequently pay a visit to Volta House
and smoke a cigarette, whilst I am being charmed by the Virginals
and the puppets into the most delightful fairyland that ever was.
So now here's the best of good luck to yourself and to Eve …

Then, as suddenly as it had begun four long years ago, the war was
over. The German pack of cards collapsed. In November the Kaiser
abdicated and fled to neutral Holland. Ludendorff, the symbol of
Prussian military aggression, went to pieces and suffered a nervous
breakdown. An armistice could at last be negotiated.

On the morning of 11 November, Eve heard the sound of yet
another air raid and opened her window. There was gunfire, followed by anti-aircraft fire and the banging and clattering of
warning signals from high exploding bombs. For a brief second she
experienced the old dismal, sinking, here-they-are-again feeling, but
only for a second. The all-clear went up. In the distance she heard
the glorious ringing of church bells – they had been silent for four
years. Somewhere close by a wheezy old gramophone began to play
'God Save the King'. Out she rushed down towards Hampstead
High Street.

The news came swiftly, mysteriously, confusingly from all directions. Groups of people were talking excitedly; the air was charged
with emotion. 'The armistice has been signed and firing ceased at

11 o'clock', her butcher shouted. One moment she was one of a passing crowd, the next she was submerged in a howling wave; heads leant out from every window (and bodies, at some risk); people poured out of offices, spilled out of shops and buildings, shouting, even screaming with joy. 'We won the war! We won the war!' Startled pigeons circled overhead. Hampstead was transformed into a place of joy; at last the dream of peace had become gloriously true.

The moment the news reached de Havilland's, William was released from work. On arriving at Volta House he needed no persuading to go back to the High Street and to the heart of London. He pressed through the growing crowd on to the omnibus, past wild figures hanging from the sides and perching on the mudguards. On the upper deck people were toppling, roaring, flag-waving, horn-blowing, cheering down to the people in the streets, and the people in the streets were cheering back, laughing, running and waving little flags. Where the flags came from was a mystery. They sprang up in millions. Everybody had a flag and everybody waved it. Everybody cheered everybody else.

The omnibus ran wildly off route; William and Eve took to their feet among the thousands and thousands to join the wave pouring down the Strand, passing Trafalgar Square in a united purpose to acclaim the King. Strangers smiled at each other in the street and many kissed. The stolid English flung reserve to the winds.

Disorder broke out; every vehicle was invaded for jubilation. Soldiers in vans were driving around waving flags in uproar. Taxi cabs balanced a dozen military on their roofs, or on running boards; no methods of making a noise seemed too eccentric: guns firing, engines whistling, motor horns hooting and, from the river, ships' sirens shrieked among a babel of human voices. They came across captured German guns, broken and burnt by the crowds; men were marching, holding up rough black-and-white cartoons ridiculing the Kaiser. The city had erupted into celebration, and the scenes of triumph, joy and relief grew wilder.

William shepherded Eve down into the Mall towards Buckingham Palace. Dancing was everywhere. People danced to the rhythm of their own handclaps; they danced round in a ring and anyone in uniform was pulled into the centre. And the London bobby rose to the occasion. People clamoured to dance with a policeman. One after another, their faces stolid and impassive, they danced with everyone in turn on the narrow pavements.

The King and Queen acknowledged the crowd below them and joined in the cheers, singing the 'Old Hundred', 'Auld Lang Syne' and American war songs. At one point a military band played 'Tipperary', 'God Save the King' and 'Home Sweet Home'; then the bandmaster paused, raised his baton and played it again. Tens of thousands of people, caught off guard, suddenly burst into tears, Eve among them.

Late in the afternoon it began to rain lightly. No one cared. Searchlights roamed at random all over the city. An early closing order went out for restaurants, music halls, clubs and theatres, their lights ablaze among the delirious celebrators. They returned at dusk in a heavy downpour to find part of Hampstead Heath converted into a dancing lawn and a bonfire lit for the first time.

CHAPTER 13

Call of the Cotswolds

1918–1919

'A map of the world that doesn't include Utopia is not worth even glancing at, for it leaves out the one country at which humanity is always landing. And when that humanity lands there, and seeing a better country, it sets sail. Progress is the realisation of Utopias.'

Oscar Wilde, *The Soul of Man under Socialism*, 1891

The war left an indelible mark on the nation, so full of pain, so bitter, that for many years it was seldom referred to. The world had changed utterly. Ancient continental dynasties and empires had fallen; the red flag flew over Moscow; many of the British political and social elite believed it only a matter of time before Bolshevism consumed their country. Within months of the armistice, the conflicts of the pre-war years erupted anew. Thirty million working days were lost as result of industrial disputes, fought out in a world transformed. Earl Haig's anxieties were on the returning armies and the demobilisation of four million men. In the four years on the Western front, five out of every nine in the army had been killed, were missing or wounded. The peace that the returning troops had long looked forward to could only disappoint.

William, who was apolitical, did not pay too much attention to any of this. If anything informed his social attitudes, it was a nineteenth-century sense of civic duty imbued subconsciously from his childhood, with his first loyalty to the country of his birth and to its institutions. The war's end left him disorientated, with a feeling of sadness over something lost. His perspectives had altered; he had become more open to fresh ideas about art and music. No longer a painter, he had shed the strict Royal Academy conventions and freed

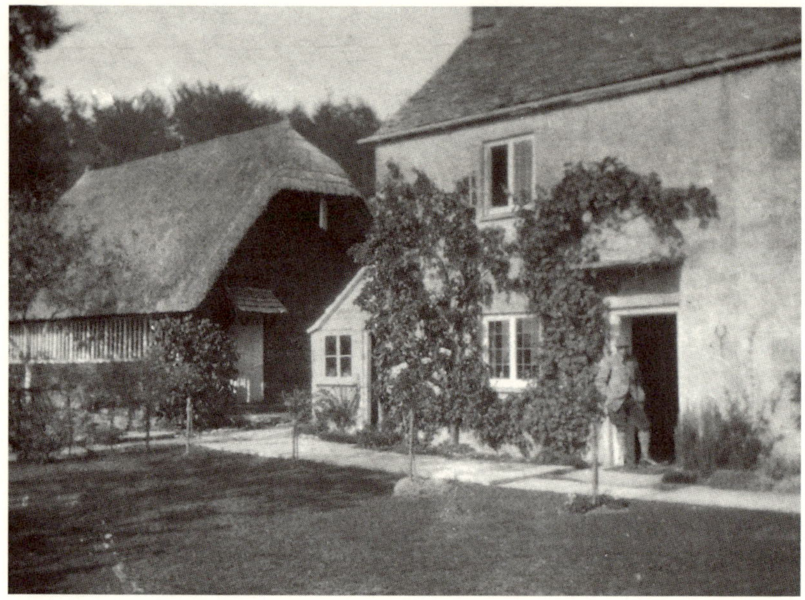

William's thatched workshop beside The Frith where he worked from 1919

himself from the spell of Edwin Abbey's mesmeric character. He had found a distinctive personal style, expressed in two different fields – sculpture and puppetry. And during the war years he had been drawn to a new, different circle of friends, many of them shaped by William Morris's aversion to all that was ugly in the world after the Industrial Revolution.

Quite soon William and Eve made up their minds to leave London. From his Fairford days with Abbey, William had formed a lifelong attachment to the Cotswolds, and his love of its hidden swathes of woodland and valleys had only been increased by his intermittent visits to the Powells in Oakridge Lynch on the edge of the Golden Valley, west of Cirencester. An added attraction was not only Alfred and Louise, but Ernest Gimson and the Barnsley crowd. After the war, Gimson, in failing health and perhaps from a premonition of early death, sought to realise his dream of coaxing like-minded friends to form an artistic commune on the land he had bought close to his house in Sapperton. He wanted to build on the revitalisation that he had brought over twenty-five years to his villages, spreading the Arts and Crafts philosophy further afield.

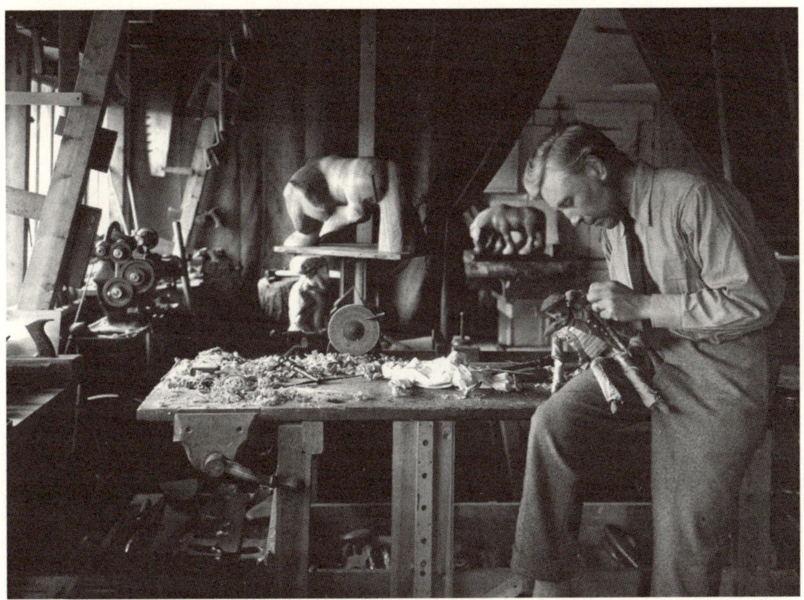

William in his Oakridge workshop carving a puppet, photographed by his assistant, Catherine Cobb. An early stage of *Black Mare* is in the background

The first to make a practical suggestion to bring William to the Cotswolds was Charles Gere, who lived further afield at Painswick. A member of the Birmingham Group of Artist-Craftsmen, Gere had illustrated books for the Kelmscott Press, achieving early fame with the frontispiece to William Morris's *News from Nowhere*, and now devoting himself to landscape painting. In January he sent a note to William to say he had found a promising place for him and Eve called Cromwell House, just below Haresfield Beacon. 'Main part of house good and old, and could be made very attractive' he wrote. There was a paddock and a nice orchard: 'the highest house in that part ... with great views but very cold when the wind blows ... a favourite haunt of ours.' The asking price was an affordable £300, but Eve put her foot down. It was too exposed for her fragile health.

The place William and Eve finally fell for in the spring of 1919, where they were to settle for the rest of their lives, was Far Oakridge, one of five tiny villages close to Sapperton. Tucked away in a meadow in the fold of a hill, The Frith, a cottage or rather two tiny workmen's cottages made into one, was a mile from the Gimsons and the Barnsleys and equally close to the Powells. It had a piece of unkempt land in front that would make a garden for Eve and a barn – very dilapidated – for William's studio, large enough to take a long table, sculpting tools and a puppet stage, as well as to store his specialised wood.

In July 1919 Dorothy wrote to ask what Eve was up to. She was now in Bengal, teaching in Calcutta and taking short breaks to live with a family in a village of Giridih to learn Indian block printing and dyeing techniques. The arrival of news from her 'dearest Eve', with photographs of William's puppets, had her emotions in turmoil. She longed to be updated, pining for a cosy gossip with Eve.

She had sent Eve some of her special drawings that she wanted forwarded on to Ananda Coomaraswamy:

> I am so glad you want to have that drawing of the woman leaning forward but you may not buy it. I rather like that one myself and was rather pleased with the easy line of the two women seated …
>
> I have been very interested to hear news of the cottage. I know exactly what you mean when you say it might be 'a little aimless' – as regards position you mean of course.
>
> But then I think that feeling will go, when you have got in there. I am convinced it was better for you to settle on it and not go on any longer looking and waiting (it is such an exquisite country there) … I should like to be having tea in the kitchen-sitting-room this very afternoon & having a good talk and a laugh.

Dorothy relied on Eve's aesthetic judgment on her paintings and drawings as much as on William's and Coomaraswamy's:

> I rather wanted to know what you thought of [the drawing of a group of pilgrims] … What does William think of them? I am glad you think I have improved … Yes! You would know how much I should like William's puppet 'the 'L o L' [Light of Love]. She is a perfect creature. I need not try to explain to you how much, & in what way she is so good (or rather bad, as you say!!). Of course I have been trying to imagine exactly what her walk is like, that you say is 'hardly respectable'!! How did William come by such an offspring? He lives with you, you know!! Hush!! How sweet of Dolmetsch to call her 'Little wretch'.

Dorothy had slipped a note to William into the envelope – not a letter but only a puppet paean. She was already the proud owner of a Simmonds Harlequin and was excited to receive the new photographs from Eve.

My Dear William,
How can you do such perfect puppets! I think Light of Love is as Eve says your top note in many ways, but the baby elephant is such a darling that he reaches far also. L of L seems scarcely the work of an individual mind, but rather a production of the best period of puppet making. She is a perfect creature … I long to see her and of course I love the fauns … the boy one's face … I want to pet him very much, but I am sure he wouldn't stand much petting, he would be off in between little bushes and undergrowth at once, playing baby tunes on his little pipes. In this photo the face and tout ensemble of the Dryad gives a much better idea of her. Also the young centaur. What a sweet, soft, furry tummy he has, and that pretty little mane & the wisps of hair & thick feet and legs. Really, William!

You can't know how much the puppets mean to me. I take them out and look at them so often. Don't you make the knee joints in a different way now? I imagine all the movements. I hope you still have that ridiculous little black thing (that hopped & leaped) that you had just before I left England Must see that again. It makes me laugh to think of it.

* * * * * *

One of the first callers at The Frith was John Drinkwater. He had not forgotten his fleeting encounters with them in war-torn London, nor an early puppet show at Volta House. He promptly bought an ashwood biblical carving, named *Eve Repentant*, and was so excited by his purchase that he dashed off a sonnet:

The Wood Carver
To W.G.S.

Out of his ash did he conceive her mood,
Repentant Eve, her pale face bowed among

cascades of hair, her limbs, that had been dewed
Lately in Eden where the apples hang,
Now carved for ever in a lovely sorrow,
All love, all grief, all kindred with the flowers
That now flush wood and meadow, and tomorrow
Are ghosts, are tears among remembered house.
O little Eve, bowed in your loss for ever,
Bowed bosom and clasped hands and hidden
We are your sorrow too, and master never
The loss of spring and the wild April grace
We love, and sin, and lose, as you to be
An image carved in beauty from the tree.

In the gentler pace of country life their friendship deepened. He was going through a difficult time with his wife Kathleen, and in William's studio he could escape; the two men also shared a love of the theatre. Drinkwater's ideas as manager of Birmingham Theatre were highly innovatory: he had overseen Britain's first purpose-built repertory theatre, and put on modern-dress performances of Shakespeare, dispensing with the traditional fussy style and breaking new ground with the simplicity of his staging and costumes. Fascinated by William's sense of the theatrical, his sculpture and his latest puppets, he had a brainwave. Why not work together on a short play, J.S. Martin's *Cupid and the Styx*, recently produced by him in repertory? He was about to give up the lease of Rothenstein's cottage – his play *Abraham Lincoln* (already a success and soon to take him to fame and fortune in America) was going into rehearsal in London – but they had time to lay the groundwork.

William was torn between his two passions. He was ensnared by his puppets but driven far more to sculpting in wood and stone. If he was to achieve something of significance, let alone earn enough for himself and Eve to live on, he needed a period of quiet to build up enough sculpture for a London exhibition. May brought a particularly inconvenient interruption in the form of a letter from Colonel Crompton forwarded by Louise Powell. The Colonel had been told that William had returned to his original and lucrative profession of artist (the language alone infuriated Eve) but, nonetheless, he had a request. The history of the development of the Tank was being investigated officially. A commission had been appointed by the Treasury that would award a sum of money to those with a valid claim for its invention. William had been with Crompton not only as a draughtsman but in the preparation of the early Tank models. Since the originals had been destroyed or lost, would William help him reproduce simple models and diagrams illustrating the part he had played in the Tank's development? He and Legros believed William, too, would be entitled to claim something for himself. But the reproduction would involve a great deal of hard work.

A week later Colonel Crompton asked William to swear before the Commission that the model he was making was a fair copy of those that had been destroyed: 'You and Phillips are the only reliable people who will be able to swear their correctness … You see it would never do for a model to be made by a third party on my information alone. For naturally my recollection of its original form would be held to be biased in my own favour.'

It was to no avail. The Commission's lawyers conceded that Crompton's design had contributed materially to the emergence of the rhomboid, lozenge-shaped tank that eventually went into mass production, but other contenders had, in their opinion, even higher claims. At least William was allowed to keep the model, which twenty years later, with characteristic generosity, he gave to Crompton for his ninetieth birthday.

* * * * * *

In August 1919, Gimson died. His loss was a blow to William and to the small community on which his personality had stamped itself for a quarter of a century. His last work before his death was a Memorial Cross in Fairford churchyard. In villages throughout the country, monuments to the soldiers who had given their lives in the war were being commissioned from sculptors and architects. William, who would also be commissioned, attended the Fairford installation in August. Gimson's eighteen-foot piece rejected the clutter of Victorian decoration. Its slim octagonal column, leading upwards to a delicate crucifixion in the form of a young tree, with leaves budding from three posts of the cross, had the same simplicity as Lutyens's contemporary war tribute in Whitehall. William was jolted to see the name of his landlady's son, Frederick Wade, inscribed on the upper plinth, together with the names of several other acquaintances from the Bull Inn days.

As if to replace Gimson and affirm the new turn William's life had taken, William Rothenstein turned up out of the blue on his doorstep in the summer of 1919. He was back in Oakridge, having returned from painting the aftermath of the war – his last war artist assignment, in France and the Rhineland.

In his book, *Men and Memories*, Rothenstein is cavalier about time. Letters from distinguished people are often undated and entries move casually backwards and forwards in time. He offers a hazy picture of coming across William in London during the war: 'heard of Simmonds as a painter and a carver of puppets', but it was not until the two met as neighbours in Oakridge that they came to recognise their unexpected affinity. This close and improbable friendship would last to the end of their lives.

Now still only in his forties, Rothenstein had lived so many different lives and experienced so many changes in circumstance that he seemed to encompass the entire intellectual firmament of the early twentieth century. Highly intellectual and self-confident, he had arrived from Bradford to study in London at the age of sixteen, a tiny man with the energy of a raw, provincial prodigy. Remaining barely a year at the Slade under the tutelage of Alphonse Legros, he had set his mind on Paris, where he was swiftly lionised in France's artistic and literary circles. After four years, still a mere twenty, he had exhibited in a Paris gallery and had been befriended by the most important artists of the time – Henri de Toulouse-Lautrec, Edgar Degas, Camille Pissarro, James Abbott McNeill Whistler (who teased him cruelly) and Aubrey Beardsley, an intermittent visitor to Paris. He was as much at home with Stéphane Mallarmé, Émile Zola and Paul Verlaine (who dedicated a poem to him) as he was with Oscar Wilde and Henry James on their visits from London. His diminutive stature, his ugliness and his vigorous self-promotion made him a magnetic figure, and when he returned to England to take up an assignment to draw the great Oxford intellectuals, he soon attracted as wide a cultural circle as he had in Paris.

Rothenstein's painting dominated his life, but with a generosity and disinterestedness unlike that of any of his contemporaries, he would dedicate time and energy to furthering the careers of other artists and writers. Wherever he went, he swept in like a tornado, engaging in dazzling, witty conversation. He would light on any subject; he held no bias in any form of art (except music, which meant little to him) and was no doctrinaire critic.

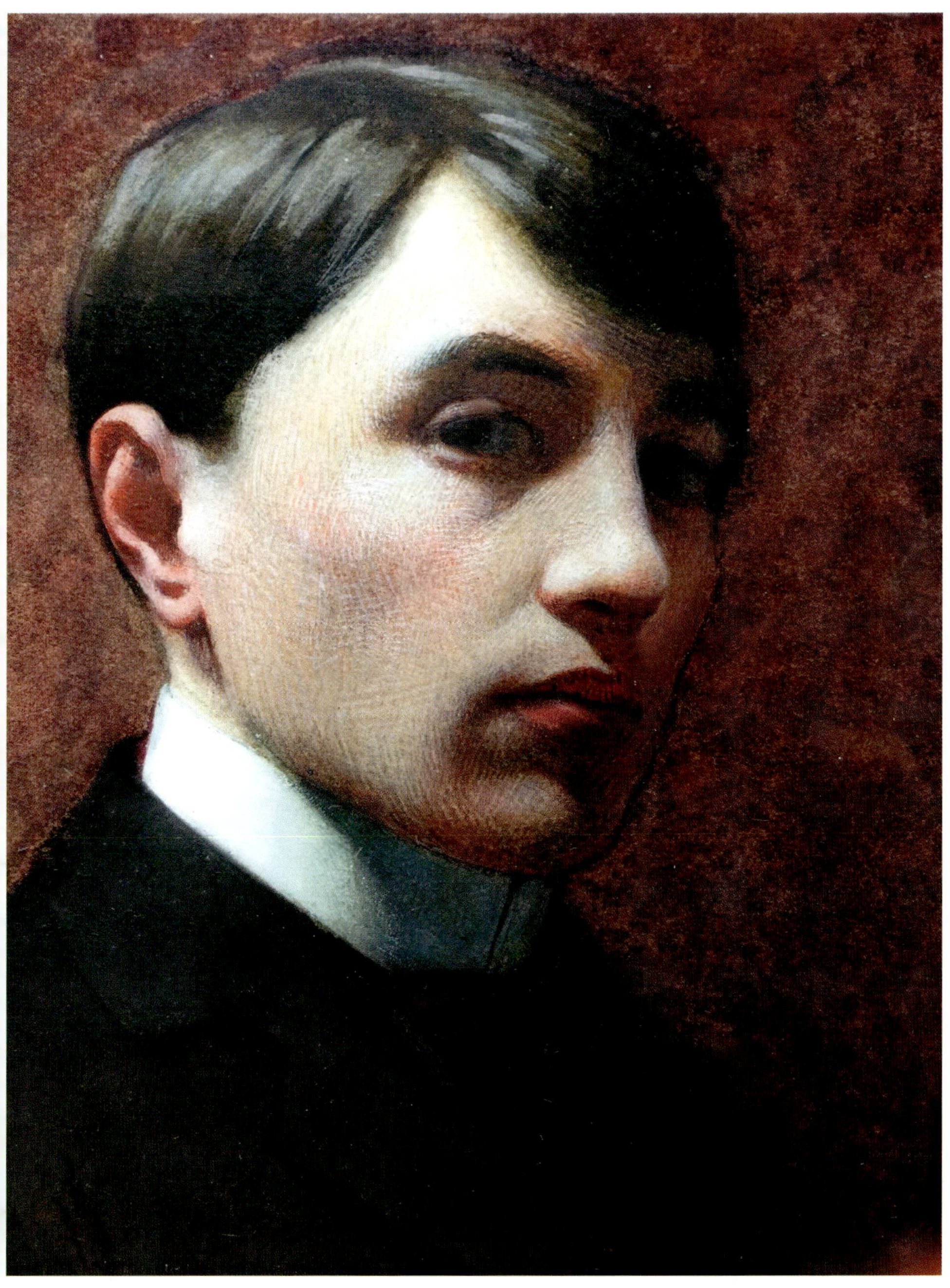

1. *Self-portrait* by William Simmonds, aged twenty-six

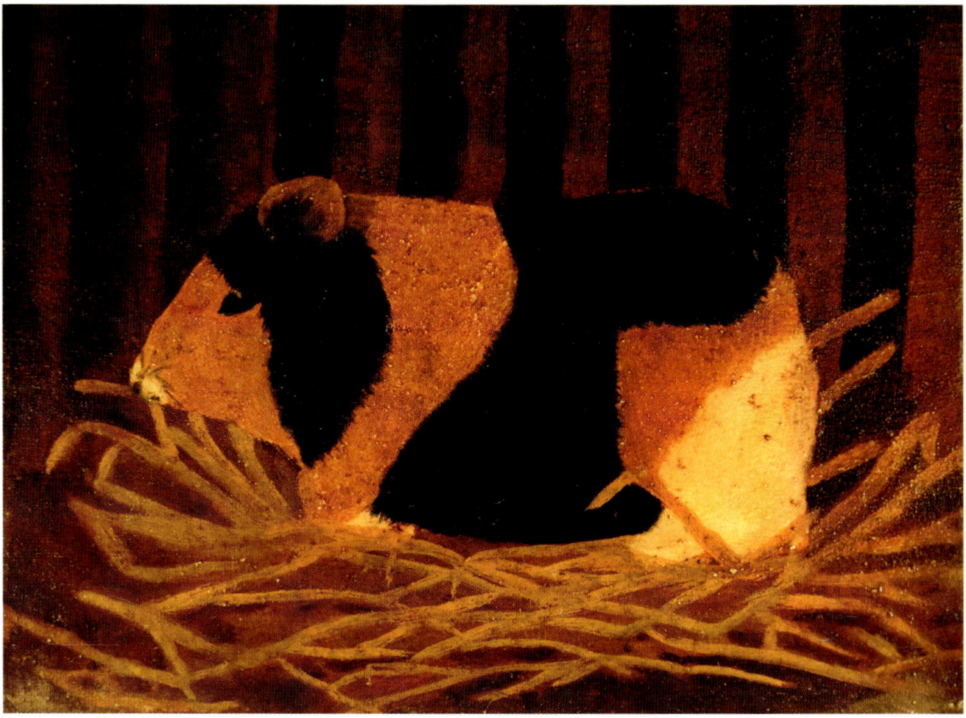

2. William's house-trained pet guinea pig, painted in oil by William, aged nine

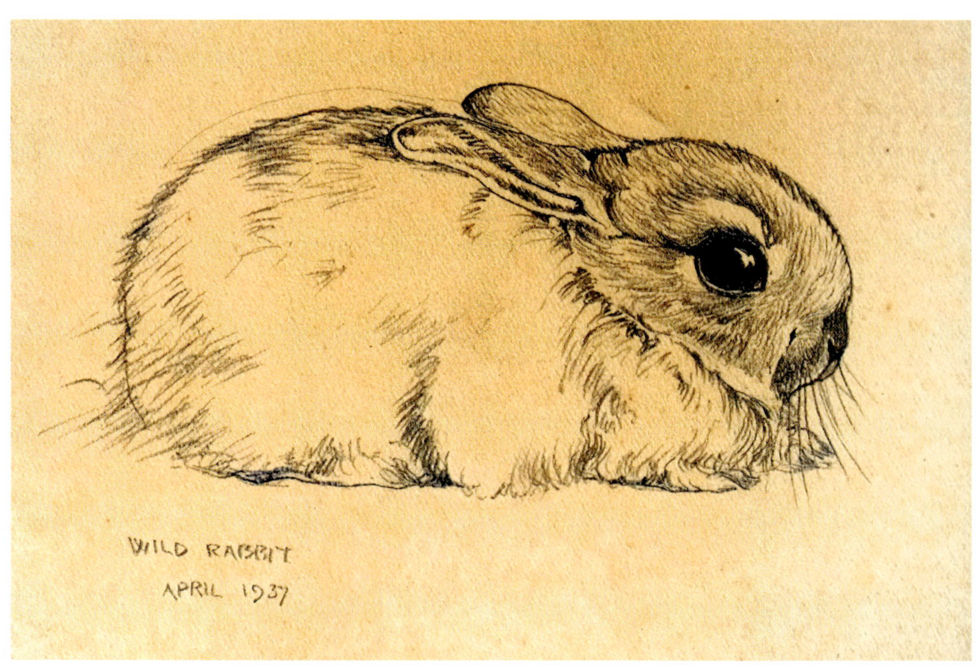

3. *Wild Rabbit, April 1937*, pen-and-ink drawing by William

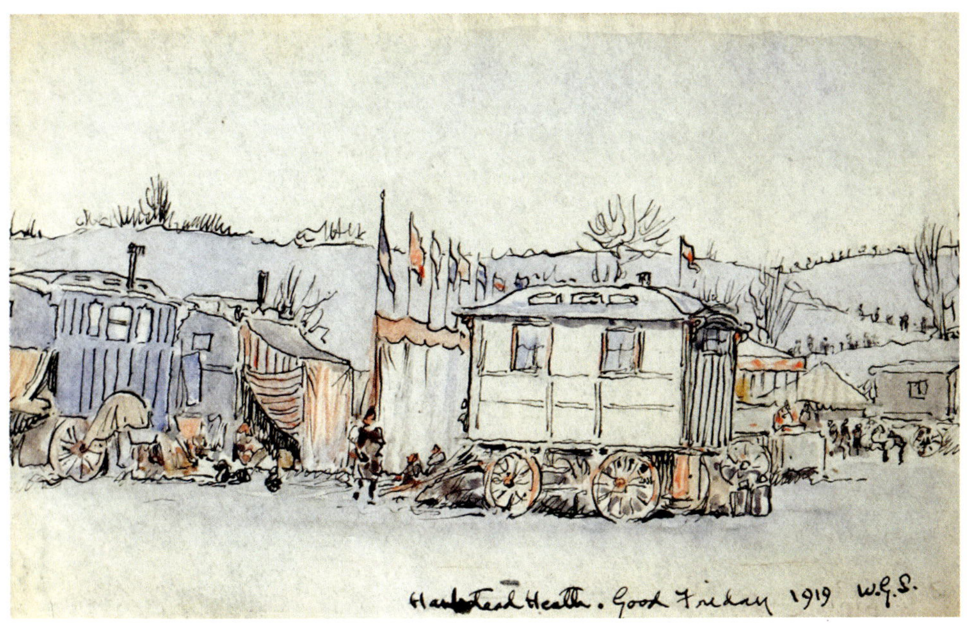

4. *Hampstead Heath, Good Friday 1919*, watercolour sketch by William

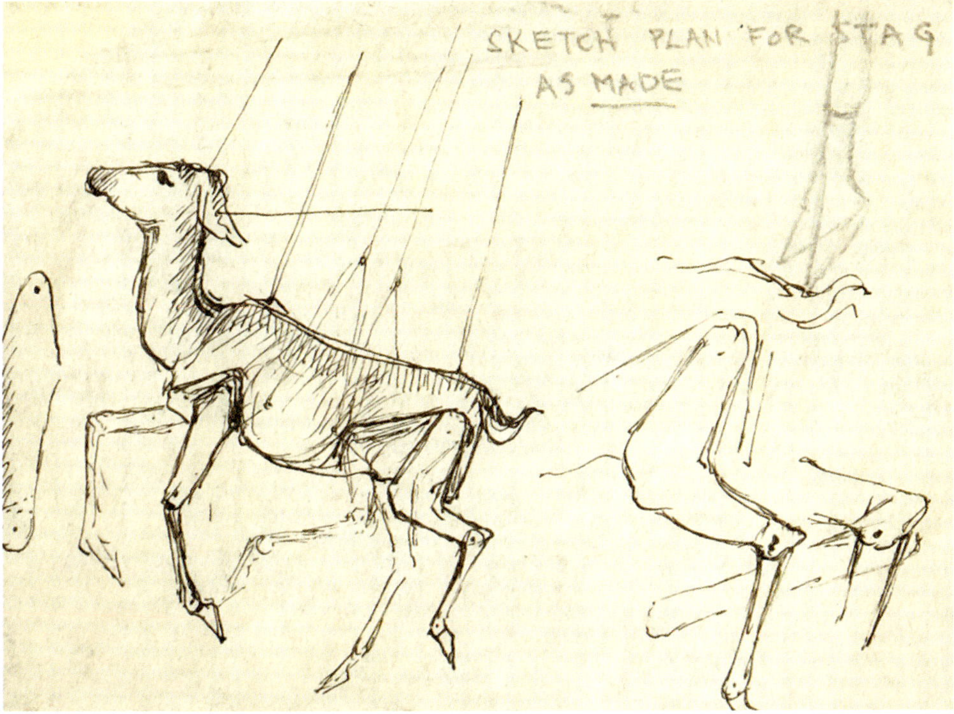

5. William's sketch of *Little Faun*'s mechanism – the art critic of *The Times*'s favourite marionette when he first saw William's show in 1921

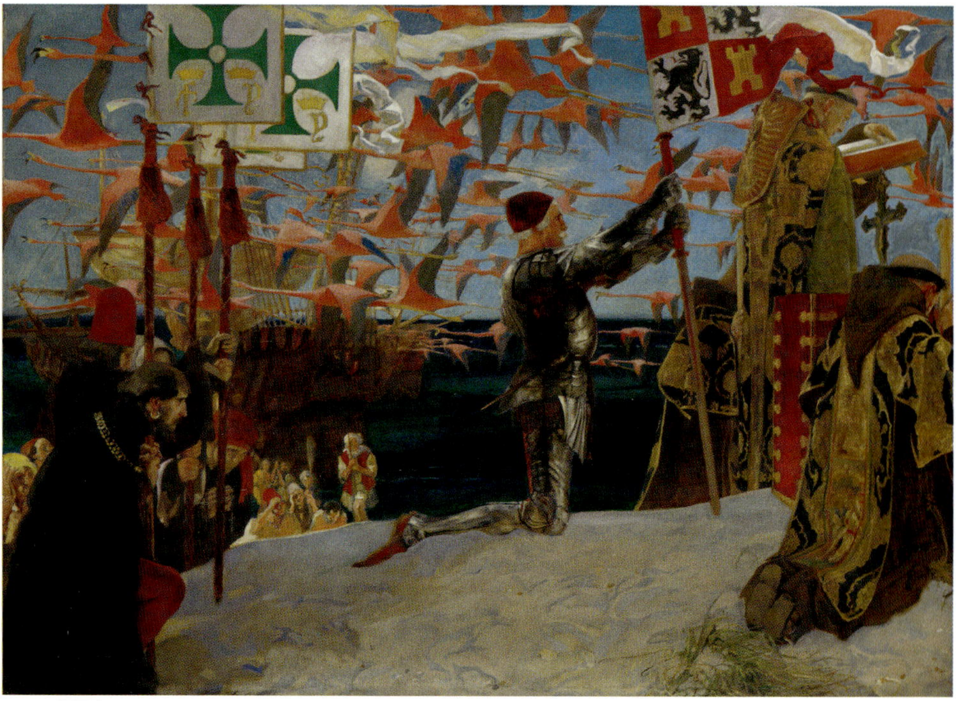

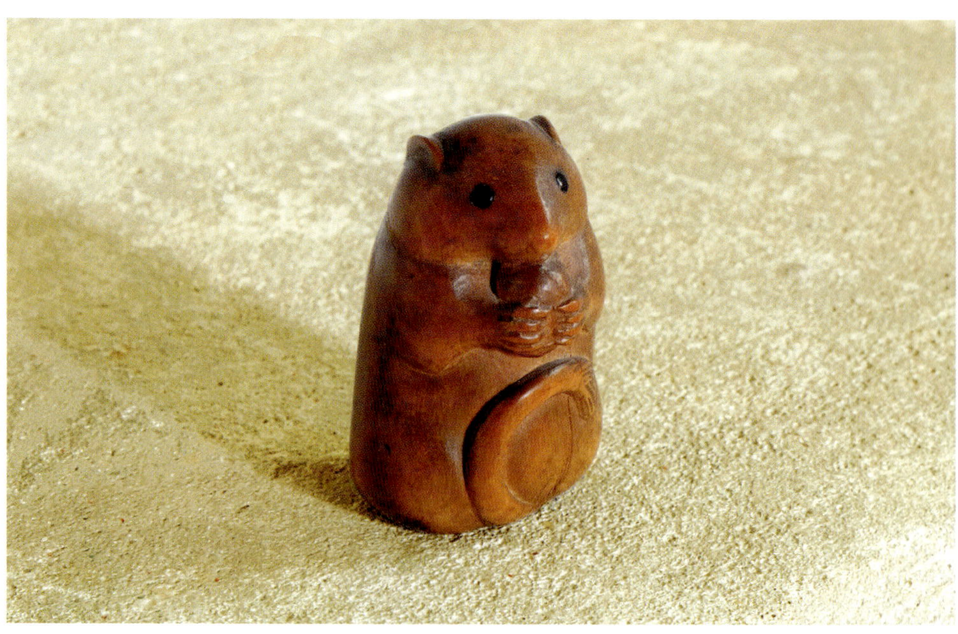

6. *Columbus in the New World* by Edwin Abbey, oil on canvas, 1906. Worked on by William during his years at Morgan Hall, Fairford

7. *Dormouse* carved by William

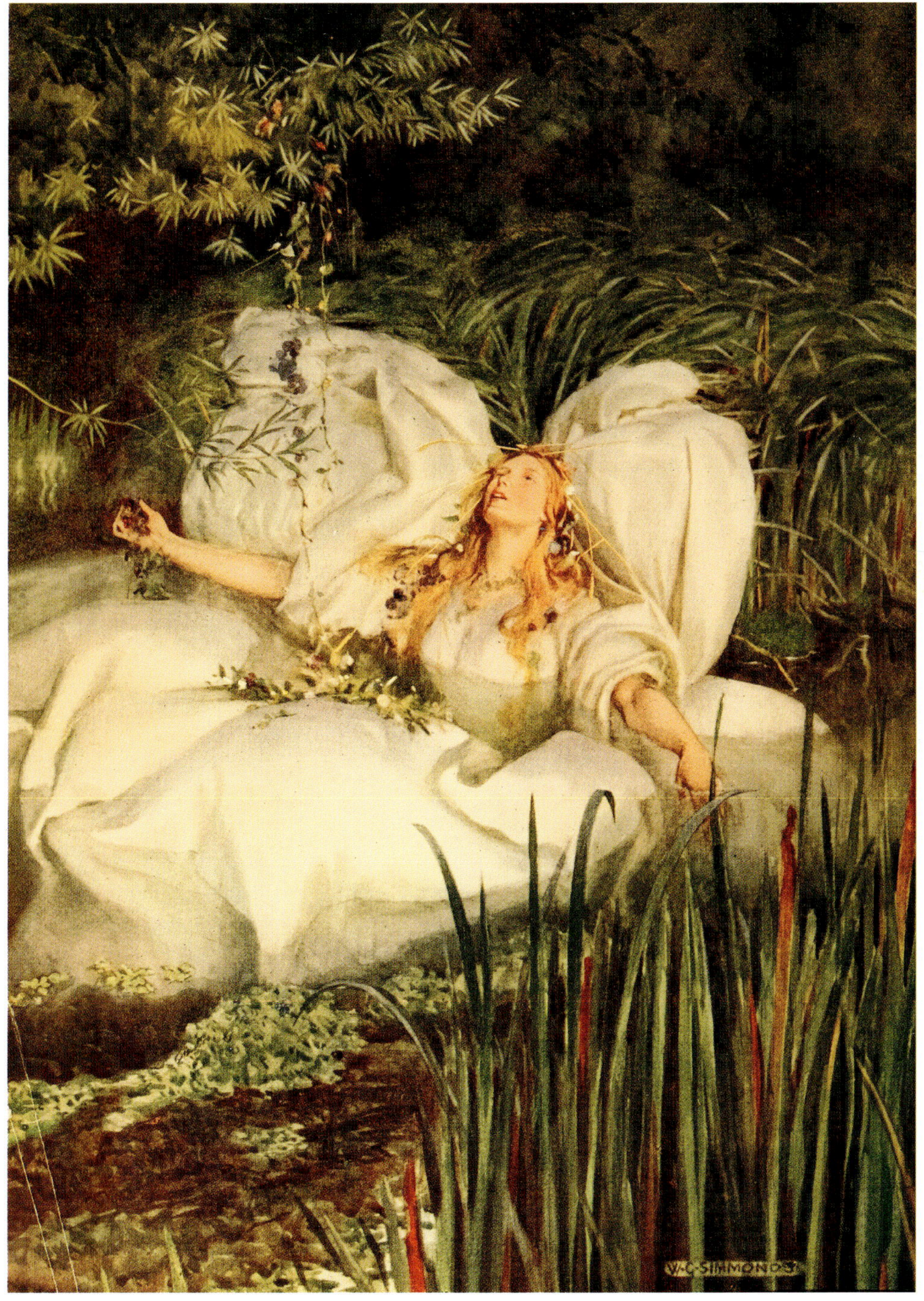

8. *Ophelia*, one of thirty illustrations by William for Shakespeare's *Tragedy of Hamlet* (Nelson & Son, 1907), inspired by his walks along the River Coln, Gloucestershire

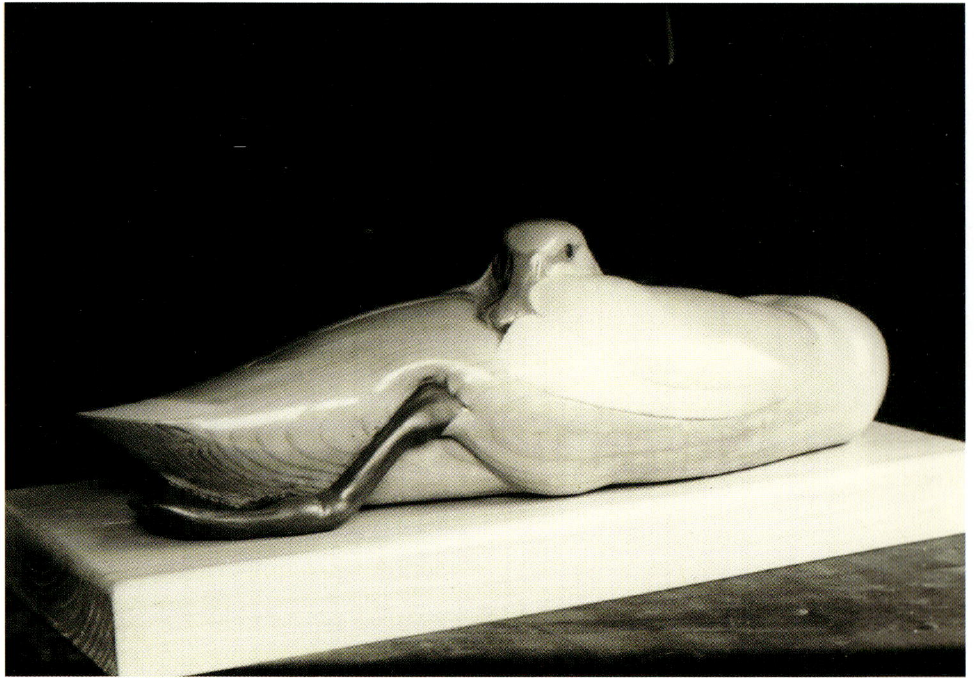

9. *Swan* by William

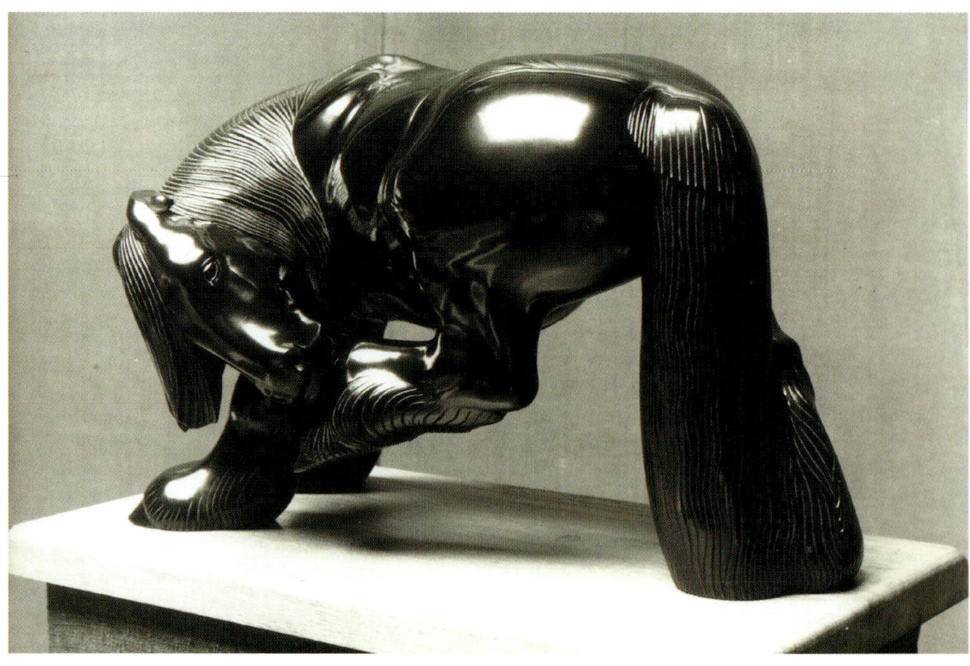

10. *Black Mare* (laminated mahogany) bought by the Greek art connoisseur, the banker George Eumorfopoulos, for his museum in 1926

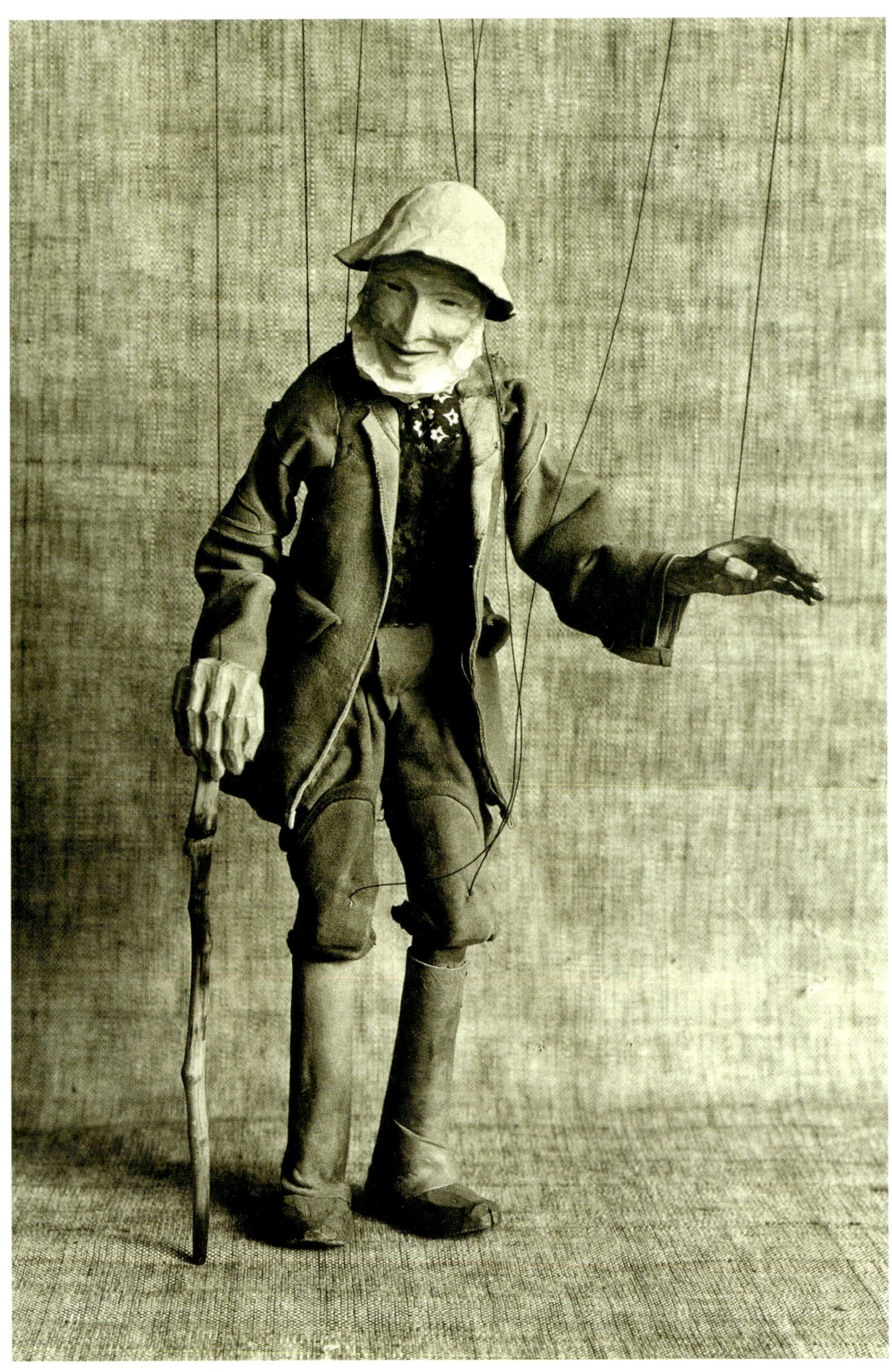

11. *Old Man* puppet: a secret portrait of one of William's friends in Oakridge, 1920

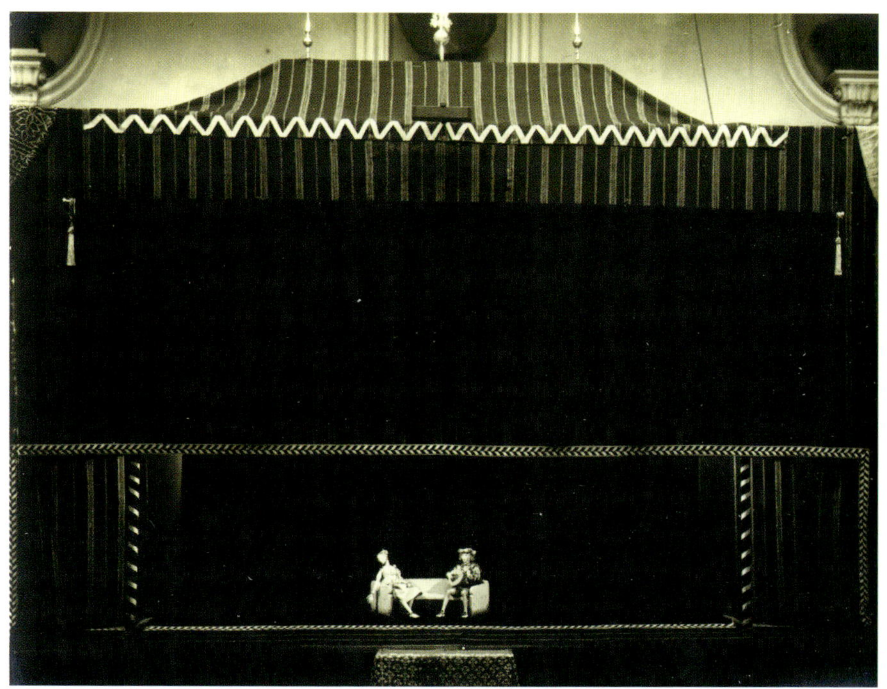

12. Stage set for *Harlequinade* show at Rodmarton Manor in 1934

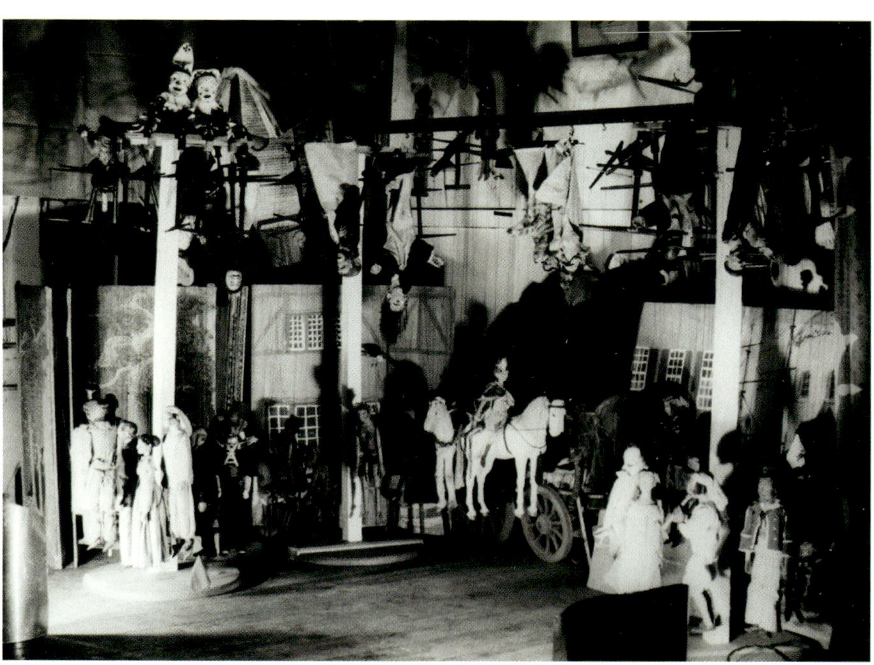

13. William's puppets waiting to perform before the show at the Duke of Westminster's house, Eaton Hall, Cheshire, 1929

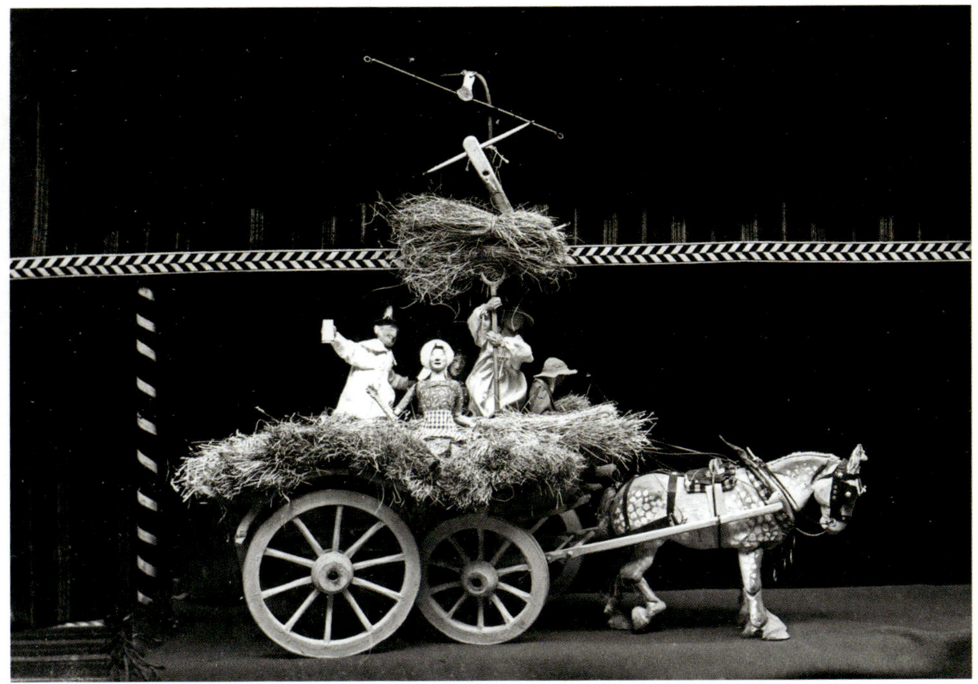

14. Horse and waggon in *Farmyard*

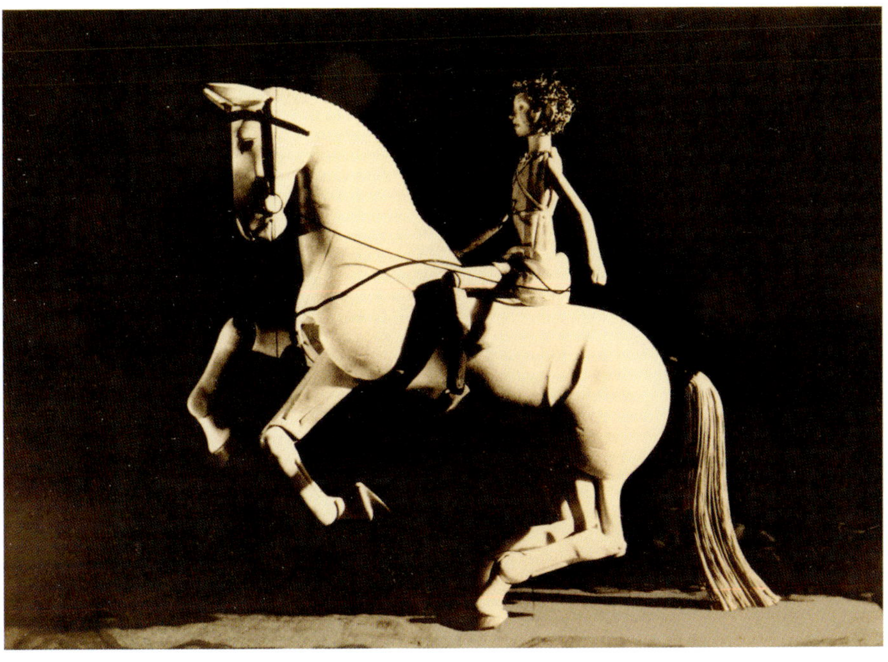

15. The puppet Estella on Snowball before being dressed by Eve. Compare with the dressed puppet on page 215

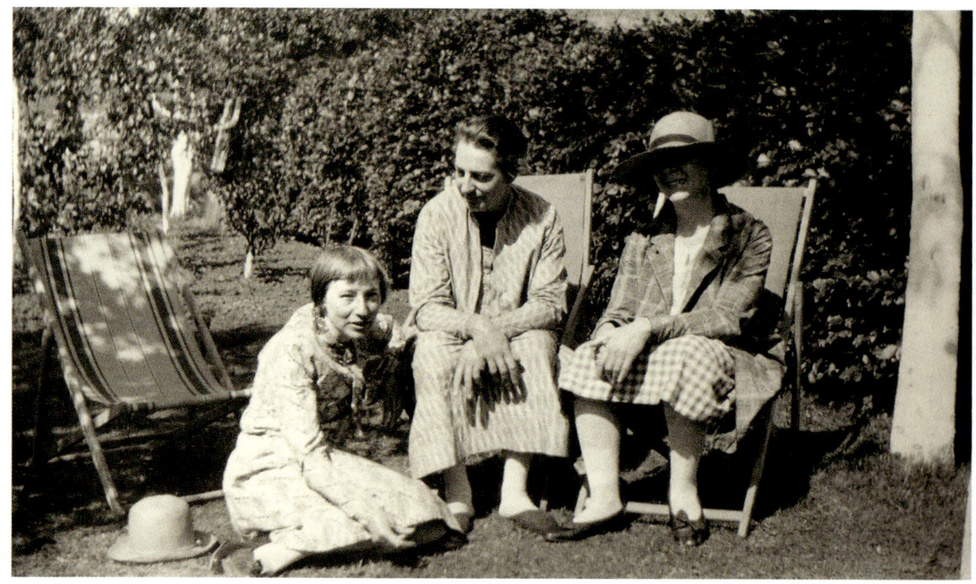

16. Eve sitting on the grass in her Frith garden with Phyllis Barron and Dorothy Larcher

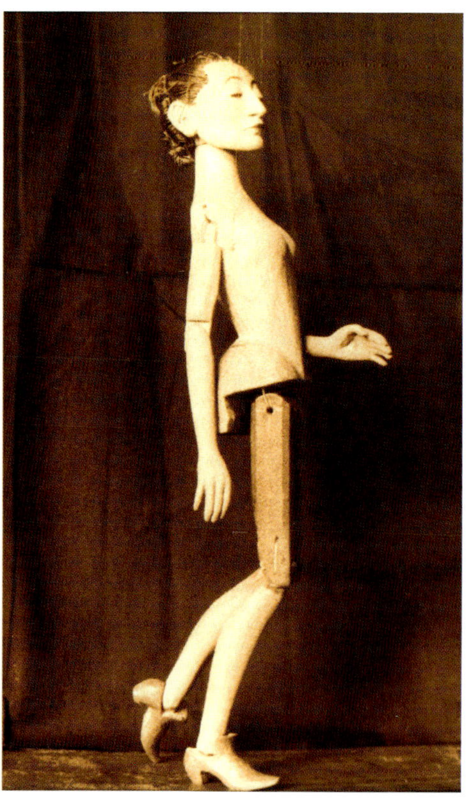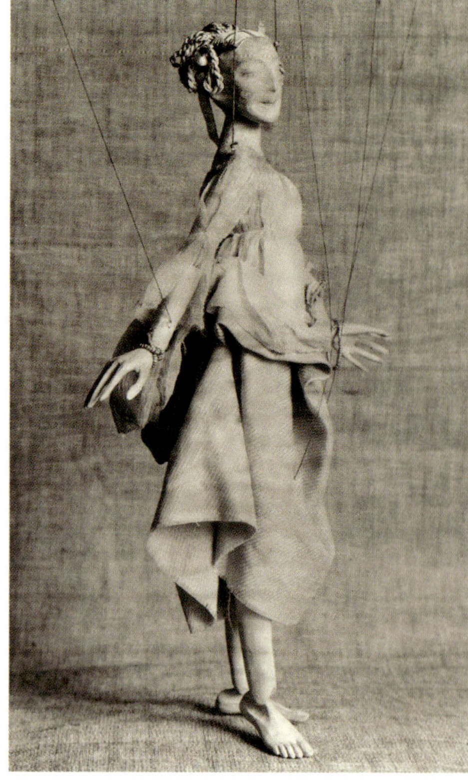

17 & 18. One of William's puppets before (left) and after (right) being dressed by Eve

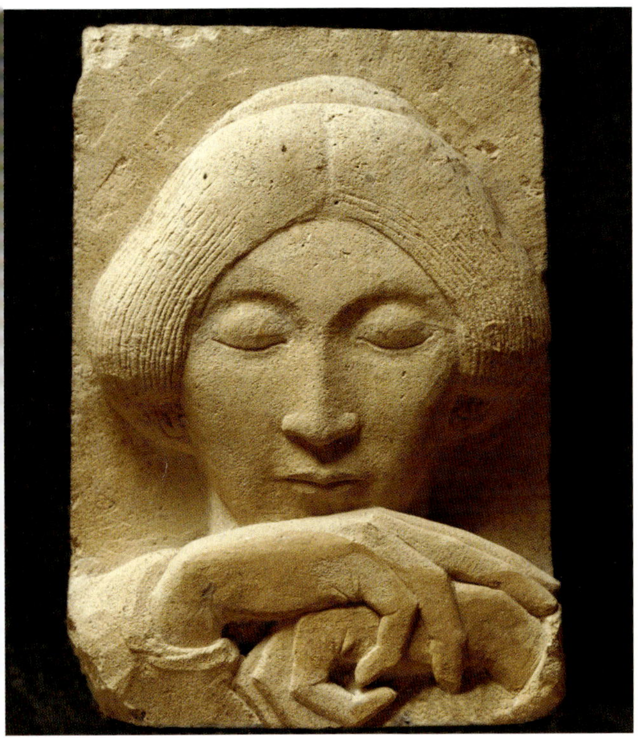

19. William's stone-carved relief of Eve

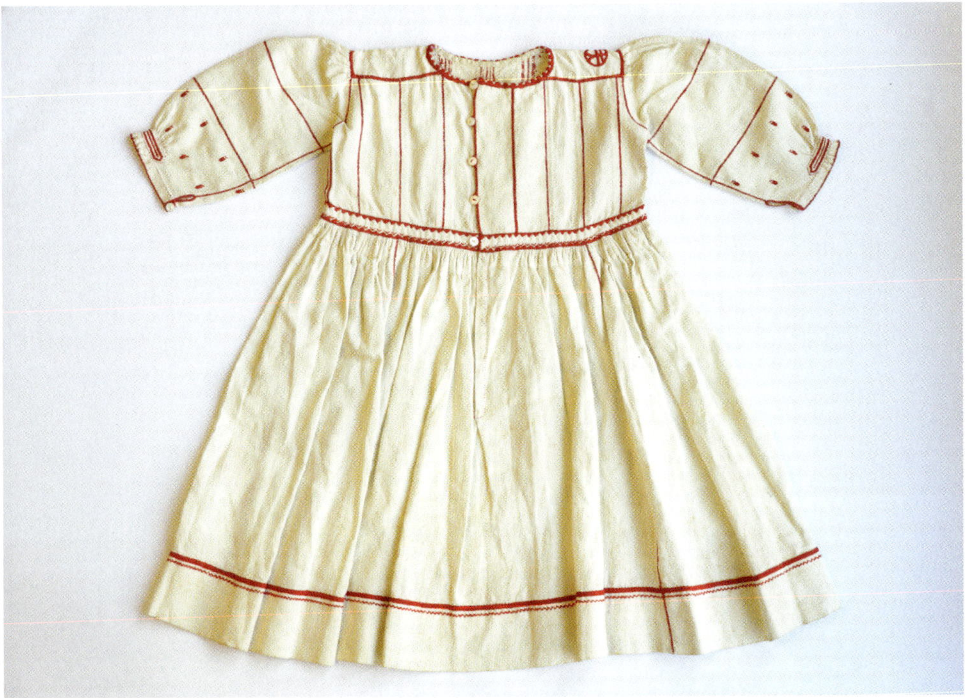

20. One of Eve's first pieces of embroidery – a smock made for her niece in 1915

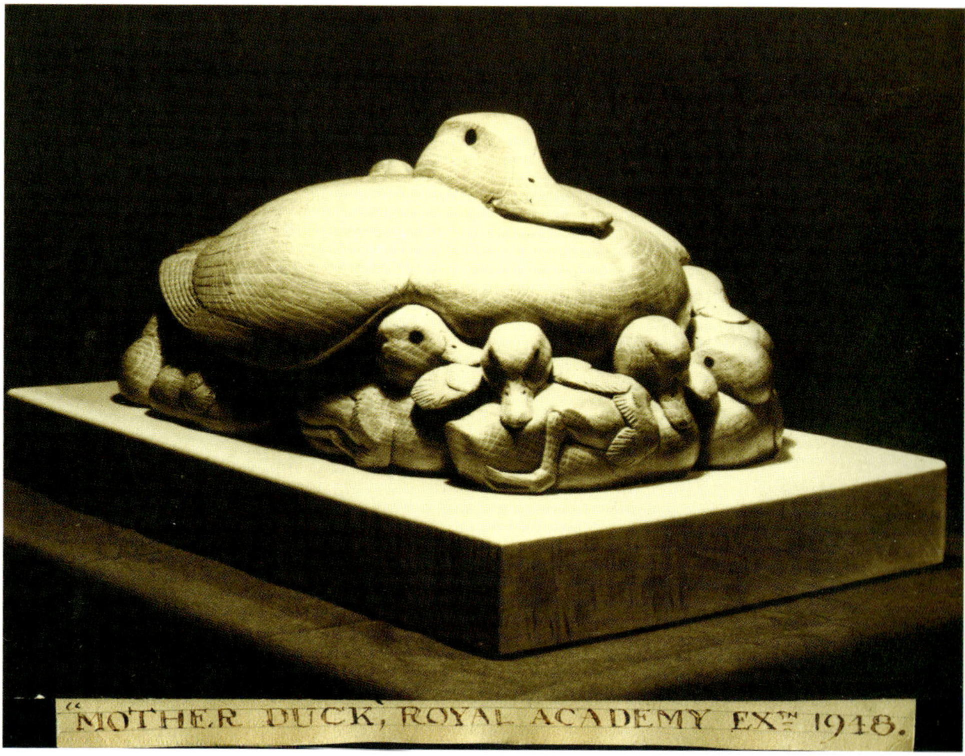

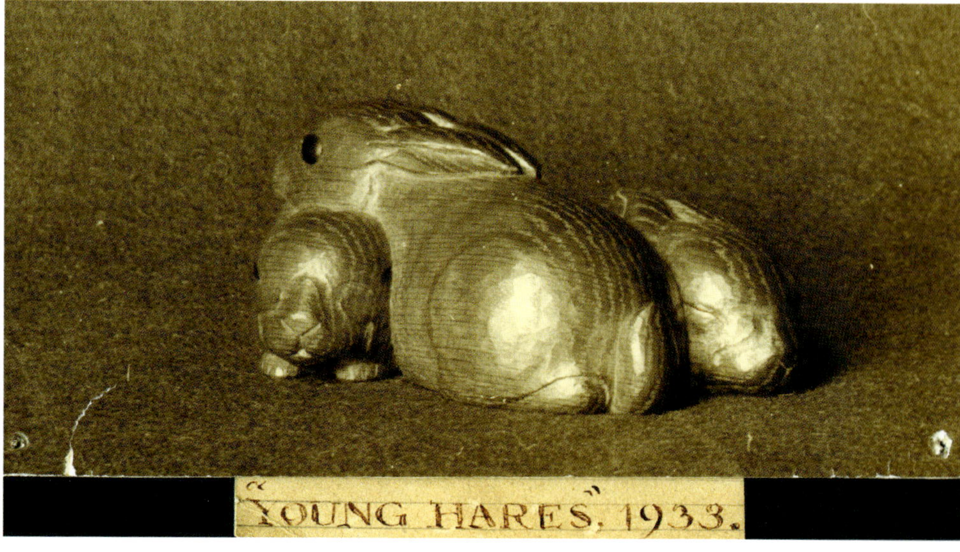

21. *Mother Duck* carved, photographed, labelled and placed in an album by William. Shown at the Royal Academy 'Winter Exhibition' in 1948

22. *Young Hares* by William, 1933. Violet Gordon Woodhouse bought this piece from the Royal Academy

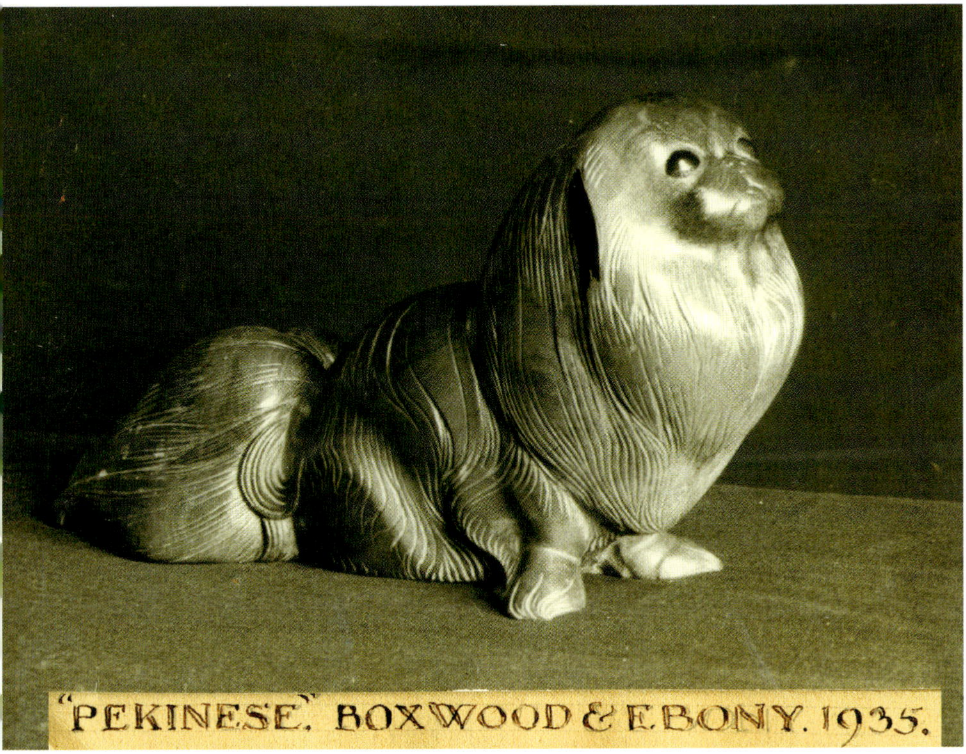

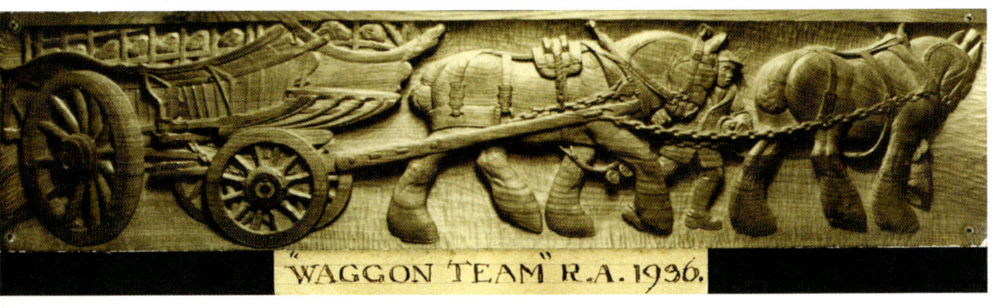

23. *Pekinese* (boxwood and ebony) by William in homage to Violet's dog, 1935

24. *Waggon Team* (carved chestnut) by William, exhibited at the Royal Academy in 1936

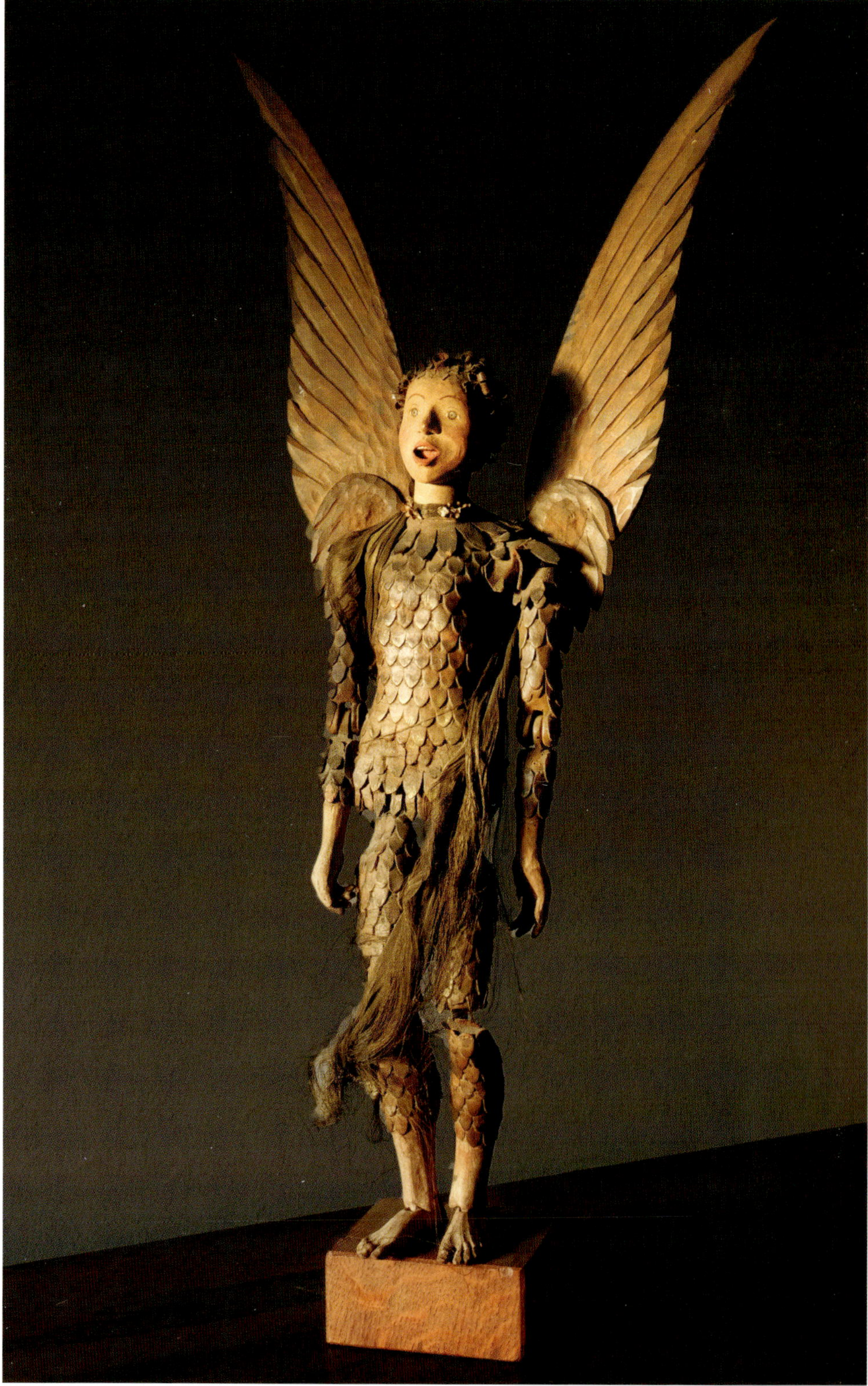

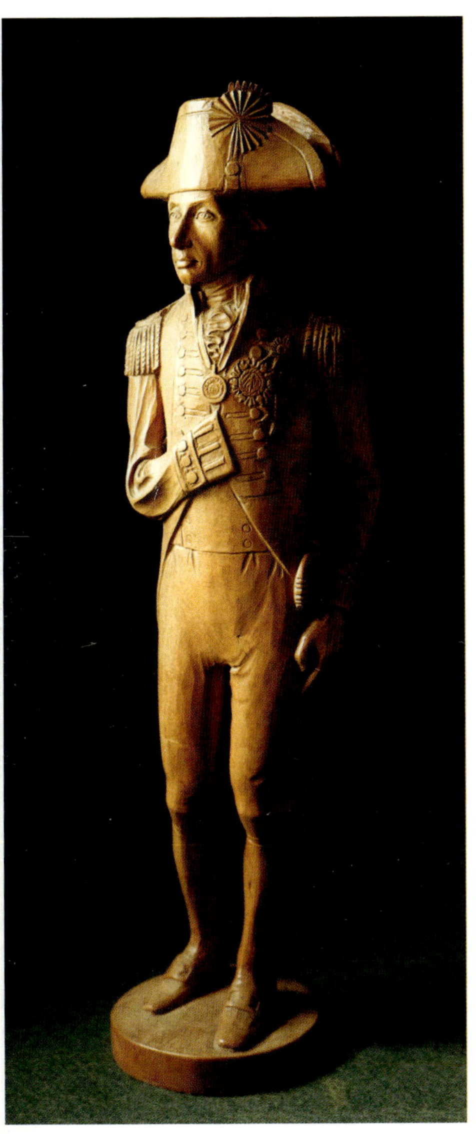

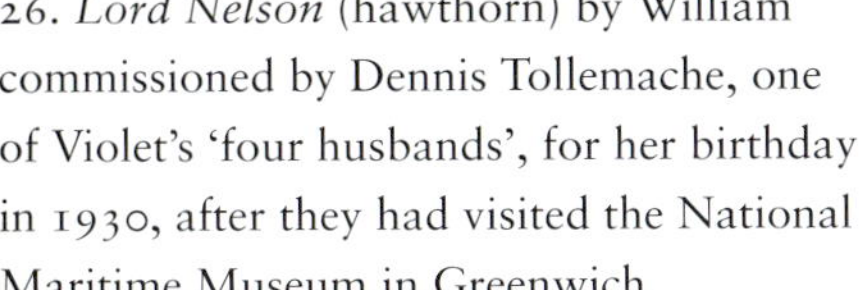

26. *Lord Nelson* (hawthorn) by William commissioned by Dennis Tollemache, one of Violet's 'four husbands', for her birthday in 1930, after they had visited the National Maritime Museum in Greenwich

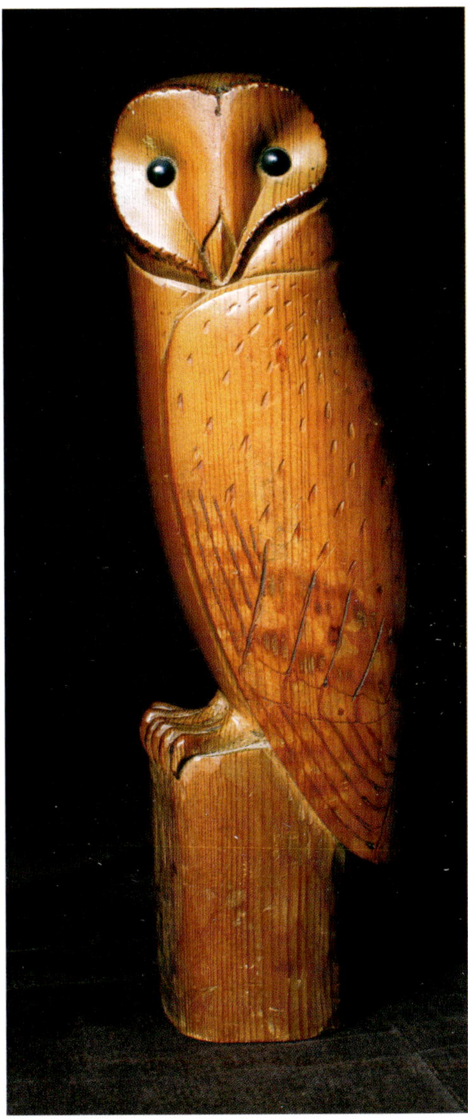

27. *Owl* by William: 'I have had the pleasure of rescuing an Owl from the chimney in the spare room – a most beautiful creature … most exciting to see near to and such wonderful dark eyes', William in a letter to William Rothenstein

(opposite) 25. *Archangel Gabriel* by William: his curls made of wood shavings and leaf-shape costume in leather

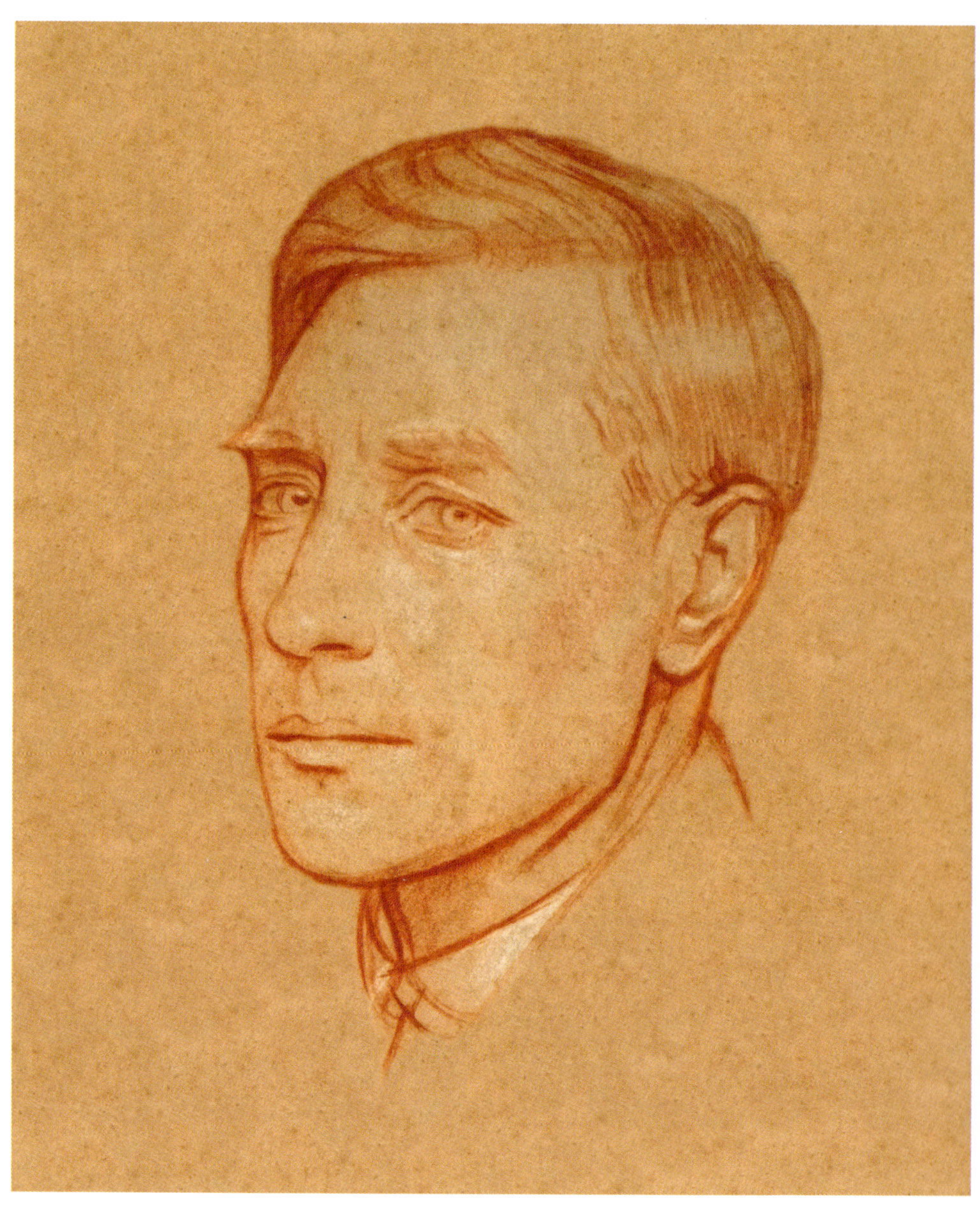

28. *Portrait of William* by William Rothenstein, 1920s

The stream of brilliant men (seldom women) who passed through the doors of his Cotswold and London homes in the 1920s and 1930s reads like a turn of the century cultural history – Bertrand Russell, Max Beerbohm, Bernard Shaw, the Indian poet Rabindranath Tagore. Once committed to their work, he would move heaven and earth to help them on their way. He saw them as co-partners in a continual, rummaging exploration into life's truths.

Before the war Rothenstein had called on Gimson and the Barnsleys in Sapperton, fallen in love with a derelict house and out-buildings nearby called Iles Green Farm, and become a convert to their village-crafts philosophy. He embraced the Oakridge villagers' life. To its characters, he gave the same appreciation as to his intellectual friends. To him, Eli Gardiner, hedger, thatcher and part-time undertaker, 'looked like Tolstoy, contained the wisdom of the ages, knew his Bible by heart, especially the Old Testament, and could interpret the sun, the clouds, the flight of birds and the secret life in field and hedgerow'. The beautiful Mrs Seth Gardiner (everyone in the village seemed to be called Gardiner, but seldom related) had a stream of strikingly handsome sons, of whom one, Jack, with a shrunken leg and a crutch, could leap on and off a horse, ride a bicycle, play cricket, keep a shop, bake bread and cakes, and tend sheep and poultry. Each year the villagers performed a play in the village hall. However wayward their rehearsals and attendance, Rothenstein saw their talent as exhilarating. In 1914 he formed the Far Oakridge Dramatic Society and took over the group's production, direction and scene painting.

Rothenstein shared William's interest in marionettes. During his Bradford childhood the enchantment of the annual Christmas pantomime had left a profound mark upon him. He adored the stage plots' intricate joke motifs:

> the Villain coming up and down through the trap door creating fire, lightning and thunder as he chose ... the transformation scene, the Harlequinade, the clown with toes in and frills out, making fools of everyone and then being fooled himself by Pantaloon; the beds falling on top of him, and the clocks moving about, ghosts haunting him, burglars threatening him, and all the while Columbine and Harlequin dancing and gliding with noiseless elegance.

Before long William and Eve had been swept into Rothenstein's milieu:

> I was henceforward to become intimate with a beautiful character
> and an enchanting artist ... Simmonds endowed every figure he
> carved with something of his own nature, yet each possessed with
> an individual soul. It is this inner life, be it lyrical or dramatic,
> which outlasts that of its creator, and distinguishes a fine work of
> art from a merely skillful one. Whether this last resembles a Bou-
> guereau or a Cézanne, a Canova or a Rodin, matters not; for if the
> quick soul be not within, it is but a doll to be thrown aside ... now
> and again a man's work is assessed at its true value. A.E. Hous-
> man's 'Shropshire Lad' became an English classic. Similarly the
> purity of Simmonds's puppets is recognised by all who see them,
> young and old.

William quickly became friends with Rothenstein's youngest children: the musical Rachel, her father's favourite, Billy and Betty. The
outcome of close acquaintance was, however, no foregone conclusion with Alice, Rothenstein's larger-than-life Balzacian wife. A law
unto herself, Alice entered into violent loves and hates, knowing no
caution and holding contemptuous antipathies of which she made
no secret. Reason did not come into it. She could adore with a frantic devotion, elevating on a pinnacle her father's late employer and
friend, Dante Gabriel Rossetti, as well as Algernon Swinburne and
Oscar Wilde. William and Eve passed the test known only to her – for
the moment at least.

Ironically, within weeks of William and Eve's arrival, Rothenstein
announced he was to sell his beloved house (no doubt under pressure
from Alice). He would move the family to London to further his
three children's education but would keep one tiny cottage. On his
departure he bequeathed his role of Director of the Oakridge Theatre
to William. He also determined to find a London gallery for William's carvings and if he took up the role now on offer of Principal
of William's old college, the Royal College of Art, William would be
one of the artists he would ask to teach there. Eric Gill, Jacob Epstein
and Henry Moore were also on his list of protégés. Once he and Alice
had moved into their new home in Sheffield Terrace, Kensington,
they would be in touch. In a whirl the Rothenstein family were gone.

The only letters in William's archives that show a glimmer of emotion (none survive to Eve) are to Rothenstein. The rest are practical

and down to earth. Bereft of Rothenstein's company, William wrote: 'You have been much in our thoughts and we feel the sudden change to quiet loneliness, especially these last few days while the Drinkwaters have also been away. Fortunately Mrs D and her mother are now back here and the great John is coming today.'

CHAPTER 14

New Theatre Director for Oakridge

1919–1921

*'The only thing in my mind at present is Lady Gregory's
Spreading the News ...'*
William Simmonds, letter to William Rothenstein, 1921

Solitary and cast low by Rothenstein's departure, William reverted to his love of walking. He came across a long network of footpaths weaving between the cottages, linking different levels before crossing the valley by the old pack horse road where the stream emerged into the River Frome, famous for its centuries-old part in the dyeing of scarlet cloth. On and up he strode through hamlets and villages to the source of the Frome at Brimpsfield, past barns, smithies and churches, through Caudle Green with its tiny church's saddleback tower and on past the little Norman church at Syde, returning via Edgeworth, Miserden and Daneway, then down the hill and back into Sapperton's Siccaridge Wood beside the canal.

In that first country summer of 1919, on mist-filled mornings, he studied insects and butterflies, and the footprints of animals and birds, absorbing every detail of the wild plants – periwinkle, pink-flowered wood sorrel and bluebells – glimpsed below the tree trunks. They reminded him of heraldry and of illustrations of legends and fairy tales.

The badger was the most difficult of the wild animals to catch sight of. He saw four fox cubs fooling around like kittens outside their earth, rolling each other over and playing hide and seek in the bushes, and a family of weasels capering on a dry stone wall and running to and fro along the top of an adjoining gate. And always horses; within a radius of six or eight miles he came to know every one of the cart horses, plough horses, stallions, mares and their foals.

With so many trees about, there was a rich variety of birds. In The Frith garden, the lesser spotted woodpecker, hawfinch, redstart, blackcap, tree creeper, long-tailed tit, coal tit and bullfinch; on the neighbour's shrubbery a tawny owl nested in the trees and a barn owl in the farm buildings. The green woodpecker was common in the meadows, and a kingfisher perched watchfully by the stream in which a dipper bobbed up and down on a submerged stone. Every now and then a pair of herons came to take prey in the Pinbury fishpond.

In Sapperton, a splendid oak stood twenty feet in spread and twenty-five feet in height before it branched out. Just beyond was an immense elm, then a finely shaped plane tree. Grand walnut trees grew in cottage gardens, one of which housed a giant Scottish pine. In the churchyards were ancient yews. The woods were thickly populated with mature chestnuts of both kinds, wych elms and sycamores, which astounded William with their line and grace. Further afield he would walk through a beech wood in Oakley Park and on into the Bathursts' estate deer park, scattering red squirrels and a herd of fallow deer, one of which was pure white. At the gates at the top of Cicely Hill, keeping to the main avenue, he walked the whole five miles, pausing to admire the grass-covered annexes known as the Ten Rides, which met at a great circle. Looking back he could see the tower of Cirencester Abbey at the vista's end and southward the church at Coates; he passed 'Pope's Seat', in a stone arbour where the poet wrote some of his best-known work, and came out along a footpath descending into Dorvel Wood.

William was looking urgently for carpenters and masons to restore his cottage – and with the high price of tiling, a thatcher for the roof of his studio barn. Stepping through the always-open village doorways he discovered each labourer's trade. When work was slack the men doubled up – most could build or repair dry-stone walls, dress stone tiles, build sheds, make windows and more. The cottages William entered, some very small indeed, revealed a patina of daily routine settled over centuries. In the main room, kitchen and living room combined, a permanent fire burned in a large iron fireplace, its hot range the means of heating water for washing and cooking and of warming the bread oven, a semi-circular projection on to the hearth. On one side of the fireplace, narrow stairs wound up to a bedroom. In the centre of the kitchen stood a sturdy wooden table where evening meals were prepared, bread and cakes made, vegetables chopped, ironing done. Once a day the square stone flags were scrubbed, boards polished and rugs beaten outside. For light, there were paraffin lamps and candles.

Beside the front door stood layer upon layer of stacked wood, sawn over winter. Water, never wasted, was collected from the rain in a drum or brought by women from streams and wells in heavy buckets large enough to carry several gallons at a time. On the road between Tunley and Far Oakridge, the Simmondses learnt of the spring where the water sparkled to produce a special cup of tea, and of another where if you dipped a bucket to a special level, the water was said to be good for the eyes. In some wells you could store your fresh dairy produce for days. Seeds were sown and planted in every smallholding in spring and the vegetables picked or dug up in summer.

Walter Gardiner built bikes and Mary Anne Gardiner ran a shop selling cotton and lace. A mile away in Waterlane another Gardiner, Jim, bartered rabbits and chickens and ran a carrier service to Stroud and Cirencester. Pipe tobacco and cigarettes could be bought in the Nelson Inn. Needlecraft was practised in every cottage.

Eve easily found a girl to help her in the house. The quest for a thatcher for William's workshop roof was also easy. Rothenstein had pressed for Eli Gardiner, whose skill was endorsed by John Drinkwater: 'the last of the great thatchers ... his long, stormy beard and thick hair, itself like thatch ...' Even in the post-war wage inflation, Eli had never increased his £1 a week wage. William watched mesmerised as he gravely and silently performed the secret rites of the trade, working the yellow thatch fast and even under his hands.

In his role as the Oakridge Society's new Director, William, unlike Rothenstein, wanted music to play a central part. It was astonishing how many of the Gardiners were musical. Quite easily he found a pianist, a drum player, two violinists (Frank and Fred Gardiner), a clarinetist (Tom Gardiner) and Austin Gardiner, a seven-string G banjo player until he lost his front teeth, to form a miniature orchestra. As for the actors, Rothenstein had forewarned that they were a law unto themselves, but had left William a valuable sprinkling of information about who lived where. Blithely ignoring the warning, William found widespread enthusiasm and booked up the ones that seemed most committed.

The villagers were leaning towards a farce for their high-profile play at Christmas time. This was against all William's instincts. He drew a strong distinction between farce, which irritated him, and comedy, which he enjoyed. Rothenstein had avoided both: his last production, Charles McEvoy's *Village Wedding*, written specially for village theatre, had been admired by Bernard Shaw but was rather too serious for Oakridge. For the moment William refrained from consulting Rothenstein (who was constantly asking for village news and still thought of the Society as his baby), partly to establish a break with the past and partly feeling that it would be an imposition given his London commitments. To get the villagers on side as much as he could, William suggested they pool ideas and was pleased when they asked for his puppet show alongside the monthly skits. In the meantime, he searched his bookshelves and asked around for suggestions for the Christmas production.

* * * * * *

Rothenstein had finally accepted the offer to head the Royal College of Art. He wrote to William about his life in London and confided the gruesome details of the uproar that had followed his appointment. Protests and deputations from entrenched art masters had descended on the President of the Board of Education; questions on their behalf had been asked in the House of Commons. Quite untroubled, although accepting that his qualifications might appear 'unusual' to the Teachers' Union, he was confident that the furore would die down. He was seeing much of Rabindranath Tagore and was painting T.E. Lawrence. He had also had further sittings with the Anglo-Argentinian ornithologist and writer, W.H. Hudson, who sent his best wishes to William and had warmly praised the puppets' post-war London debut at the Rothensteins' house-warming party. Rotherstein relayed to William: 'Hudson heard constantly from people who saw your performance – one and all say the most enchanting they ever saw. Alice and I were all more grateful to you both than we can well say … I hear there is some chance of your joining us in Norfolk.'

After William's puppet show for them in London an impulsive invitation came from Alice to join the Rothensteins at the seaside in Norfolk. They accepted, and the holiday in primitive Happisburgh, or Hasbro as the cognoscenti called it, cemented the friendship. The war had left its mark on the village population, but William saw instinctively why for a century or more the place had been the favourite haunt of artists, bishops, explorers and writers streaming in to spend their summers in the ancient seaside cottages. William's tiny Kodak snaps show beach life with Alice and the children, a visit to St Mary's Church and its fifteenth-century octagonal font with carved figures of lions and satyrs and another visit to the oldest working lighthouse in East Anglia, an eighty-five-foot tall tower with lights to alert mariners to the treacherous Happisburgh sands. Taking a break from a surfeit of family life on the beach, he took a bus to the Norwich Art Gallery archives to do some research for John Drinkwater on the Norwich painters. In a letter written on 11 August 1920, he said he found the paintings 'refreshing' but had not discovered what he was looking for, adding that they had 'settled into this free and easy life quite successfully and don't seem to miss our daily jobs … bathing chilly … all Rothenstein family in good health'.

Work was crowding in. The most unnerving and probably the most important of the gifts Rothenstein had showered on William since their Sapperton meeting was his arrangement with the prestigious Alpine Gallery to hold a Simmonds exhibition in February 1921. Without anyone spelling it out, part of the deal was for Rothenstein to give William a leg-up by showing his own landscapes and portraits alongside William's carvings. The exhibition would coincide with the publication of Rothenstein's book *Twenty-four Portraits*, which contained several drawings of Sapperton characters. Unbeknown to William, the book was dedicated to him, along with John Drinkwater and Max Beerbohm.

Well before their seaside holiday, Rothenstein had observed that William had a lot on his plate. Would there be enough sculpture to make a proper impact, he wondered? As far back as May, William had warned that it was unlikely that *Wood Nymph* or any new puppet carvings would be ready. He would try and fill a display case with woodcarvings, but it was the ivories that were taking the time. Admittedly, the ebony case Sidney Barnsley was making for them, a mere eighteen inches in length, would take up very little room.

No doubt it was partly Rothenstein's own fault for bequeathing William the Oakridge Theatre. His anxiety was well founded. During the autumn and winter there were twice-or-thrice weekly village meetings in Oakridge Parish Hall, a rundown corrugated hut among beech trees close to the vicarage; there was a regular band practice; the choral group on Thursdays; the Players on Fridays; and a whole range of director's obligations: scenery to be designed and made, tickets to be printed and distributed, props, scripts, costumes, setting up the stage, accounts and raising money through jumble sales. But the worst of Rothenstein's 'poisoned chalice' lay in a cast who might or might not perform well on the night and who turned up for rehearsals only when they felt like it.

Towards the end of September, William, still dithering about replacing the idea of a farce with a Lady Gregory play, tactfully half-sought Rothenstein's advice:

> I am afraid if they get it [the play] themselves it will be very poor … I have asked John Drinkwater and another friend and trying to recall anything they have ever seen that might be suitable … the only thing in my mind at present is Lady Gregory's *Spreading the News* but I don't feel safe in facing the Irish language … it is just the sort of thing and would amuse them very much.

Lady Gregory was a writer, scholar and a friend of Yeats, with whom she had founded two of Ireland's great theatres. Her short plays are little classics. For her a comedy stood by its characters; she was fairly unconcerned with the plot, which she often left hanging. *Spreading the News* depicts a small village in Ireland with a bumbling new magistrate who inspects stalls at the fair, looking for the worst – a suspicion that the inhabitants unconsciously live up to. Deafness and gossip are some of the elements that culminate in an arrest for a non-existent murder. The satire ends abruptly, without resolution, leaving the audience to ruminate on people's readiness to think ill of their neighbours.

Far from coming up with an idea, and still worried that William was over-committed, Rothenstein replied breezily after a three-week delay, 'Oakridge wants to perform a farce, and to see a farce, & it is right Oakridge should have a farce … I hope to come to see the performance' … 'We want to see you soon' and added 'you are not forgetting next February [the Alpine Gallery exhibition] I hope.'

William was not best pleased with Rothenstein's advice, especially given his complaints on how 'trivial and characterless' the villagers' choice of plays had been in his day: 'Heaven knows where they got them.' But William compromised, successfully he thought, by having two plays; and to accompany them he had persuaded the villagers to let him use some Percy Grainger choral music:

> I think the two we have started will do very well ... *Spreading the News* seems just the sort of play for them and very good but rather short so we have chosen a farce as well – *The Area Belle* – which some of them jumped at and were more anxious to do than anything else. So James Gardiner is going to take charge of the farce and I am taking the play which seems a very satisfactory arrangement because luckily each set of players seem to like the things they are doing and the people who were so anxious for farce have got what they want.

William shook off all the difficulties. His pre-war experience with Edwin Abbey in Fairford and his London puppet shows had accelerated his love of theatre and, influenced by Yeats, he believed that the villagers' voice was the theatre's most authentic form. He was surrounded by a group of avant-garde poets, thinkers and writers, and it was now invaluable to him that the movement included many of Rothenstein's friends: Rabindranath Tagore, Max Beerbohm, Walter de la Mare, John Masefield, W.H. Hudson and, of course, John Drinkwater himself. Thomas Hardy, too, was to collaborate with William in allowing an adaptation of *Under the Greenwood Tree*, and also helping was the now almost-forgotten author Eden Phillpotts, famous at the time for his novel cycle about Dartmoor, as well as the Chipping Campden artists who remained after Charles Ashbee, the group's founder, had left and his commune had broken up.

The role of literary village impresario was to capture William for the next twenty years. Unlike his future friend and collaborator, the poet John Masefield (who had established his own village theatre in Oxfordshire, where he put on plays in verse), William did not share the load with his wife. Eve felt that managing the ticket sales and accounts was inappropriate for her status. She would give her all to establishing her new garden, entertaining on her terms and, of course, creating the puppets' music and their clothing, but no more than that. Masefield wrote:

We were the last of the Pre-Raphaelites followers. All of us were … deeply under the spell of William Morris … These were the days long before detractors had begun their malice; … we felt we owed our souls to them [and were] a living part of the fellowship they had made … Yeats gave us some share in [their] kingdom.

CHAPTER 15

Annus Mirabilis

1921

> '*When a man has fine passions to start with and whose mind
> is trained to observe and retain his impressions, and his hands
> to express them, then everything will be full of meaning;
> so that really [William Simmonds'] sculptures can show but
> half of the hundreds of beautiful ideas which form the daily
> life of William Simmonds.*'

Exhibition catalogue, Alpine Gallery, February 1921

Despite the distractions of the village play, William had man-aged to organise himself in time and fill the vitrine with enough old and new work. The Alpine Gallery exhibition opened with fanfare on 9 February 1921. *The Times* reviewer wrote 'W.G. Simmonds carvings are so small that the visitor might over-look them; but they are unique in our time for their combination of exquisite finish with large and intense imagination … The Chinese themselves have done nothing better, yet there is nothing imitative in them … admired by a master of any age.' And on 14 February, the *Westminster Gazette* wrote 'tender and perceptive studies as simple as elsewhere he is complex … he is so familiar with animal life that he can achieve what may be termed generic portraiture of the beasts he loves and knows … and a glass case of tiny ivories … it is not too much to say that WGS has caught the essential greatness that makes medieval European and Chinese ivories respectively things of gran-deur and of delicacy.'

These were not the only critics to recognise a centuries-old tra-dition expressing itself in William's work – a tradition epitomised by the Netsuke artists of Japan, where men worked for love of the object they were carving, in anonymity, oblivious to recognition, let alone self-promotion. The *Evening Standard* saw 'A case of carved ivories whose work approximates that of a Japanese Netsuke worker although the feeling and conception is entirely his own.'

To William's embarrassment, the critics were dismissive of Rothenstein's work. '[Simmonds's pieces are] exquisitely satisfactory in that they spoilt the eye for the parched co-location of some of the [Rothenstein] portraits – not that they were entirely lacking in interest', wrote the *Connoisseur*, 'One in particular – Elie the Thatcher – though lacking in volume as regards the body ...' Rothenstein had promoted the private view and William's sculpture to as many people as possible; William was touched that George Clausen and Sylvan Boxsius from his Academy days came on the opening night. But collectors were disappointed that so few pieces could be bought. *Shepherd Singing*, an early ash carving from the Fovant days, went quickly, as did the exquisite *Small Cat*.

In the week that followed, his diary filled up with invitations, some from patrons commissioning work, others from would-be lionisers. The much-decorated Scottish Lord Lieutenant, Lord Carmichael, who had bought the cat, wanted an iron weather vane with two figures; Darcy Braddell, the architect, introduced him to Winifred Tennyson Jesse, a beauty and a writer whose Tudor watermill he was working on; Claud and Margaret Biddulph commissioned a private troupe of Punch and Judy puppets and booked William and Eve to perform with them at Rodmarton Manor, their house not far from Oakridge; Lady Orpen and Lady Montagu invited the Simmondses to tea in London; and Albert Rutherston, Rothenstein's renamed stage-designer brother, organised a lunch with the Powells and his actress wife to discuss his sets for an ancient Chinese play. Unused to this social attention, William took time out to visit Rothenstein at the Royal College of Art, after which he took Rothenstein's daughters Rachel and Betty to *A Midsummer Night's Dream* at the Royal Court.

In retrospect, the years 1921 and 1922 – three years after he had given up painting for good – were a landmark for William. The originality and imagination of his sculpture brought him a national reputation as a minor genius, one whose art could stand comparison with the miniatures of Nicholas Hilliard and the watercolours of John Sell Cotman, or the poetry of A.E. Housman.

Towards the end of his show, William ran into the egocentric 'genius' Gordon Craig of the Alpine Gallery. Now firmly established as the world's leading expert on every aspect of theatre, he had been asked to curate an 'International Theatre Exhibition' in Amsterdam that was to transfer to the Victoria and Albert Museum. It was to be a huge undertaking, and the first exhibition to concentrate on theatre designs, drawings, masks, plans and models for the modern stage from all over the world. Craig's particular interest, marionettes, would be prominently on display. 'There is only one actor … who has the soul of the dramatic poet … the true and loyal interpreter of the poet, he would proclaim; this is the marionette.' He asked William to contribute pieces for the British Room, as long as he could ensure delivery by December. Something about the encounter rubbed William up the wrong way. His diary remarks with an uncharacteristic sting: 'Gordon Craig tells us what is wanted on the English Stage and we find at the end … that what it wants is Gordon Craig. Does it? And if it does, why doesn't it get him?'

Despite the exhilarating experience of the London show, it was a relief to return to The Frith. William now set himself a hard routine for the year ahead. Rothenstein, however, interrupted his concentration by announcing his intention to come and stay on Good Friday; and on the Monday could his two youngest children, Betty and Billy, come to stay too? Followed by Rachel? Apart from the urban-loving Alice, who had endured enough isolation in the country throughout the long war years, the rest of the family were pining to return to their idyllic village and Rothenstein determined once more to have a foothold in Oakridge. So while staying with the Simmondses he intended to see whether somehow the little cottage beside his old house could fit them all in. It had suited the childless Beerbohms and Drinkwaters happily enough, but a family of six was another matter. Poor John Drinkwater, although no longer impoverished, indeed rather well off with his theatre contracts and his Abraham Lincoln lectures in America, was in marital difficulties. On one of his frequent journeys to New York on a passenger steamer, his wife Kathleen had fallen for the Ukrainian pianist Benno Moiseiwitsch. In retaliation Moiseiwitsch's wife Daisy had succeeded in trapping Drinkwater into an affair.

With a month to go before the opening night of *Spreading the News*, Rothenstein could not resist attending one of William's rehearsals, to see how he was dealing with a recalcitrant cast. He was deeply impressed with the production. Up to then he had thought of William as 'a carver in wood and ivory … a Little Master, in the old German sense'. Now he saw him as an avant-garde producer-director of a new genre. Seeing that William had set his heart on Lady Gregory's one-act comedies, he was converted and would back him for another of hers, *Hyacinth Halvey*, for the end of the year.

With typical generosity, Rothenstein determined to launch William on a parallel career. He wrote privately to Lady Gregory to tell her that he had promised William that he could get the performance rights for him in time. Her delayed reply from her home in Galway was friendly:

> I must honour your promise for this performance of 'Hyacinth' and will make it right with Samuel French [her agent], who has 3 plays in his hands – The puppets sound delightful … I once helped start a [marionette] Company … in turning out old cupboards yesterday [I found] a model puppet I had bought in Paris. 'Hyacinth' is quite up in the world: it was given at the Birmingham Church Congress before 8 Bishops and I know not how many lesser lights … Please send the permissions on to WS.

Rothenstein's next target was John Masefield, a man of gentle disposition who despite being over the compulsory service age had volunteered to work in a French military hospital when war broke out. Once peace came, like William, he moved as soon as he could to the country, where he kept bees and raised goats and poultry.

At one with Oxfordshire's people and their rural ways, his mission now was to create not just a more closely knit local community but also, bit by bit, a better society through village theatre. He shied away from the stereotype of the poet as a man apart from his audience, with long hair and velvet jacket. As a devotee of Yeats, he believed the music and rhythm of words should not be confined to the printed page but communicated more directly through the living voice.

Masefield's theatre at Wootton, near Oxford, could not have been set up without his wife, Constance. But for all her efficiency and their fervent belief that they were creating a higher form of drama, and despite their occasional use of professional actors, mishaps occurred from time to time, as when an imported King Lear cried off on the opening night, leaving Masefield to read his lines as best he could from a script. A man of surprising energy and a prolific writer, he found time to combine his role as Theatre Producer with the writing of a mountain of plays, lectures, speeches, novels, essays, articles, children's stories and, above all, poetry. This last would in 1930 lead to his becoming Poet Laureate, an honour that most had expected to go to Rudyard Kipling.

By June Rothenstein's introduction to Masefield was bearing fruit. The two were collaborating over a three-day festival in Stroud with the Cotswold Players – another village theatre group, of which Masefield was Honorary Chairman and which had been founded by the husband-and-wife team, artist Maxwell Armfield and writer Constance Smedley, both committed pacifists. All the proceeds went to help war victims.

After Armfield and Smedley had set up the Cotswold Players and staged their first show in Amberley, they continued with simple comedies in Gloucestershire dialect and featured local places and legends. Spurred on by success, the Players spread further afield, travelling by wagon or bicycle or on foot, into the villages around Stroud. Since 1918 the group had become more professional and more ambitious. At its zenith the company included in its repertoire plays by Jerome K. Jerome and John Galsworthy and was referred to in national newspapers as the most distinctive amateur theatre company in the country.

The Stroud Festival arrangements began in businesslike fashion with letters arriving at The Frith regularly from the Committee Secretary. Would William's and Masefield's two companies perform together with a short play each on 6 September. Masefield – whose literary fame bestowed on him hallowed status – was given a separate slot to perform Euripides's *Iphigenia in Tauris*, as was Constance Smedley with her *Cheerful Tramp*.

As the weeks passed, the lack of financial control became a nagging anxiety. William had confidently signed up to sharing all expenses and profits between the participants (after a deduction of twenty per cent of the revenue to cover general costs). But bills for poster designs, newspaper advertisements, programme layout and print run increased by the week. He was forced to intervene personally and another theatre group, the British Drama League, was brought in to share the costs and give more publicity to the festival. Surely the venture must end in debt.

The first night was reasonably well received. The Stroud theatre critic praised William for his choice of Lady Gregory's play, full of laughter with an element of tenderness and sympathy, but went on to pan his stage performance. Some of his friends thought that he was not a bad actor, but no one could pretend his gentle equanimity was an asset in his role as a stage villain. 'He managed the lounging, song-humming mood well, but surely he should have roused himself from his calm when he was struggling against four or five peacemakers to get at his enemy? His charmingly horrible threats lost much of their taste in his mouth.' William was not that put out. As each year passed, he could never resist taking on minor roles in his village productions.

When no accounts appeared, William's worry increased. Finally there was relief. In November the Cotswold Players' Secretary wrote to tell him that the Festival had indeed made a loss 'but we have decided not to ask Oakridge to contribute anything. We enjoyed your performance very much, and have heard from many quarters how much it was appreciated – belated and best thanks and to all the players.'

William's plans for the marionettes had been continuing alongside his theatre work. The deadline for Craig's V&A exhibition was always on his mind. The troupe had grown from the Volta House days and by the end of the year his workshop contained twenty-six puppets in all. He would jot down in his diary ideas for scenes and names of characters – Charley and Joey, Drey, Jum, Zachariah Talbot (a harmless fellow), Jeffrey, a policeman. Here and there he scribbled down jokes, based on contemporary gossip or on news items, or lifted from the romantic silent film of the day, *The Bohemian Girl*.

The dolls' characters, the storylines and changes in the script were tested out on Eve, who was lavishing her attention on the costumes but continued to have an equal say in the music, mostly to be played by her on virginals. William's songs, his sailors' ditties, his peeps, squeaks and birdcalls, his country and cockney dialogue and his animal sounds were a triumph of invention. Masefield's long poem 'Everlasting Mercy', a depiction of English country life written in Sapperton before the war, had brought him mixed fame and notoriety; its frank, vernacular language had encouraged in artists a certain freedom and given them licence.

Since his discoveries in his tank-design days about balance and traction, William had continued exploring ways to improve the swing and mechanism of his marionettes. His attitude to their manipulation, so unlike that of other showmen, had developed into a science. His diary contains lists of brown fishing twine, binding, white Sydney thread, upholsterers' twine and macramé thread – all weighted and tested to find their breaking strain. He maintained to the end that the most important and difficult side of his art was the movement of the figures. If the marionettes' string work performed without a hitch, they might be ready for the world at large.

Incrementally, William's marionette performances had been gathering more widespread attention. As editors and journalists pursued

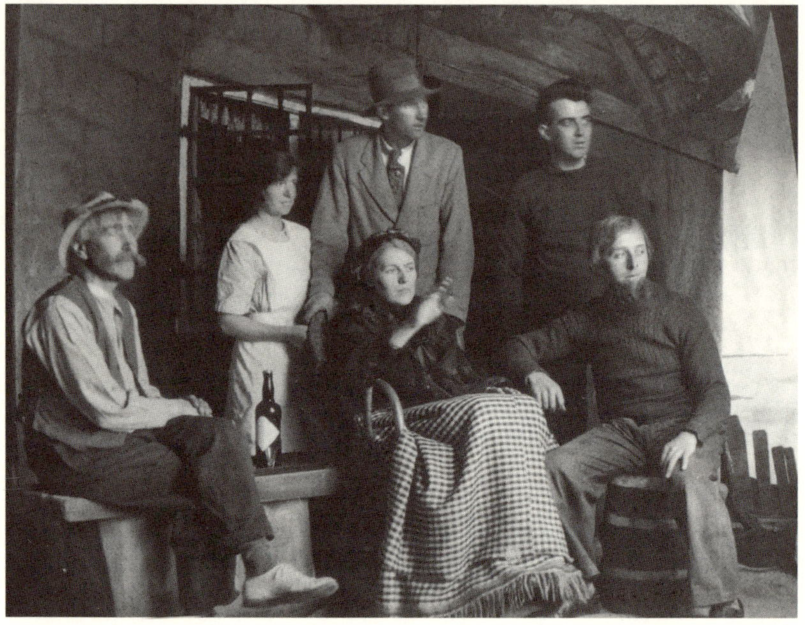

Oakridge Theatre Players directed by William in Sapperton Village Hall

him for photographs for magazines and newspapers, he felt obliged, in his modesty, and maybe with a fear of disappointing future audiences, to point out 'it is so much easier to pose puppets for the camera in elegant attitudes than it is to move them gracefully with lively and spirited action, free from the joltings and awkwardness of staggering movements. So many marionettes that photograph well are disappointing once they are seen in movement …'

Newspapers sent their own photographers for pictures of the new star. The best description of William's manner and appearance at this stage in his life comes from a *Manchester Guardian* journalist: 'a studious looking man, scholar and artist, light of figure and step, with fair hair and a smooth sensitive face, of the type that will probably never look old.'

During the summer came the first diary reference to the birth of new fifteen-inch puppets – King, Queen, Princess and Trillon – and to the new skit in which they would appear. By early December *Calico Castle* was all set to be tested on village friends.

CHAPTER 16

Second *Annus Mirabilis*

1922

*'I am not an entertainer: I am a wood carver ... I do little
else, except when the puppets break in and take me away.'*
Interview with William Simmonds,
Observer, 17 December 1922

William's second *annus mirabilis*, 1922, started unpromisingly with another of Eve's bouts of ill health. William had hoped that life in the country away from London's germs would cure her. But she was still confined to bed once or twice a year for days at a time. In William's Collins Diary, a loving Christmas present from Rachel Rothenstein, he records that Eve had a high temperature and her Peart relations had to be farmed out to the Jewsons, who lived in a converted group of cottages close by.

At first wary of William because of his close friendship with William Rothenstein, Norman Jewson, a key personality in the village, had finally befriended him. Fifteen years before, as a trainee architect, he had set out from London by donkey and trap to explore the Cotswolds. After discovering Sapperton, he had turned up on Gimson's doorstep at Daneway House and been invited into his workshop, first as his assistant, then as his friend and later as his partner in an architect practice. Eventually he married Ernest Barnsley's daughter, Mary.

Jewson had fallen out with Rothenstein when restoring his house in Iles Green. Halfway through the work, Rothenstein, until then a strong adherent of village-crafts philosophy, had taken umbrage at Gimson's attitude to their labour force, accusing Gimson of operating a closed shop by artificially keeping the cost of labour high.

Jewson, who would hear no criticism of his revered partner, was angered by what he saw as an attack on Gimson's character. The row rumbled on for years, and was further aggravated when friends attributed the falling out to Rothenstein's tiring of 'arts and crafty priggishness' and preferring 'the magnificence of machines as they produced things that could not be made (or not be made as well) by man'.

Escaping with some anxiety from nursing duties, William packed up his 'Castle' puppets and went with the Jewsons and the Pearts to perform round the kitchen table at the Barnsleys' family tea party, and the following day to the fancy dress dance in Sapperton Village Hall. There they found Catherine Powell dressed as Little Red Riding Hood and Louise dashingly disguised as her grandmother. But no Alfred. He had accounts and paperwork to settle in London. Their pre-Christmas exhibition of pottery in the Brook Street Gallery had been crowded, a year's work sold out and orders taken for more. Their money problems had retreated, but at a cost: the increasingly exhausted Louise had burdened herself further by agreeing to help Gordon Craig curate his V&A theatre exhibition. But Alfred appeared the next day and begged William to bring out the puppets once more to entertain village neighbours for a bagpipe party. A riotous evening ensued with the Sapperton men giving a sword dance and then bringing out their fiddles for Alfred to sing 'The Cheerful Arn' accompanied by a horn, and a Somerset air, 'The Blacksmith's Song'.

By the end of January, Eve was well enough for a weekend visit to the Wilkinsons at Cromwell House in Haresfield. This would be their first meeting since the Wilkinsons' move to the house that Eve had turned down in 1919. She was keen to see what they had made of it.

Having heard how happy the Simmondses were in the Cotswolds, Lily had been longing to cut loose from the Garden Suburbs. They must put the prison year behind them and take the plunge into what she saw as the fashionable 'Natural Life'. No matter if it were Sapperton, Painswick or Chipping Campden: a house in the heart of the blossoming Arts and Crafts movement was the place to be. And Eve was clearly the linchpin among the burgeoning network of artists, musicians, writers and craftsmen.

Far from fading away after the death of Gimson and the departure from Chipping Campden of its central figure Charles Ashbee, the Gloucestershire fraternity was experiencing a late flowering of considerable force. It was no longer in London and Birmingham that the protagonists wanted to live but, perhaps as a result of the war, in deep countryside, enveloped in the unassuming simplicity of village life. It was the Cotswolds that attracted the greatest number of them. Close by was the artist Charles Gere and his half-sister, Margaret, and the architect Detmar Blow, one of Ruskin's last disciples, who had just completed his own house, Hilles, in Arts and Crafts style. In the small town of Chipping Campden were the etcher and scholar F.L. Griggs, the furniture maker Gordon Russell, the silversmith Oliver Baker and the gardener Lawrence Johnston at Hidcot. The garden designer Harley Butt lived nearby in Chalford, near Stroud, and the stained-glass specialist Edward Payne with his son Henry at Amberley. Gimson and the Barnsleys' disciple and colleague Peter Waals, the furniture designer, would also set up in Chalford. The Sapperton crowd was reinforced by Emery Walker's commitment to Daneway after Gimson's death (he finally took over its lease in 1926). This was only a start. The list of artists who came in the 1920s and 1930s grew and grew. But would the Wilkinsons fit in? Previously they had been thought of principally as eccentric nomads with a Fabian interest in the cooperative movement.

The Simmondses found that the brothers' time in prison had done nothing to dampen their relentless cheerfulness. Late Christmas presents were exchanged on arrival and hot cider appeared every evening, followed by exuberant dancing, initiated by William, on the mouth organ given him by the Wilkinsons. Inordinately proud of the children, Arthur and Lily were teaching them at home, helped by their uncle Walter. Pino was musical and Bimbo artistic; both were turning out to be even more precocious than the young Rothensteins. Arthur had set about restoring Cromwell House (with Walter as general dogsbody), taking special care with the medieval fireplace in the drawing room.

As for Walter, it seemed his pre-war dream of roaming on his own and escaping the role of subservient younger brother had been lost to sight. But it lurked. On the Sunday walk to the Cromwell Stone on Haresfield Hill, erected in memory of a Civil War siege, he buttonholed William. He planned to make puppets for himself, breaking away from Arthur. He was now once more in the grip of his recollections of William Morris's book *News from Nowhere*, which had made a vivid imprint on his early adolescence with its romantic description of Cotswold life seen through the lens of Morris's special brand of cultural socialism.

Eve noticed Walter and Arthur's excessive interest in William's new marionettes, particularly after Charles Gere gave *Calico Castle* high praise over supper on the last evening. When Eve casually mentioned that the Biddulphs might book them for Rodmarton Manor, Lily pressed hard for a date to come and see the new creatures. Were the Wilkinsons, Eve wondered, beginning to think of William as a rival? It would be impossible for them to plagiarise his puppets – they were too original and too well known wherever they went – but Lily's rivalry could harm William in other ways. Eve had by now established herself as the 'business brain' of the family. One was very much needed. Apart from what William might earn, their income, from a few shares that she owned, barely covered their household expenses.

Eve understood the crucial role played in William's circle of creative artists and craftsmen by their patrons: the Bathursts in Cirencester Park, the Wills family at Miserden Park, the Bensons at Stanway and the Cadbury family, who took houses in various villages. But closest to Oakridge were Claud and Margaret Biddulph in Rodmarton. They had been impressed by William's Alpine Gallery show and were as keen as ever to commission his work. Intensely loyal and protective of her husband, Eve determined to ensure that the Wilkinsons did not invade his territory.

In spite of their growing number of admirers, and their value as a source of income, the puppets were of less importance to Eve than William's serious sculpture. Eve placed any new piece ostentatiously on show in the sitting room to catch the eye of a potential buyer. She felt it was the pieces he submitted to the Royal Academy each year that gave him the proper status to which he was entitled. She did not change her mind after the furore the marionettes caused at the 'International Theatre Exhibition' at the V&A later in the year.

To the Oakridge villagers, Eve was aloof; she was careful whom she invited to The Frith and into whose house she and William were received as a couple. She enjoyed supper with the Jewsons and the Emery Walkers, and tea (with games of tennis for William) with the Barnsleys in Sapperton, and of course visits from the Powells. William remained oblivious of such social subtleties. He was an accepted part of the villagers' lives, always in and out of their houses, immersed in and fascinated by their work and talents. A 'foreigner from London' he might well be, but he was never perceived as patronising. He was one of them, and he met them on equal terms, just as he did with his more well-off friends.

In early spring Margaret Biddulph showed William round Rodmarton Manor, its courtyards, outbuildings, the emerging private chapel and garden, and the hall to find the best space for the puppet performance. For the first time he was able to grasp the scale and importance of Ernest Barnsley's masterwork. The huge project had been under construction well before the war and was already becoming as a talisman of the Arts and Crafts movement. Claud Biddulph, a London banker, had pledged £5,000 a year to work slowly on the house and was exerting no pressure to rush its completion. It had been conceived not just as a family home, but to embody the ideal of community spirit, with space and buildings for village life, as well as for their estate employees. Only local materials were used. Stone and slate from nearby quarries were brought to the site by farm cart, and cut, shaped and laid by local masons; oak for the roof timbers was hewn from the Rodmarton woodland and seasoned in Rodmarton barns. The interior, also carried out by local labour and entirely designed by Ernest and Sidney Barnsley, had become a centre for reviving the crafts education of the villagers. William chose the hall for his puppets and, after negotiating a £3 fee, Margaret signed up the Oakridge Players to perform Lady Gregory's *Hyacinth Halvey* in the Rodmarton schoolroom. She also commissioned some puppets for the villagers as long as William gave them lessons in how they worked.

Having taken on board Drinkwater's suggestions on how best to deal with the play, William at last achieved a successful village production of *Cupid and the Styx*. In May Jewson brought the recently married Nina and Fred Griggs to The Frith during a break in sitting for their portraits by Henry Payne, which had been given them as a wedding present. Something of a hero to William, with his *Highways and Byways* book on the Cotswolds, Griggs came over again the next day to examine the puppets' movements in detail, and spent an hour drawing them.

William had sculpture commissions from outside as well as inside the charmed circle. After a struggle, he managed to finish carving an oak piece for the most seductive and unlikely of all his patrons, 'Fryn' Jesse, crime writer and great niece of the poet Tennyson. Jesse was restoring medieval Cut Mill in Sussex, romantically situated in Bosham Creek. She had fallen in love with it sailing up Chichester Harbour with her husband, who kept his marriage secret to avoid offending his mistress but took the risk of discovery by generously buying the house for Fryn. She was spoilt and elegant and had been wildly beautiful: 'I have never seen a lovelier girl', said the travel writer Rebecca West. But by the time William met her in her thirties her looks were already fading. After a joyride in an old-fashioned plane with its propeller at the back, she had crashed. Six operations and many pain-killing injections later, she had turned into a morphine addict.

* * * * * *

The 'International Theatre Exhibition' at the V&A was opened in a roar of publicity by Gordon Craig's mother, the illustrious actress Ellen Terry. In Craig's foreword to the programme, he wrote that with 900 exhibits from Europe, Russia and the United States, he hoped to set new standards before the public eye:

> a new way of looking at an old thing – no hideous revolution, no pompous reform – we just made some most ordinary and desirable changes. We based our changes on some of the best and oldest traditions known to mankind, though we rejected that ancient, and for some unknown reason respected, tradition that orders you to 'do as was done last time'. We began to build our theatres differently, to set our stages with different scenes, we acted our old and new plays differently not in every land or in every city – but in nearly every land and in most cities.

The Simmonds pieces were tiny in the huge exhibition space. William was proud they were there, but was wholly unprepared for what was to come. As the exhibition was coming to its end, he received a newspaper cutting from John Drinkwater's wife with the scrawled words 'Hullo? Love from Kathleen' at the top. An article in *The Times*, headlined 'Adorable Puppets' was devoted to his work.

The Times was the world's leading English language newspaper and the weekly column of its theatre critic, A.B. Walkley, was the first page turned to on a Wednesday. A friend of Bernard Shaw, Walkley, who was given to slipping graceful scholarship into the lightest of sentences, specialised in rare and subtle forms of art. One afternoon in July 1922, he was passing through the V&A in a depressed frame of mind, which he likened in his column to the 'Melancholie de Paquebot' in Flaubert's *l'Éducation Sentimentale*. Dismissively acknowledging designs by Lovat Fraser and Gordon Craig, he suddenly stopped short: 'blush to say that what chiefly delighted me there was a vitrine of marionettes, the work of Mr Simmonds ...'

Walkley describes how the sight of William's artistry in carving stimulated his imagination and ran riot in his head. Among several favourites, he singles out the *Calico Castle*: 'The quiet humour ... so expressed in the set and the surprised puppet faces ... makes my description of it vulgar by comparison.' He laments the absence of anyone in the museum's room to work the puppets,

> an immobile puppet has something mysterious about it ... capable of many strange things ... the demure but expectant girl labelled 'Light of Love'; the 'Old Man in Black', in decent black in so prim and Victorian a cut ... Is it a cynical story that will be told when the puppets move, if they ever do? Will the old man make advances that reflect shame on his grey hairs? The courtesan looks as though she thought so.

This was no more and no less than a wide-open invitation for a London public performance. Despite his daily painting and his absorption in reorganising the Royal College, Rothenstein energetically set about helping his new friend. Shamelessly, he was using his new position to speak out for causes he believed in. In a lecture on Art and Industry to the Royal Society of Arts, he laid into the lack of respect given to present-day creative genius. He told William the Art Workers' Guild would be fine as a setting for a puppet show in December and following that, over Christmas, he would give a party for the marionettes.

Alice had moved the family to a house with a relatively large studio on the top floor in Sheffield Terrace – the perfect place for a live show. He would invite as many influential people as possible, including journalists: the *Daily Mail* came out first with an article describing: 'A select gathering in Professor William Rothenstein's studio to witness a private performance of a WGS puppet show ... an artist of such rare versatility that only his modesty could prevent his fame from spreading throughout the land.' Bernard Shaw, so caustic at William's puppet show in Volta House during the war, grunted his approval every other minute and told all and sundry

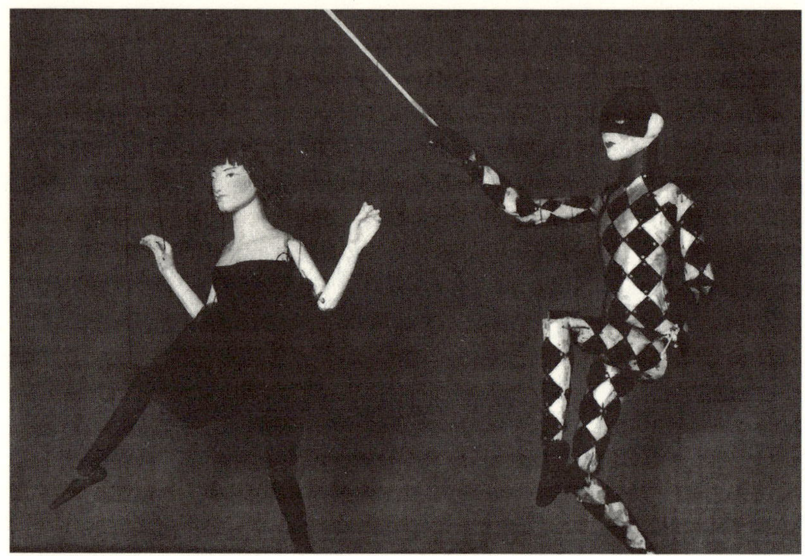

Colombine and Harlequin enter dancing to the 'Greensleeves' overture in
Harlequinade

that he was 'completely charmed with the Marionettes'. Arnold
Bennett agreed.

Soon after, the *Observer* (17 December 1922) commissioned a
highly complimentary interview with William, beginning with his
early life and artistic training and ending with a detailed description
of each of his four playlets: *Harlequinade, Woodland Scene, Street
Scene* and the fourth episode, a village fair at which a puppet show
is one of the attractions. 'As the scene opens the showman is waiting
for the people to arrive; characters we have already seen come to the
fair and take their seats for the performance – to virginals with the
help of trumpets we add the noise of the fair. Then the little curtain
goes up and you see the smaller puppets playing to the large puppets.'

Six months after discovering William, A.B. Walkley devoted
another 1,000-word *Times* article to William when at last he found
the puppets 'at work'. Walkley felt relief that 'in a world of ever-ceas-
ing change', his fascination with William's puppets had increased
rather than disappeared.

Of the four plays, Walkley was most charmed by *The Woodland*;
he compared William's faun to a tree-nymph from Greek mythology.

It was 'a Chaucerian play of mythological nymphs, fauns and hamadryads – which suggested a picture by a cinquecento artist illustrating a short story from his medieval legend series by Anatole France'. And here he found genius in William's technical expertise:

the dying stag's chest heaves and falls. Little Faun twirls high in the air and squats on the ground as a faun should, but as you would suppose no puppet could. Young Centaur kicks out with his hind legs. The Forester kneels behind his bush as easily as though he were flesh and blood. The wild dance of joy between the two fauns is wild indeed, but in perfect unison. It is almost impossible to think that these tiny figures are all wire-pulled: they seem to be endowed with life. But what after all is the great delight is not so much the nimbleness of Mr Simmonds's figures as the delicate freshness of his fancy … reminding me of Hazlitt's Table Talk 'On Landscape by Nicholas Poussin' and his picture of the shepherds in the Vale of Tempe going out on a spring morning and coming to a tomb with an inscription: *Et Ego In Arcadia Vixi* … in this semi-classical scene I glimpsed that I too had been in Arcadia. Fielding's puppet master boasts that his 'figures are as big as life and they represent life in every particular'. Not so Mr Simmonds's … These are not more than a foot high, if as much, and though they represent life in every particular, it is not ours but theirs. There is something uncanny about it, because while their limbs move, their faces are set. It is a life in which while it is the easiest thing in the world to dance, to spring your own height or more in the air, to twist your limbs into knots, it is difficult to walk, still more difficult to sit down, and quite impossible to pick up a handkerchief or hand a letter. You cannot have a puppet show *Macbeth*, because when Lady Macbeth has to say 'Give <u>me</u> the daggers' she could only drop them with a clash which wakes up the whole castle. You cannot have a puppet show of *Hamlet* because Ophelia couldn't carry her flowers, still less distribute them. Difficult as it is for the puppets to sit down, Mr Simmonds manages it in Puppets' 'Holiday' when they all take their seats at a puppet show – puppets looking at puppets more minute than themselves, a puppet show within a puppet show, puppetry so to speak mathematically, with the square root extracted … these microscopic puppets are as neatly articulated and dance as accurately as the larger ones … puppets have, whatever their dimension, this advantage over

human actors – they are made for what they do, their nature con-
forms exactly to their destiny.

Walkley registered relief that his first encounter with Simmonds's
puppets had not played him false, as once had happened with his
early love of Ibsen and Thackeray. 'Simmonds puppets ... are little
marvels of the sculptor's art, as delicate in their miniature elegance
as figures of Tanagra. The plays have a literary quality, a sense of the
past, and at their best a touch of poetry ... sheer enchantment.'

The Tanagra comparison was apposite. Fifty years earlier, great
quantities of small terracotta figurines, dating from the fourth
century BC, had been uncovered by Greek ploughmen in tombs
near the ancient city of Tanagra. Their poise, refinement and realism
appealed to nineteenth-century European ideals and the 'Tanagra
figures' had entered the cultural vocabulary. For the French their
elegance represented 'the Parisienne of the ancient world' and Oscar
Wilde's protagonist in *The Picture of Dorian Gray* likens his love,
Sybil, to 'the delicate grace of the Tanagra figurine that you have in
your Studio'.

William's success did not end here. After the puppets' four public performances at the Art Workers' Guild, a full-page article with
photographs appeared just before Christmas 1922 in the *Manchester Guardian*. 'William Simmonds has returned to his village of Far
Oakridge in Gloucestershire, a famous man ...', the article began.
'His audiences had included many of the most fastidious and influential figures in intellectual and fashionable society – booked seats
days before the production – and much intrigue went to secure them
– an extra performance given ... WGS had raised puppetry to an
undreamt of picture of loveliness and delight.' Eve too was praised:
'her delightful playing on the virginals of old English airs quickened
the beauty of the show.'

Thus two shining years – years of unexpected recognition, of new
friendships and intense hard work – came to a close. William knew
by now that woodcarving was his true life: 'I do little else except
when the puppets break in and take me away. I am not an entertainer, I am a wood carver.' But the ephemeral art of the marionette,
from whose power he claimed to seek escape, touched people with
stardust. Another critic wrote of 'The articulation of the puppets,
devised with such ingenuity that every movement is a humorous
representation of real life ... his several years of devotion to the

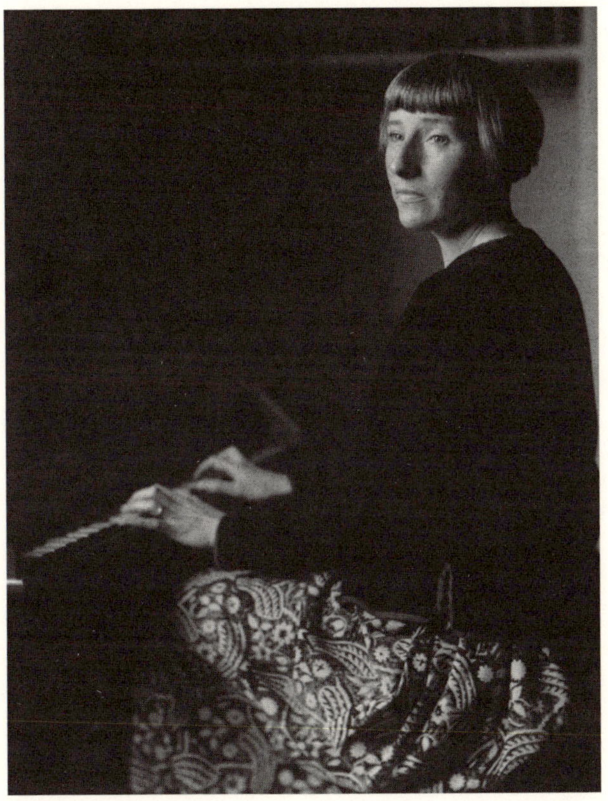

Eve playing the clavichord for the marionettes at the Art Workers' Guild, 1922.
Her skirt is made from Barron and Larcher material

development of his Puppet show ... brought to a wonderful degree of
perfection thanks to his independence from outside help. The marionettes, costumes, scenery, the working of the strings, the invention of
the scenes and episodes, the dialogues and the singing being entirely
his own. The result of this concentration is absolute artistic unity.'

CHAPTER 17

Professors on the Road

1922–1923

'... puppets – referred to by Eleanor Duse as "guided by a soul" – are the only artistic protagonists of drama – that impersonality is an invaluable asset in dramatic performance'.
Interview with Gordon Craig, *Observer*, 1923

Critics continued to treat William less as an artist nearing fifty than an up-and-coming young man to watch. Readers of the *Morning Post* in January were told that at the Royal Academy 'WG Simmonds must again be mentioned for his extraordinary "Duck" and "Drake" carved in Sycamore with ivory inlay' and *Country Life* did a full-page spread of his carvings. The glorious years seemed to be continuing.

Much of his early recognition had been owing to Rothenstein's help. He was fortunate to have had four years of Rothenstein's friendship and unwavering support before a change came: at first sudden, as Rothenstein was hit hard by his daughter's devastating illness, and then more gradual as his own condition slowly deteriorated and finally led to his collapse. It would be eight years before he returned to a semblance of his old self.

Late in 1922 Rothenstein's beloved daughter Rachel, who had just got into the Royal College of Music, developed undefined symptoms and underwent a major operation. Alice, in her customary state of nervous anxiety, was unable to be of much assistance, and the burden fell on Rothenstein alone to give Rachel the full measure of the loving attention she needed. The outside world saw his marriage to Alice as at best a *modus vivendi*, at worst a rank mismatch. Perhaps rightly:

they had little in common and exasperated each other. With time they came to live increasingly separate lives.

In February 1923 Rothenstein, clearly distraught, brought Rachel to convalesce in Oakridge. His friends rallied round. Dolmetsch made her some virginals and Walter de la Mare visited, along with a stream of other sympathisers. William did his best to find gentle ways of amusing her through the one thing her father could not provide, a shared love of music and song. He hoped she would be well enough to go with him to see an Italian troupe of marionettes, the Teatro dei Piccoli, which was coming to London in March to perform at the New Scala Theatre. They were renowned for their performances of Shakespeare, and the purists huffed that the wooden figures sacrilegiously degraded the Master's genius, mutilating *The Tempest* for children's amusement – and in Italian at that. If one wanted to see a Shakespeare play, one went to the English theatre.

But by the time the famous Teatro dei Piccoli finally arrived in London, Rachel's health had deteriorated again and she had to be sent to a nursing home. Before the summer was out, Rothenstein would put aside everything else in his life to take her to Switzerland for 'sun treatment' in the Alps. 'Two people wrapped up in love in a great warm cloak', his novelist friend Fred Manning described them. Hearing of her critical state, William was deeply concerned for her father: 'After seeing Rachel look so much herself,' he wrote to him:

> it was a terrible shock to hear the news last night from Sidney Barnsley. What a terrible, anxious time it must be for you waiting for signs of recovery … we can think of nothing else. I feel miserably helpless to do anything that can be the least bit of help … all I can do is bother you for news, which we shall be very grateful for and to send a very deep wish that it will be to tell us of some improvement
>
> From, very affectionately, William

There was nothing much William could do except offer practical support. He took the two younger Rothenstein children, Billy and Betty, to see the Italian puppets. Some of the figures were 'very good indeed', but what astonished him was the scale of the production. The company had five hundred marionettes (each about four feet in height), with twelve operators able to control twenty-four figures at any one time on stage. In their repertoire they had five ballets, several variety turns, five plays and twenty-five operas, with music adapted for the Teatro from Purcell, Donizetti and Wagner. *The Sleeping Beauty* was chosen for the London debut. Ottorino Respighi conducted a full orchestra and nine singers, with the dialogue and arias in English.

The marionettes became the rage of London. The critics were impressed in their Anglo-centric way, the *Observer* taking the opportunity to push Gordon Craig:

> a particularly interesting experiment … the marionettes make great play with their hands – they do not seem British by birth … Mr Gordon Craig startled the world some time ago by coming to the logical conclusion of his theories that puppets – referred to by Leonora Duse as 'guided by a soul' – are the only artistic protagonists of drama – that impersonality is an invaluable asset in dramatic performances.

The Times promoted the British version through William: 'We just do not know in England what a puppet show can be. Punch and Judy is our solitary example. One Englishman has tentatively manned a puppet ship and launched forth – It would be a great thing if Mr Simmonds could set up an English Guignol.'

The Teatro dei Piccoli's publicity brought William himself further into the limelight. Lydia Lopokova, the prima ballerina, wanted to see his puppets 'near to', and he would bring some over for her to see. After Diaghilev's lavish production of *The Sleeping Beauty* at Covent Garden in 1921, where she danced the Lilac Fairy and Princess Aurora, Lopokova's years with the Ballet Russe were coming to an end. Maynard Keynes had fallen in love with her and she was waiting for her divorce to come through. Marionettes had been central to her artistic life. In her first captivating appearance as Columbine in 1910, her tiny five-foot frame reminded the critics of Hoffman's *'poupées'*. Nijinsky, as Petrushka, was the imprisoned genius through his portrayal of the wooden puppet struggling to become human again. Oppressed by his fate, scrambling for a vestige of dignity, meditating on the precariousness of freedom and the tragedy of its loss, in his final failing gesture he is left outside and alone – a Hamlet of puppets, a mythical outcast in whom was concentrated all the pathos and suffering of life.

* * * * * *

Meanwhile Walter Wilkinson had no intention of poaching on Williams's territory. Chafing at his role of junior brother, he was pushing William hard to join him, having decided for a second time to throw up his conventional life and follow Morris's call to live a simple existence. In this promised path to happiness, Walter confided, he sought the rebirth of his self. He would take to the road, like the wandering puppeteers of the pre-war era, popularly known as 'Professors'. While keeping the traditional Punch and Judy routine, he would take a sideways look at contemporary society, and update the puppets' characters with impromptu plot lines, leaving the show open to change at every village.

It did not escape Walter that he could also use some practical help from William in finding his inner soul, for the details of getting everything together in time for the summer season began to overwhelm him: choosing the size and colour of the boxes for the puppet theatre, buying the camping equipment and designing the wheels for the cart to ease the task of pushing, pulling and climbing hills. And then there were the puppets themselves. Glove puppets were less onerous than marionettes, but he had to create their characters, carve their heads and hands and make their clothing. For the Farmer he had earmarked some old corduroy, for the well-dressed Parson a piece of an abandoned riding jacket, and for the Monkey's skin he would chop into an old Jaeger coat. But he had yet to complete any of them.

As March turned to April (1923), to calm Walter's growing panic, William promised to accompany him on the first part of his West Country tour and take two of his own puppets to perform. Even more generously, he offered to make the truck with which Walter would travel and the two boxes for the puppet theatre equipment. Being the man he was, he turned it into a minor work of art in balance and traction.

Walter set out a day or two earlier on his own to Miserden to rehearse the puppets at a settlement he admired called the Whiteway Colony, where a few of its original settlers remained. Founded twenty years before in a wave of Socialist idealism, the small community had renounced private property and lived a peasant life on Tolstoyan principles. In spite of some disillusionment

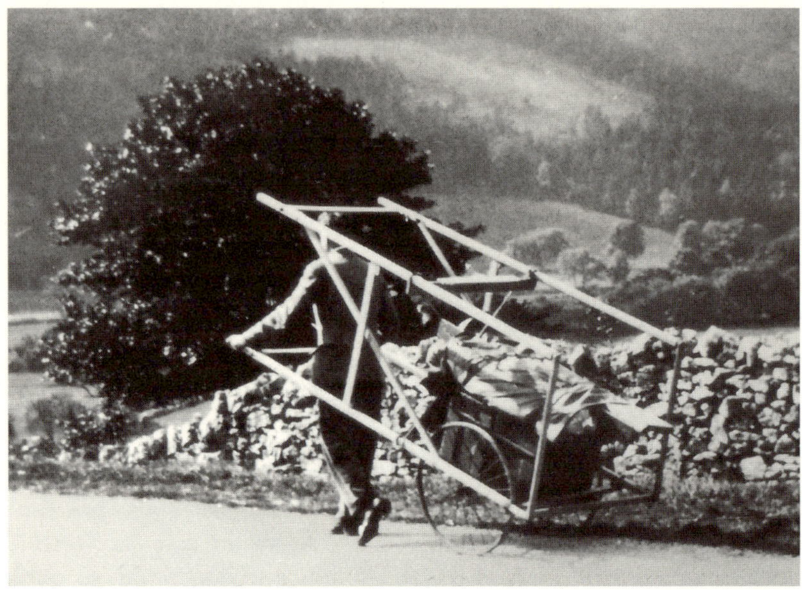

William made Walter Wilkinson's cart for the puppet shows that he performed all over England

(the members were lazy, the stony ground hard to grow crops in), they had recently built a communal hall and a school – the perfect place for Walter to try out his new vocation. The settlers were enthusiastic at this break from monotony. Two days later Walter moved on, preening himself on his success, to meet William on Painswick Beacon, on the slope half a mile above the Adam and Eve Pub.

Eve had brought her sister Dorothy and the Sapperton bunch en masse – Sidney and Lucy Barnsley, the Jewsons and, of course, Arthur and Lily Wilkinson and their two children – to cheer William and Walter on their way. The new cart looked promising. True to his word, William had brought along his two puppets, as well as some tobacco and chocolate, a flageolet (an ancient trumpet) to announce the performances, a new pair of simmoman's boots and *The Complete Works of Shakespeare*. He had bought this edition with his own pocket money as a child and it travelled with him everywhere

After a wine-filled picnic and a farewell performance on the Painswick hilltop, Eve presented her husband with a large notebook and made him promise to keep a diary. The pages that follow are lifted in part from William's own account, and in part from Walter's book, *The Peep Show*, published in 1927. Walter's description of their journey (where his companion is nameless, and at the end resented) portrays him as a Professor leading a lonely and courageous life on the road. As for William, if one reads between the lines of his account, it is clear that though the experience was one he did not regret and at times greatly enjoyed, he was clearly relieved when it was over.

The two men left the group towards evening, slightly drunk, for their first night in the open. They pitched tent – six feet long, four feet wide and three and a half feet high – looking toward the River Severn, which glinted in the setting sun as it snaked its way in a haze of mist across the plain and out to the sea. As they set off, Walter kept to himself the uncharitable thought, which he later admitted in his memoirs, that William might not do his fair share of pulling. It showed how little he understood his man. Keen to test his new wheels, and very fit, William had pulled the load almost the whole way.

Next morning at 11 o'clock they reached the Gloucester and Sharpness Canal, hauled their equipment over the bridge railings and clambered aboard a barge, their destination Sharpness docks near the top of the Bristol Channel. Here they would catch a boat to Bristol, then on further south to somewhere, anywhere, in Devon or Cornwall.

At Sharpness, pulling the load over rusting cables and railway lines, along cinder paths, among ramshackle offices and lumber yards, they missed the Bristol steamer. Walter turned down William's suggestion of boarding one of two other boats on the grounds that they looked 'dirty, untidy places, with rough, swearing crews who would only provide bloaters and tea'.

They took a train to the centre of Bristol and rattled through the cobbled streets to its outskirts to spend the night in a field on a haystack. Next day they tracked down a boat to Minehead. This time they were treated like royalty. At the sight of a Punch and Judy Show, the sailors sprang into life, flung out a special gangway, ushered them to the front of a long queue, lifted their paraphernalia aboard and lashed it to the mast – then stung them for seven and sixpence.

But at Minehead Pier a high tide and violent waves prevented their boat from docking level with the platform. Over an hour after arrival, exhausted, they eventually shouldered the cart down a steep gangway and up a slippery iron staircase to a higher deck, from which they were able to disembark. Once on the pier they coughed up a fourpenny landing fee – a tiny sum compared with the boarding charge, but by now they could barely afford it: after two days on the road without one public performance they were running out of money. They had to stage a show as soon as possible.

Their trade advertised itself. As they made their way towards the coast lane, pushing through barking dogs and horses shying, past advertisements for teas and blaring announcements for charabanc trips, children ran ahead of them and spread the news. The whole town stood still in the street and stared.

Where the lane widened, they lit on an open grass space with a fountain, and set the show up against a small tree to give support. Soon buskers with violins, guitars, mandolins and banjos appeared, eyeing up the situation. Undeterred, William gave six rousing blasts on his trumpet. John Barleycorn, Walter's favourite puppet, danced left, right and centre in the theatre to signal the start of the performance. All went well, undisturbed by the buskers. But afterwards, as William was collecting the last of the takings – a healthy few shillings – a tough-looking man with a mandolin on his back and a hostile manner pumped Walter on his future plans. Another roughneck was more direct: 'get out of town, far better trade in the villages'. At that point a photographer from the pier pushed through the crowd shouting and swearing in the foulest language at the top of his voice, 'don't listen to them. This place is a ****ing gold mine. People will love your stuff here. Stay, just bleeding stay …'

They had taken over the buskers' pitch. Serious trouble was in store. Walter foresaw days of plotting and sabotage in a world of raucous commercial competition. This was not the Utopian Socialist dream that William Morris had promised, the life of poetry and philosophy to which Walter had pledged his soul. 'We're going anyway', he said and without more ado, he grabbed William, hastily packed up and took to his heels.

In truth it was rather liberating to run away. To be stuck in a town was the last thing either of them wanted. Two miles out of Minehead they pulled up a steep bank and pitched their tent in a meadow bright with buttercups overlooking a valley with the downs beyond. They pottered about: mending the puppets and touching them up with dabs of paint, spilling methylated spirits into a lantern and preparing a supper of buns, cheese and cocoa. As the moon rose and the stars appeared in a clear sky, a deep satisfaction, a fulfilment of a long-felt need, enveloped them both. 'We live in a poem', William said as he pulled out the flageolet and played an Elizabethan air. They fell asleep on clumps of thyme and low scrambling trails of lady's bedstraw.

In the first crystal clearness of morning, they made their way along a winding road to Porlock under a panoply of oak and ash trees like a tunnel above them. In Porlock, past the church with its strange beheaded spire, they searched out a carpenter's shop. It was taking far too long to assemble the theatre, so they had decided to screw its framework permanently to two long wooden battens, ready for immediate use.

Porlock turned out to be the biggest success so far. The show began on the village green in front of the Castle Hotel with Walter's slap-stick puppets. John Barleycorn's wife Martha fell out of the window, a monkey defeated the light heavyweight champion Joe Beckett with head butts and an umbrella and Barleycorn appeared again with an attempt to turn worthless articles into gold and diamonds by putting them in Tutankhamen's enchanted chest.

After a ten-minute interval, Walter went to sit in the audience, relinquishing his role as Professor to allow William his turn. Through Walter's reminiscences we have a detailed description of a Simmonds puppet show in the open:

The chattering crowd became quiet, closing in around the theatre: the scene began with a discussion on music between an old coun-try man and a modern artist. The yokel sings an ancient folk song which the artist despises as a primitive relic of the past – for his part he only sings the very latest compositions. In overblown caricature, he sings 'Come into the garden, Maud' which does not impress the old man in the least. When the song is finished, the yokel wants his portrait painted, whereupon the artist produces his easel and canvas, and with real brush and real ink draws a good portrait of the old man, who complains it is nothing at all but a lot of black lines. This leads to an argument, and then to a fight, which is ended by the old man seizing the canvas and smashing it over the artist's head, so that he finishes up wearing it as a collar.

The brilliance of William's cameo and the nonchalance of his man-ner were not lost on the villagers, who began to ask him what was his real profession – evidently he was more than just a travelling performer like Walter. His nose out of joint, Walter put this enquiry down to William's behaving as if they were doing the show 'only for a bit of fun'. 'It was either his dignified way of collecting as he strolled round smoking his pipe, or it may have been his new gold boots from Piccadilly, an unusual shopping district for Punch and Judy men.' No matter, the hat was brimming over with coins. It was their biggest haul yet.

With renewed energy and an exhilarating belief in their powers, they took a precipitous track out of Porlock, each step a good stiff pull. They were warned that this route was the longest and steepest in Devon. As the lane took them higher and higher, trees and hedges disappeared, and in one final effort they lurched on to the open moor. In astonishment they came to a standstill. A vast stretch of immense beauty lay before them, the land ablaze with sheets of gorse, heather, foxgloves, bilberry and bracken, and below them to the right far ahead, the sea blue grey merging in the distance with the Welsh coast. Wild ponies and their foals darted away from them as William pulled out his sketchbook while they ate their picnic.

On they travelled over the wild and silent Exmoor, feeling a sense of life and purpose, entertained by flocks of white geese in a great stony sky and the chilling cry of peewits in the wind. Away from the grandeur of the moors, down steep hills and ravines, they came across remote moorland settlements, lonely hamlets and farms, then, on down into Lorna Doone country, to villages signposted Oare, Oareford, Brendon and Cheriton, then southwards to Barbrook, East and West Ilkerton, Shallowford and further south to Lynton, Lynn and Lynmouth.

At every stop the country people gathered around them as they bought milk and cheese and put up the proscenium. The farmers' wives laughed at the puppets' jokes, the children shrieked with joy and babies in arms yelled. But the most they earned in any village was 3s. 10d.

Sometimes they lost their way and were forced to climb on to mounds or walls or shin up trees to spy out the territory, which revealed nothing but bewildering stretches of plain in an ever-changing purple, grey and beige, and distant roads of a cruel steepness. Plunging on again, bumping down steep paths into moorland valleys, past woods of beech and pine, they splashed through streams, in water up to their knees, over rocks and boulders, through bracken and across two rivers: Weir Water and Chalk Water. Here they pitched camp under a young ash tree by the water's edge, lit a fire, brewed tea, fried eggs for supper and smoked. William would have stayed forever, wherever the gods arranged, he told Walter. He wanted for nothing save carving tools, a turning lathe, a chest or two of his books and (to Walter's chagrin) his friends.

On the edge of Exmoor, they emerged from the woods sunburnt and gnarled, with knotted hair, and dropped down into the pretty, shadowy cliff village of Lynmouth. It was here they would perform their last show together. They clattered through the narrow streets pursued by children in a surge of excitement and set up in front of two lime kilns beside the Edwardian railway ticket office. The spectators perched on the promenade wall and the puppets entertained them until night fell.

While William and Walter were packing up, the children crowded round, peeping anxiously inside the set. But when at last William dismantled the outer corner of the house, they were shattered to see how empty it was. Where had the little people gone to? 'All travelling on to the electric car', William replied pointing to the cliff railway. The older children developed the story 'with great zeal until the smaller ones quite believed it and turned their attention to the car gliding up steeply above Lynton'.

Leaving their cart in Lynmouth, they turned back up the village road in light rain and continued up the hillside, climbing across boulders and overhanging trees, every foot of ground at an impossible tilt. Picking their way like cats, they reached the patch where they had been obliged to settle earlier in the day – no more than three yards square and close to a ravine. After a bun and cheese, Walter demonstrated how to put on pyjamas in such cramped conditions: sitting thus, kneeling thus, bending the body in a reclining position – thus and thus. He accidentally hit William on the nose; an argument followed and William fell to one side, John Barleycorn fashion, bringing the whole tent down.

Patching up the quarrel, William lit a lantern and played his whistle pipe to the accompaniment of the tumbling waters. Soon he fell into a deep sleep. But Walter, thoroughly put out by the prospect of William's departure next morning, lay staring at the tent's roof fuming, gloomy and resentful as his companion, sleeping bag rammed up next to him, snored peacefully.

Years later, as Walter wrote in his memoirs, his resentment had still hardly cooled:

The man had only been a Showman for a week; he travelled for pleasure; he cared nothing of earning money and of the impecunious plight I would be left in – cut off in Lynmouth, cut off from every-where … financially, this was a CATASTROPHE, bankruptcy in fact – no more jaunts on steam ships, jugs of cider or tea with jam and Devonshire cream in elegant tea shops … I must now in grim earnest, settle down to the job … show here, there and everywhere, live upon the takings and clear off my debts …

William's diary postscript was characteristically laconic, with just a hint of the relief he felt: 'woke at quarter to 6 up in time to catch the 7.30 cliff railway to begin the journey home. Walter came to station to see me off and I left him to continue his wanderings alone, while I return to my beloved wife and workshop at Far Oakridge.'

CHAPTER 18

Puppets Claim Centre Stage

1923–1925

'Alice Rothenstein's folie de grandeur *continues.'*

Eve had her own news for William on his return. Dorothy Larcher, at last permanently back from India, had come to stay at The Frith. She had noticed Phyllis Barron's printed Lizard material in Eve's bedroom, and cried out 'Who did that? I should love to meet whoever it was!' A few days later Eve had taken her to the opening of Barron's exhibition at the Brook Street Gallery and introduced the two.[1]

To Eve's surprise, so different were they, Larcher and Barron had instantly hit it off. Barron would say to close friends 'so Eve found me for her'. The dominating Barron, forthright, warm, outgoing and masculine, and Larcher, an equally strong character, but quiet, introvert and hidden behind a veil of reserve, had a world of things in common.

Events had moved fast. Barron had quarrelled with her assistant and invited Larcher to move into her new flat in Park Hill Road in Hampstead – 'the ugliest studio in the world' – to work with her on a huge project. Detmar Blow, now agent and Architect in Chief for the Duke of Westminster, who had also been at the Brook Street Gallery opening, was so taken by Barron's designs that he and his wife Winifred had talked her into furnishing the Duke's new yacht, *Flying Cloud*, the world's largest schooner, 282-foot long and originally

built for the Italian navy. The offer was to design and print materials for the yacht's immense saloon and its forty cabins: new divans,
bunks, cushions, blinds and curtains were needed. The deadline was
a ridiculous three weeks away. But with Larcher's help and luck on
their side, thanks to the captain's delays, all was accomplished within
three months. Barron found time to enter several designs for the
Royal Academy exhibition and Dorothy some 'small embroidered
caps' and an embroidered hanging.

As for Arthur Wilkinson, he too was pursuing William, but on
a different track from Walter's. He had been worrying away about
the decline of British puppetry and was working out a grandiose
scheme to form a Marionette Society. Through this group he felt
sure more puppet masters could be recruited and theatres spread
throughout the country. He would launch the plan with a London
performance at the famous Poetry Bookshop. Its founder, the poet
Harold Monro, had bought an eighteenth-century garret above
the shop, and this was where Arthur's demonstrations would take
place. He and Gordon Craig would promote the evening with the
message that puppetry was now on the threshold of a genuine and
far-reaching national revival.

The event was a disaster. William had kept his distance and
missed it; he had to knuckle down to his work for the Royal Academy exhibition. Worse still for the Wilkinsons, when Craig went
into overdrive with the journalists, he reserved his highest accolades
for the absent William: 'It was not the Italian puppets at the Scala
which stimulates interest in these little people', Craig proclaimed in
the *Star* (5 September 1923):

> The Italians came to the Scala because of the puppet revival in
> England, which has been perceptible for some time. Acting, much
> of it, is so bad just now … and the actor often is so commercialised,
> or so absorbed in his own personality, that there is relief to see a
> marionette, which can be made a perfect model and never does
> anything you don't ask it to do. There is an English carver named
> Simmonds who, like the Gair Wilkinsons, lives in Gloucestershire.
> As a puppet maker and manipulator he is without question the
> greatest living artist, and I do not exclude the Italians.

Even if in this case overwork served as an excuse, it was important to
William to produce pieces for the Royal Academy. He was banking

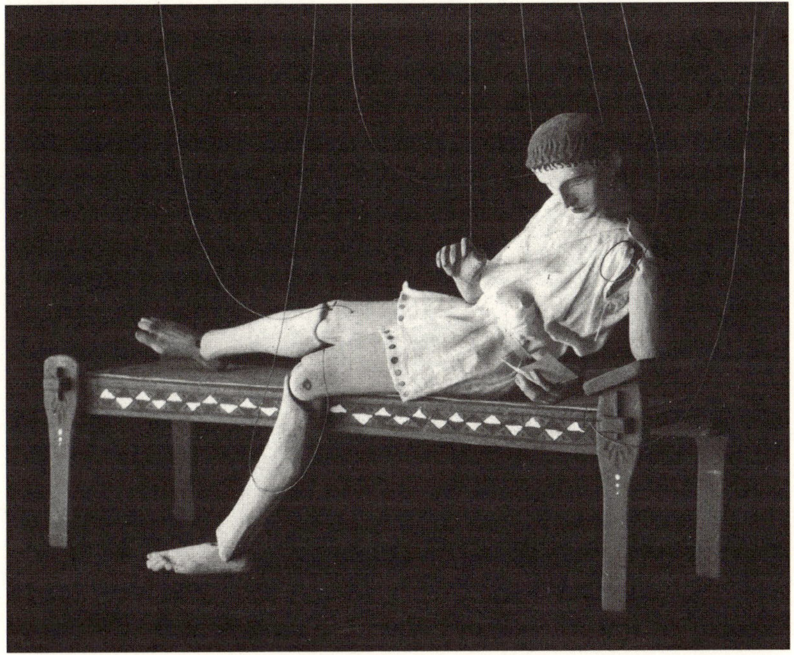

A Greek: lead character in William's adaptation of John Drinkwater's one-act play *X=O*

on selling his sculpture to maintain some sort of income; but it was equally essential to keep his work in the public eye. It was not only in Britain that the Academy was seen to be the most prestigious institution in which to exhibit, but in Europe and America. Moreover he was a newcomer in the flourishing movement to which he was now aligned: it was a mere three years since he had been launched by Rothenstein. Here he would be exhibiting alongside Sidney Barnsley, William de Morgan, Arthur Gaskin, Ernest Gimson, Bernard Leach, Edwin Lutyens and Charles Voysey. In the end he entered his *Duck* and *Drake* in sycamore and ebony inlay (already sold to Rothestein's elder brother Charles Rutherston) and *Wood Nymph* carved in ivory. Eve too was entering her 'embroidered flowers on black silk', which would be in the same glass case as Dorothy Larcher's and May Morris's work.

When in London, William and Eve now stayed in the Powells' new two-floored flat in Mecklenburgh Square. The transition from Volta House had been relatively painless. With Catherine away at boarding school, there was room enough for the Simmondses; and Alfred generously offered the large drawing room for a trial run before the marionettes took off for a second ten-day season at the Art Workers' Guild.

Sydney Cockerell came during the first week and a second time with more friends, this time to a full house. He wrote that everyone had been spilling over with compliments for the puppets but if William could bring them to Cambridge, he insisted he included the missing *Holiday* skit. William joked back that with such praise he could 'only hope their heads won't swell and refuse to turn' and agreed they could travel to the Fitzwilliam.

On the last three days there was standing room only in the Guild's room and with difficulty Eve found seats for a last-minute request from Dolmetsch and his whole family. The puppets were turning out to be another valuable source of income.

Ten days later on 12 January 1924 the puppets performed for the League of Arts. The league had been founded in 1919 in a spirit of post-war optimism under the motto 'To bring the arts into everyday life', and was proving valuable to artists and writers in William's circle. In Margaret Morris's studio, it had got off to an illustrious start with lectures on painting by Wyndham Lewis and on poetry by T.S. Eliot, and in small galleries, were exhibitions of work by Duncan Grant, Cedric Morris and John and Paul Nash. Of special interest to William was its troupe of travelling players who performed in village halls throughout the country.

* * * * * *

Rothenstein had yet to succeed in persuading William to come and teach at the Royal College of Art, courting him there with lunches and teas whenever William was in London. Always pushing himself harder than others, overworking at the Royal College and worrying about money and Rachel's mysterious illness, Rothenstein began to wilt under the strain. But still he was unceasing in his efforts to help William. His latest goal was to ensure that William's piece *Farm Team* should be bought by a major museum.

Having failed with Leicester Museum, he reproached its trustees several months later in 1925 in a public lecture at Manchester

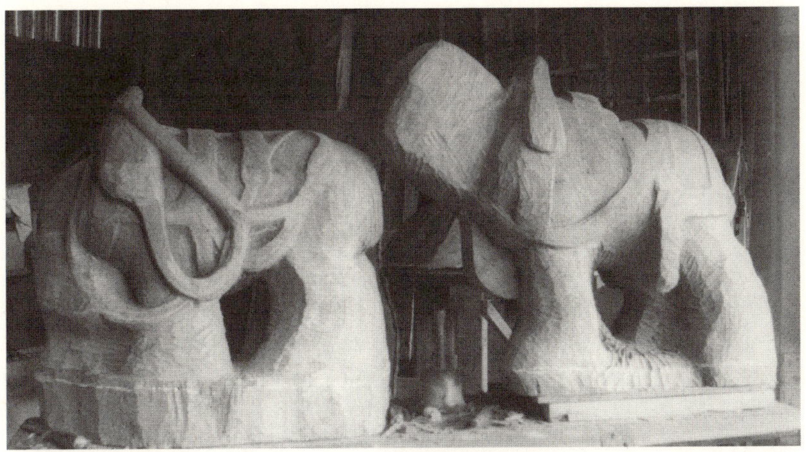

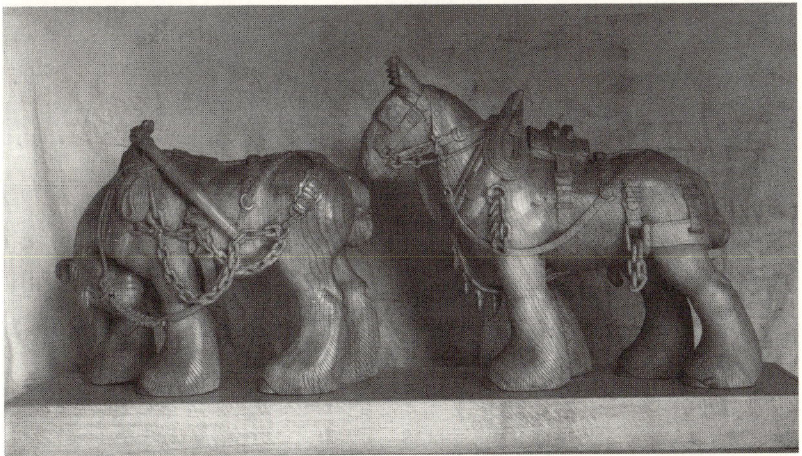

Above: *Farm Team* (wych elm) in William's workshop before completion
Below: *Farm Team* was bought by the Tate Gallery from the Royal Academy

University for their short-sightedness in letting such an opportunity slip: Simmonds's work, he argued, compared with the finest wood-carving of the Middle Ages. He did not let the matter rest and began negotiating for the horses to be bought by the Tate Gallery. Then he pressed the banker George Eumorfopoulos. A Londoner whose grandparents had fled Greece during the Turkish massacre of 1822, Eumorfopoulos was an expert on Eastern art; he had recently founded the Oriental Ceramic Society and now had bought a house on Chelsea Embankment to convert into a museum for his enormous collection, which alongside Japanese and early Chinese art contained European medieval and Renaissance art and eighteenth-century ceramics. Rothenstein encouraged him to spread his interests further afield. When a year later he saw William's *Black Mare*, a magnificent, twelve-inch high black lacquered beast with massive stylised mane and tail, its head straining down to scratch his leg, he instantly bought it.

Meanwhile, Alice Rothenstein's *folie de grandeur* continued. Determined to entertain on a larger scale, she had found a large mansion for the family with grand, high-ceilinged rooms near Sheffield Terrace in Airlie Gardens. Her husband's pining for Oakridge would be appeased by the illusion of living in the country: the magnificent balconied drawing room led down to a sweeping lawn and on into a communal garden with borders of shrubs and flowers, and massive ilex trees and cherry trees. Alice's 'At Homes' started at teatime and carried on with a new wave of guests for drinks, then, for the chosen few, for dinner. As her energy and social ambitions grew, her husband's vitality seeped away. Staying with the Rothensteins, Max Beerbohm noted how his old friend – amazed at the vibrancy of his all but grown-up children – sat and watched their bright and animated antics, smiling and quietly reflective.

After a gap of several months without hearing from Rothenstein and no way of knowing how badly his health had deteriorated, William blithely wrote letters thanking him for his help over the Tate's acquisition of *Farm Team*, regretting that he would not see him at Easter but was looking forward to the arrival of Betty and Billy. He followed up with another long letter describing a holiday in Holland with Alfred Powell. In September he wrote what in retrospect seemed a poorly timed letter, again declining the offer to teach at the Royal College of Art.

The Frith Far Oakridge Stroud GLOS
9th September 1924

My dear William
I hate persisting in my refusal to take on the teaching of wood-carving at the College, but I really can't see my way to do it under present circumstances. I have thought about it very deeply, and feel quite disturbed at the idea of the opportunity passing, when you

have a clear chance to begin with a scheme, teaching wood carving in its broken traditions. I feel [you] must think me lacking in enthusiasm for the students, not to be willing to give a little time each month to them, but although this means little time, it means, if it is done properly, a great slice of my attention and that is the part which would 'moider' me, added to the many other things that attract me. I can't dismiss things from my mind and not to work on the thing of the moment, so that the variety of my enterprises already rather overwhelms me, in spite of the general impression that I live a quiet and simplified life.

This winter I have planned to settle down to work here on carvings I want to get done, and I have Robert Payne, Henry Payne's eldest son, coming to work with me (and for me in return for instruction) and I want to get something done for the Arts and Crafts show fixed for next year. Also I have 'put my hand' to the Oakridge players and we are going to do the adaptations from 'Under the Greenwood Tree', 'The Mellstock Choir', not a light undertaking for me. We have had to strike hard at it to do it justice.

I know you won't expect me to excuse myself for my decision, but I should not like you to think that I refuse without good reason or without much consideration. I think we shall probably give the puppets a rest this winter, but we have not quite decided yet.

Yours affectionately William

Taking on Robert Payne as an assistant seemed to have given William a new burst of energy. Far from giving the puppets a rest, he looked around for new themes. Nor did he abandon the Oakridge Players. After correspondence with Hardy's wife, he was given permission to use *Under the Greenwood Tree* and to edit the text for his purposes; there could have been no more suitable subject for William's devices than Hardy's gentlest and most pastoral of novels. Rehearsals began with a vengeance. By the turn of the year into 1925 he and Payne had converted one end of his workshop into a small auditorium. They lined the barn with stone and boarding, hung up Indian printed linens and curtains on the walls and covered the floor with Eastern rugs, transforming the space into something inviting, warm and comfortable.

Eve rose to the occasion to entertain with supper and tea parties. She took her entertaining seriously. A photograph of her sitting beside the fire sewing, in her unusual dress, with her elegant,

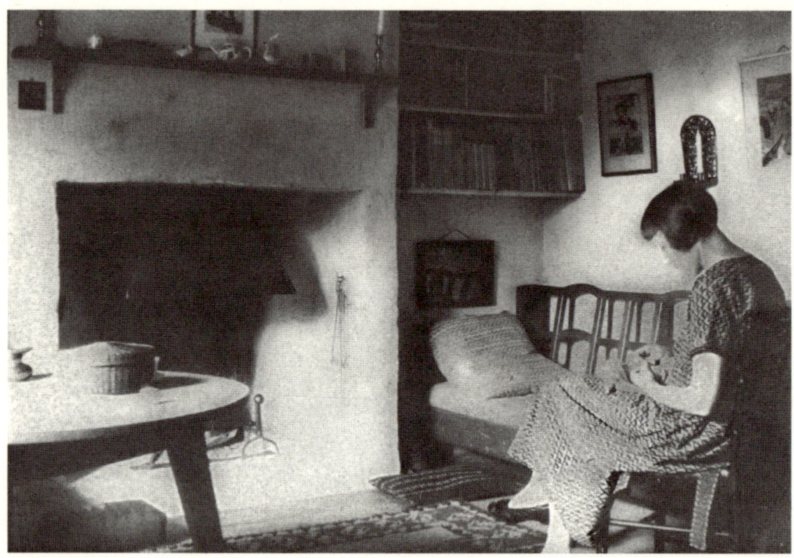

Eve embroidering in her Frith sitting room. On the wall is her framed needlework, above her head a sconce made by Alfred Bucknell. The cushions and the cover on the Ernest Gimson settee are in Barron and Larcher material

severely cut hair, gives a sense of her poise. Fastidious and perfectionist, she had a well-earned reputation for good taste and good food. Her teas were an artistic display. On 2 January the Barnsleys, the Powells, W.H. Davies, Alice Rothenstein and her bevy of youngest children crowded in to see the opening performances of *Harlequinade*, *Woodland* and a new piece, *Farmyard*. Norman Jewson brought Fred Griggs and his wife Nina, and the Blows came with more friends from Painswick. Eve invited a new acquaintance – soon to become close neighbour – for the weekend: Emery Walker's daughter Dorothy. Emery's Hammersmith house, with its historic Morris archives, was run by Dorothy. There she kept open house to entertain for her father's friends; in Sapperton she would do the same and within four years become a central piece of the jigsaw in Eve's altered life.

William's diary for that year was crammed with notes, sketches and snatches of dialogue for puppets and for the Oakridge Players. Edward Payne was painting the scenery of moveable screens and taking the role of the vicar in Hardy's *Under the Greenwood*

Tree. The takings had improved: £19 8*s*. 3*d*. and, after expenses, a profit of £10 14*s*. 5*d*. In an unusual burst of pride William noted that Alfred Powell reported bumping into Fred Gardiner, 'and heard great praise of my work for the Players; that I was "such a good teacher", I "could tell them how to do things without offending anyone, and so get on"'.

Still unaware that anything was seriously wrong with Rothenstein, William wrote to him from a holiday with Barron and Larcher in France, commiserating with him about the 'chill' he was rumoured to have caught and remarking on how wearing the last year must have been for him. His own news was filled with happiness and interest.

Barron had wanted to go to Paris to visit the 'International Exhibition of Modern Industrial and Decorative Arts', where her work was on show. The French were using the event to feature pavilions devoted to different manufacturers and department stores – a series of *grands magasins* – displaying every aspect of French excellence: an affirmation that after the disasters of the Great War, Paris retained its former glory and still reigned supreme in the art of design. The displays of Art Deco, Art Nouveau and decorative Cubism were attracting massive attention; special controversy was engendered by Le Corbusier's *Esprit Nouveau* pavilion, where he promoted his theoretical *Plan Voisin* project, a collection of identical 200-metre tall skyscrapers and rectangular apartments designed (but mercifully never built) to replace a large section of central Paris. Other rivals for stealing the show were the Russian pavilion's display of Constructivism, the Germans' Bauhaus and examples of the Italians' Futurism. Also among the 15,000 exhibitors was the work of the sculptor Ivan Meštrović, so admired by William during the war, who was awarded the Grand Prix. Edwin Lutyens had been chosen to design the British pavilion, though its contents were less exciting than the explosive innovation on display elsewhere.

Apart from the exhibition, what Barron and Larcher most wanted on their French holiday, as did Eve, was to rummage through market stalls for linens and materials. On the Channel coast they visited the charming walled town of Montreuil-sur-Mer, where they stayed in the Hôtel de France 'mentioned in Sterne's *Sentimental Journey* … a very entertaining place to stay even without that link'. William and Eve had found a simple cottage to rent with a maid in the tiny village of Sangatte, close to Calais.

William was in his element. Whenever he could he left behind the slow-walking party of middle-aged girls to stride 'through field paths … I have never seen so much corn in my life, hundreds of acres of it and beautiful heavy crops.' The scattered villages and towns all seemed to have small farms in the main street, a daily market and, to his discerning eye, 'surprising methods of making and doing things'. In Coquelles, he set about drawing an unusual windmill, meticulously recording its traction, inner components and mechanisms; in comparison, his Kodak photographs give but a hazy impression of its magnificent complexity.

* * * * * *

The pains in Rothenstein's chest in the summer of 1925, long assumed by him to be indigestion, were now diagnosed as heart disease. He was given a year to live. As much as they could, the family kept the shock and their distress to themselves. He was given temporary leave from the Royal College of Art.

CHAPTER 19

Wilkinsons, Simmondses, D.H. Lawrence

1926

*'Mr Lawrence is here giving us a lecture on modern art,
so I think I will have to leave off.'*
Bimbo Wilkinson, letter to William and Eve Simmonds,
1926

Life in Gloucestershire throughout 1926 was tinged with a sense of both loss and renewal. On 6 January Ernest Barnsley died, leaving his most important project, Rodmarton Manor, unfinished. It fell to Sidney to complete his brother's work; but within the year he too would be buried beside his brother and Ernest Gimson.

The reviews of the 'Arts and Crafts Society Exhibition' at the Royal Academy in January were universally favourable. 'Mr and Mrs Powell's' painted plaques, 'Mr Waal's' furniture, Bernard Leach's pottery, Ethel Mairet's handwoven cloth and Phyllis Barron's hand-painted fabrics were all singled out, but William was again spotlighted 'the most outstanding feature to be found [in the exhibition] – 3 carvings – their natural rhythm and beauty … and 3 fascinating drawings of 18th century French Windmills still in use'. The *Glasgow Herald* reminded its readers how much William's carvings at the Alpine Gallery – the marble *Calf*, the lacquered wood *Black Mare* and the wych elm *Horses Grazing* – had impressed *The Times* critic and other connoisseurs. It was here that the *Black Mare* was snapped up for £500 by Rothenstein's friend George Eumorfopoulos (see plate 10).

Barron and Larcher were going from strength to strength, in spite of their difficult working conditions in Hampstead. The Duke of Westminster's yacht had propelled them to prominence. From the mid-1920s the name 'Barron and Larcher' on a design was the ulti-mate in modern chic. To cap it all, *Vogue* had chosen Roger Fry to write up their Mayor Gallery show in its April (1926) edition; he generously praised the beauty and distinction of Barron's work.

In March, Gertrude Abbey, still in Edwin's old studio in Tite Street, wrote to William out of the blue, peremptory as always, with an irritating demand. She was worried about her husband's reputa-tion, which was being undermined by a book about the Harrisburg murals: 'Write me a few lines', Mrs Abbey wrote,

> stating very clearly the facts and that you were in the studio at Fairford when he was doing the above and helped him and went to Harrisburg and saw all his designs ... carried out on the walls and ceilings for the House of Representatives and Senate Cham-ber – HUSTON said HE was the architect of the Capitol and was afterwards as you will remember imprisoned for graft etc (I did not know he was out).

William met her in London and satisfied her as best he could, but uppermost in his mind was Eden Philpot's play and negotiating with Thomas Cook's travel agency about his impending journey, planned in spite of Eve's reservations, to visit the Wilkinsons in Italy. Eve would have far preferred a holiday with Barron and Larcher, but that was out of the question.

The Wilkinsons had disappeared during the winter. Forever restless and somewhat disillusioned, feeling like fish out of water in Pain-swick, they had sold up and left their 'Gloucester village arty life' (as their new friend D.H. Lawrence put it behind their back) in search of nature, health and culture in Italy. After Christmas, soon after their arrival, they both wrote separately to William. They had found a villa in Scandicci close to Florence. It was all that they wanted. 'My dear people, if you want to come to Paradise, come here in April, May or June ... nothing can describe the beauty of it all – it has to be experienced', wrote Lily. 'The flowers, the nightingales, the glorious sunny days, the velvet softness of the nights, the fireflies – but just make up your minds to come.'

D.H. Lawrence and his German wife Frieda, who coincidentally was renting a house a stone's throw away, were trailed as a draw. Lawrence had a reputation for being intense and argumentative and his proximity might have been a mixed blessing for the Wilkinsons.

But in the event, as the only outsiders in a tight-knit peasant community, the two couples had become inseparable.

Lawrence, though he had yet to scandalise society with *Lady Chatterley's Lover*, was well known in the Simmondses' circle, though not to them personally. More of a lure were Lily and Arthur's children, of whom William was especially fond; they had added Christmas notes to their parents' envelope. It was their first experience of Florence, and they were bowled over by it. Pino, the musical son, described the operas the family had seen over the holidays – *Aida* with a splendid tenor, *La Bohème* on Christmas Day where they had been given a box as a present, *Carmen* on New Year's Eve, and a 'rather stupid' *Rosenkavalier*. Bimbo, the artistic older daughter, was ecstatic about a visit to the cinema to see *Cinderella* produced by a German company with eighteenth-century music: 'fantastically well done … I don't believe I have ever enjoyed one so much, so real, so much of the spirit of the fairy tale and so magic … all of us got quite carried away.' The letter ended: 'Mr Lawrence is here giving us a lecture on modern art, so I think I will have to leave off. Much love Bim.'

With his usual relaxed attitude to money William readily accepted the invitation and booked the tickets. He felt nonchalantly solvent after the Eumorfopoulos sale and had several puppet bookings for later in the summer.

On 3 May, oblivious to the escalating crisis in England, William and Eve caught the train from Kemble to Paddington. The situation in London was dire. The government's disastrous action of trying to go back to the gold standard at pre-First World War levels had led to a severe recession. With notice expiring at midnight and no settlement to the threatened coal strike in sight, it was less than certain that any trains would get to the coast. Installed for the night in a small hotel near Victoria Station, the Simmondses were woken in the middle of the night by a massive roar and blast, with every engine shrieking their whistles in unison. Next morning all the buses and taxis were on strike. Except for a sprinkling of independent vehicles, London had come to a standstill. The general strike had started.

Chaos reigned in Victoria Station, most of which was locked. A train for Folkestone was found, but with no engine; then one with an engine but no driver, but by midday they were able to ease out of the station at snail's pace on a deserted line. In every outlying village a guard, sometimes a stationmaster, single-handedly set the points and signals.

By a miracle, they caught the last ferry to leave and travelled for three days through France, then to Basel and across the St Gotthard Pass to Milan and Bologna, before arriving at Florence's Scandicci Station on 6 May, where they found the entire Wilkinson family waiting on the platform. Outside, farmer Mancini with his pony cart was ready to take the luggage to the Villa Poggi.

The Wilkinsons, to begin with, were thrilled to see them:

> preparing for our problematic visitors – very busy indeed. Will they come? We cleaned the windows and we sawed and we cooked and we baked, we washed the tea cosy, we saved a lot of wood … come they did!! and as large as life and punctual to the minute. It was an exciting meeting and a great relief on both sides to have them safely arrived … they had less news of the general strike than we had, having come up from the Cotswolds without realising anything about it … we gave them a cup of tea at Gilli and then came out to the Villa Poggi and a lovely evening it was, and the house inside and out looking delightful and a fine supper ready for them in no time.

Exhausted, Eve fell asleep to the song of nightingales and awoke at dawn to their same fierce call, soon overtaken by the sounds of peasants and the animals congregated around the well. She looked out from her window on to a panorama of unspoiled medieval country, farms on little green hills, pinewoods fringing the ridges, olive orchards unfolding across the Valdarno to the distant brown sprawl of Florence. The Wilkinsons brought her breakfast in bed.

Their first days were spent walking over the hills through olives and vines and among swathes of wild flowers to the local tower or to Scandicci, Giogoli and Galluzzo. After visiting the *certosa* at Galluzzo, they lunched at a riverside café near the bridge, watching the mule trains meander lazily by, bearing casks of fine wine, with red-and-white cloths on their backs and bells on their collars. Another day they went to Rosetta for the peasant festival at the sacred spring, which for William was disappointing: 'an ugly block square brick room over it with a large tap for the spring water.' Worse, the villagers who had come from all over the area were 'all in print jumpers, silk stockings and with high-heeled shoes like Oxford Street'. To cap it all the Wilkinsons' dog, John, was run over by a cart.

On one expedition deep into the hills a thunderstorm threatened and in alarm they broke up the meal to rush home. From then on Lily's diary entries became increasingly caustic. Apart from the occasional dig, William got off relatively unscathed, but she was increasingly maddened by Eve:

So William, with the least possible amount of urging set out to read us *The Farmer's Wife* by Eden Philpotts – the play which has broken the records for length of run which they have just produced (better of course than pros) at Oakridge. William reads very badly indeed! and we thought the play rotten, just a hotch potch of all the old stage jokes about country men and love-making and not a little vulgar. This reading lasted several days and was a good diversion under the circumstances, especially for them, and we others got some sewing and darning done. The truth is that during the first few days of the visit we found things a little difficult and though later we got on very sympathetic terms, it was only after a great deal of forbearance (more than we could manage sometimes) on our parts. They were both pretty sick and exhausted when they arrived and perhaps this is the explanation. But Eve especially seemed determined to let us feel how successful they were and what important people they had become since we met last and what unimportant people we were. This last mainly by refusing to take even a polite interest in our work and when Diddy insisted on them taking a look at our drawings in the studio, Eve just turned away and talked about the view and picked up photographs with unnecessary enthusiasm and William just made comic remarks as to the weather in the drawings and they were both supremely uncomfortable. Later, it is true, William was heard to say, rather to murmur, 'That is a beautiful drawing' and to hand the said drawing to Eve, but Eve never said Nuffink!! They never once asked Pino to play or asked any questions about his studies.

Was Lily's irritation in what was for her an unusually long diary entry due to a sense that her life did not quite live up to her aspirations? Or was it Eve's air of superiority that riled her?

As to their own importance it was mostly expressed in the oft repeated story of William's *Black Horse*, stained black and biting a flea. An old Greek Jew has bought it for a fabulous sum (though we never got the cold figures). Eve would keep on about it. This Popolipolis has a private museum on the Embankment, everybody

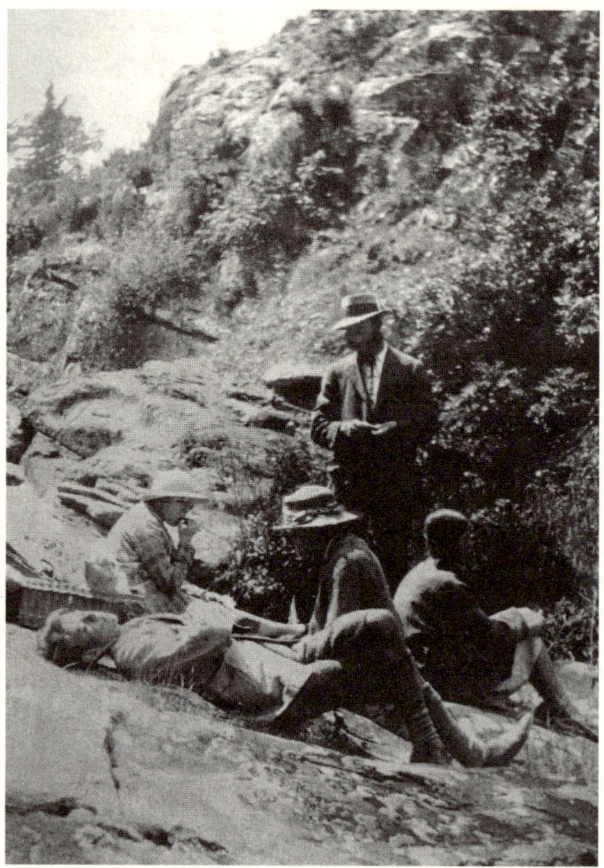

Eve and William picnicking with the Wilkinsons and the D.H. Lawrences in the hills above Scandicci, near Florence

who knows anything (excluding us) knows it's far and away better than the Louvre and the British Museum put together! (Eve's own words.) He just has the most perfect and exquisite examples. Just a very few modern works! No paintings (this with infinite scorn) only sculpture and craft work. Not 'Good' things, Oh No, nothing but the most perfect examples!! He's bought William's *Black Horse* etc etc over and over again!!

We had a lively passage of arms about picking flowers. We were finding flowers to show her the first day and she called us 'hinus' for picking them and managed to make it most offensive.

After several days, the Wilkinsons took the Simmondses by bus to the centre of Florence. For William it was a revelation. Years of copying casts in the South Kensington Museum and the Royal Academy proved a pale introduction to the power of the original works of art in marble, bronze and stone. William haunted the Uffizi and the Bargello Museum, and spent as long as he could studying the bronze Ghiberti doors of the Baptistery and the three-dimensional perspective of Masaccio in his fresco in Santa Maria Novella. But he had to yield to family plans and there never seemed quite enough time. He would find a way.

The Lawrences lived even closer to the Villa Poggi than William had realised – only a two-minute walk away. Before 'The Author', as Arthur called him (Frieda being 'Mrs Author' or 'Mrs Lorenzo'), descended on them, Arthur mentioned privately to William that Lawrence had had a haemorrhage in February, and had recently been diagnosed with tuberculosis. It was not getting any better: 'The poor chap – what a nightmare … he never refers to his illness, except sometimes to say he has "trouble with his broncs".' The only external clue to Lawrence's ill health was his gaunt face. He had adopted the Wilkinsons' dog John (happily still alive after his encounter with the cart) who went everywhere with him. As he convalesced, he enveloped himself in the May sunlight, spending lazy days lying under the trees with lizards running over him and John making smudges on his paper as he began writing a few short essays on Florence.

More often than not, they met up with the Lawrences in the late afternoon or evening. William's first diary note was of a 'rather a clamorous tea party' at their dilapidated flat on the top floor of the Villa Mirenda, an old, square, heavy building just beside the San Paolo Chapel. The furniture was sparse and simple. Lawrence had whitewashed the walls and laid thick sweet-smelling rush matting on the red tiled floors. Most importantly, he had hired a piano, on which he and Frieda sang German and French songs. Frieda, a cousin of the First World War pilot Baron von Richthofen, the legendary Red Baron, appeared good-natured, with a large, round face and well-upholstered body with neither waist or bosom. The Wilkinsons' piano was equally acceptable: one night, after dinner at Il Poggi, the Lawrences opened their book of French songs and took control: 'we sat round the table in the salotta with bottle of Vermouth and one of Certosa and sang the chorus to Lawrence's

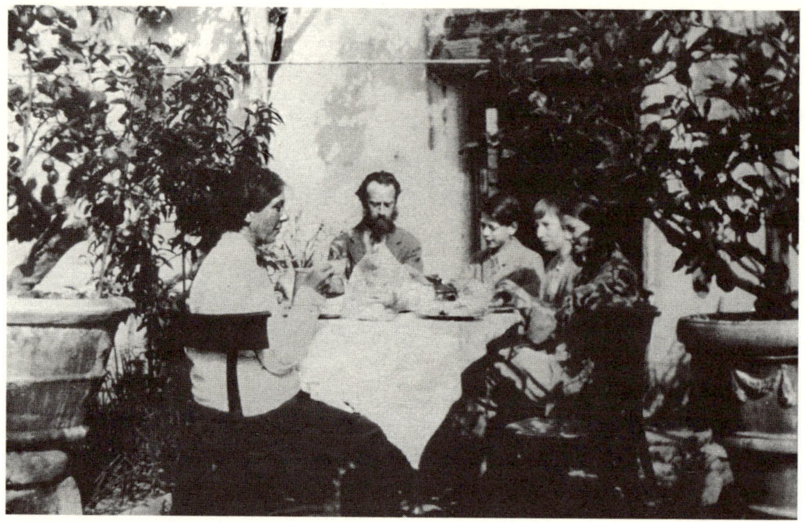

Eve breakfasting outside the Wilkinson's house where the Simmondses stayed in 1926. D.H. Lawrence stayed next door

lead. He chanted away as bold as brass in the solo parts ... evidently very familiar with French.'

Conversation was teasing and argumentative. 'Sargent is such a bad painter', Lawrence announced as he declared that he himself had recently taken up painting.[1] He was scathing about the spiritualism that many relatives of dead soldiers had taken up, reserving particular scorn for Sir Oliver Lodge, the illustrious scientist, who had written a book, widely regarded as close to unhinged, recounting his contacts with his youngest son Raymond, killed in action in 1915. According to Raymond, soldiers smoked cigarettes and cigars 'on the other side' just as they had when alive. The Wilkinsons instinctively took Lodge's side and charged Lawrence with 'defending a quite impossible position ... no harm done, though Lorenzo evidently don't like to be crossed in an argument'. In his broad Nottingham miner's accent, Lawrence laughed at Arthur's soft-left opinions, his vegetarianism and his red beard.

Yet for all the good-natured mockery of each others' ways of life between hosts and guests, 'The Author' took care not to ride his hobby horses too hard in the Wilkinsons' company. The families had formed a genuine friendship. In any case, Frieda was not partisan. She would tackle her husband's 'curious class feeling', interrupting periodically with 'Lorenzo you can't say that' as Lawrence swore by his class, with death and damnation to all other classes, and railed about modern men and women breaking the true pact (that is, unbridled sex) between body and soul, claiming they must return to balanced natural relations and that the modern world had become over-intellectualised and inhumanely mechanised. Unbeknown to the Villa Poggi household, 'The Author' was also working on the first draft of his next book, provisionally called 'Tenderness'. In three months' time it would emerge as *Lady Chatterley's Lover*.

Halfway through the Simmondses' visit, Lily took them and a local friend to the Villa Mirenda. William by now could do no wrong: 'It was William who came and helped with the washing up. William's behaviour has been irreproachable so far and he's as happy as could be. He's always singing.' But Eve could do little right:

> Sybil arriving we went to tea with the Lawrences, got the nicest of receptions, a delicious tea and the party went (with one exception) as merry as a marriage bell. Sybil having read all his works was agog to meet her favourite author and it was a lark to see the way she cut Eve out and absorbed the famous man and got him talking as happy as could be. Eve sat all alone looking v foolish and W. and Diddy and Mrs Lawrence and Arthur getting on fine together. We went down to the garden and sat on the grass talking until 6 o'clock and even then Lawrence came down the road and sat on our stone bench talking with whomsoever would talk with him.

Bus journeys into Florence were time-consuming and erratic and after ten days William tactfully said he wanted to be nearer to the galleries. For the last week before a pre-arranged expedition to Assisi with the Wilkinsons, he would study and draw in the Uffizi and decamp to the Pensione Lucii.

On Whit Sunday they were having supper at the Caffè Centrale when a large crowd appeared carrying torches; as evening fell the buildings gradually lit up. William was transfixed by the dramatic beauty of the spectacle, little realising it was a Fascist rally celebrating Il Duce: Mussolini was now into his fourth year as Prime Minister. William walked up to the steps of the *Duomo* with Eve: 'the Palazzo Vecchio beautifully illuminated with three flares placed between the battlements to the very top of the small tower and at each large window three large glass globes about 18" across, each with two large candles in it'.

Before returning home, there was the trip with the Wilkinsons to Assisi. At Easter Arthur and Lily had attended two candlelit processions when the image of the Virgin Mary, with many swords stuck in her bosom, had been carried a mile from the cathedral down to the Church of St Francis, the central point of pilgrimage, where a recumbent figure of Christ lay in state on a bier covered with a black veil. After a short ceremony, back went the Virgin to the cathedral for her next procession. It had rained halfway through, robbing the cortège of all pretence of reverence, as the priests and monks prodded each other with their dripping umbrellas, joking and roaring on their *via dolorosa*.

Arthur led them to the famous blue-domed St Mary of the Angels, which marked the place where St Francis had lived, worked and been baptised. Arthur was cynical about twentieth-century Assisi. With thirty churches, the town was overrun by them. But William was thrilled to discover this medieval town and he and Eve stayed on for a week. Registering in the modest Hotel Subasio, they set out to climb up to the ruined castle. But William preferred to immerse himself in the narrow streets, among the people who lived, worked and traded much as they had always done. He drew carts, wagons and animals – a white ox being shod and a carriage loaded with metalwork. He also drew the amphitheatre. And one day he walked 'to the call of St Francis' and then down to the river into the glorious sweep of the broad plain, 'the green heart' of Umbria. Greens of every shade: deep spring green of the oaks on the hillsides; the silver green of the 700-year-old olive groves spread across the valley; the emerald green between the grape vines.

* * * * * *

Returning to Florence, they paid a farewell visit to the Wilkinsons and had tea with the Lawrences before setting off for Milan and the long journey home. William's notes on reaching The Frith have more than a fleeting hint of Kilvert's *Diary* as he jots down his observations of the birds in Eve's beautiful garden: 'watched two little Owls on the wall, a Hedge Warbler with young in the Rosemary, Chaffinches with young in the Plane tree, and young wagtails promenading … Blacktits or Blackbirds in the woodshed feeding their young on our gooseberries, a Wren – from I don't know where.' Such detailed observations found expression in his *Owl*, *Fieldmouse* (see plate 7) and *Leveret*, his *Wren* wrapped in a chestnut leaf, leaving their tender, poetic imprint on us today.

The Times critic rightly wrote that he was 'so familiar with animal life' that he could achieve 'the essential greatness … grandeur and delicacy' of the finest Chinese sculptors. Of all the birds his favourite, and sometime friend, was the owl; William reserved a special place for it. 'I have had the pleasure', he wrote to Rothenstein 'of rescuing an owl from the chimney in the spare room – a most beautiful creature … most exciting to see near to and such wonderful dark eyes.' His idealised owl sculpted in sycamore, flat and half-abstracted though it is, enters and disturbs the heart with its ethereal face and sad ebony eyes and his symmetrical claws gripping the branch of a tree (see plate 27).

The Powells were at home working as hard as ever, painting, gilding and silvering a magnificent heraldic design on to a stone fireplace and painting ceramics for their pre-Christmas show, while Alfred simultaneously worked on a commission from Harrow for a set of tiles with cricketers on them. Their school teaching local girls pottery for Wedgwood was up and going. But within a month, exhaustion finally caught up with Louise and she collapsed, leaving Alfred dreadfully worried; she went to a nursing home, which she was not to leave for six months. Eve was at a loss as to how to help.

More cheerful news was that Emery Walker and Dorothy were now settled in Daneway. The Simmondses were immediately invited to a large tea party there, at which William went into a huddle in a corner with Norman Jewson and the architect William Weir. It had been a somewhat taxing, if exhilarating, year for Jewson. After Ernest Barnsley's death, Sidney Barnsley had briefly taken over at Rodmarton, inviting Ernest's son-in-law Jewson to help. This should have been an enjoyable prospect given that it was 'the last house of its size to be built in the old leisurely way, with all its timber grown from local woods, sawn on the pit and seasoned before use,' as he would later write. But Rodmarton Manor was not his creation. Working with England's leading restoration specialists, he had developed into an assured, original architect but longed for a project of his own. Fortuitously, over the summer he had found a semi-derelict house close by that could be truly his: Owlpen Manor. With this he would find his ultimate fulfilment.

William had been slow to realise the extent of Frederick Grigg's influence on Jewson in saving Owlpen Manor. Some time ago Griggs had become obsessed by the deserted 700-year-old house. At first known to him only by rumour, it was hidden secretly in the fold of a hill; its magical dilapidated beauty towering above terraced gardens with a parlour of vast, ancient, finely clipped yews incongruously kept intact by a lone gardener. The decaying building was close to collapse. Its owner neither lived in it nor wished to sell or repair it. Then, quite recently, news had come that the old owner had died and the property was up for auction. Jewson had needed no persuading to go and look at it. Ever since that first visit, when a caretaker had emerged from the kitchen wing to show him round what was left of the ground floor, the manor had come to dominate his mind, as it had Griggs's. The building's spirit represented to him the unspoken noble heart of the English tradition, an inheritance equal to that of Kelmscott and Daneway. He had discreetly attended the auction and bought Owlpen. For how much, nobody knew.

Over tea, exultant at seeing William back from Italy, Jewson buttonholed him in a corner to ask if he would come with him the following day to see what he had been doing at Owlpen over the summer and to draw three of its significant features for him. William was astonished to find Jewson managing a team of no fewer than sixteen local builders, all of them originally trained by Gimson and Detmar Blow, and wondered how Jewson could possibly afford it. Would it bankrupt him? He concluded that it must have been an investment: 'I think his plan is to restore it and sell it again.'

Jewson had been taking great care to preserve and document the subtleties and texture of the ancient manor's fabric, as much inside as out, surveying and recording, sketching in watercolour and photographing details, adding to Owlpen's flimsy records.

William's task was to draw the medieval kitchen fireplace, the charcoal stove and a seventeenth-century cider press. He completed the work over two days with short breaks for lunch and tea in the car. Clearly the house was safe for the moment under Jewson's care.

On 25 September Jewson took a break with William to go to Somerset where William hoped to measure up a watermill he had discovered a year earlier. They were too late. It had been gutted of its machinery and all but destroyed. Returning home through Glastonbury, Wells and Bath, they arrived in Oakridge to find Mary Jewson at the gate in extreme distress to tell them that Sidney Barnsley had died, suddenly, two hours before their arrival. William, shattered, wrote in his diary:

> He [Sidney] was on his way from his own house to Daneway in a car with some friends (motoring), and opened the gate for them of his own paddock. He got into the car and was asked to change his seat, and just as he had done so bent forward and gave three deep breaths. The car at once returned to his house but he was dead before it arrived there. He showed no sign of illness … a great blow to everyone. Sidney the finest living and most likeable of men. A great loss to me … his cheery friendship and understanding.

William's low-key words defied the depth of his feelings. Three of the Arts and Crafts movement's central figures, the most talented English architect-designers of the age, had gone. None had survived into his seventies. But of the three, it was Sidney to whom William was most deeply attached. In the evening he walked slowly to Sapperton with a note for Lucy Barnsley. She had recently married the son of the Sapperton rector, an officer in the merchant navy, but the two were 'not ready to set up a home of their own', whatever that meant. Deeply fond of her father, she had remained in her parents' house working at her pottery under Alfred Powell's tuition. Nearing Sapperton, William felt he could not present himself at the Barnsleys' house without showing too much distress. Seeing his plight, Norman Jewson delivered the note for him and accompanied him back home.

Rothenstein's younger brother, Albert Rutherston, who had taken a cottage near Waterlane and was privately bearing the anxiety of his brother's illness (still portrayed to outsiders as 'a chill'), came to share William's grief and take him to Sidney's funeral in Sapperton: 'Full church of all Sidney's old friends, the Walkers, the Biddulphs, the architects William Weir, Francis Troup and Charles Spooner, and Alfred Powell, Peter Waals, all the villagers and workmen. Jewson back to supper.' The sadness hung over William. He immersed himself in his workshop and in rehearsals for the new Eden Philpotts play, *Devonshire Cream*. There were diversions from neighbours: Adrian Stokes, a young painter renting Rothenstein's Winston's Cottage, dropped in to introduce himself and invited the Simmondses to tea. But bad news did not let up. On 7 October Albert Rutherston returned, very concerned about his brother. If

William went to see him, he warned, he would find him in a very bad state: 'a complete breakdown.'

* * * * * *

Jewson's plight compounded the gloom. For some weeks he had been deeply depressed. Owlpen was too large for him ever to live in himself. Worse still, the restoration was eating up money. In early October he finally broke. William and Eve called at his house: 'he told us that he would have to put Owlpen up for auction if he cannot sell it privately – a great shame and trouble to him.' William understood. It was the end of a love affair.

He sold the estate, its outbuildings and seven acres of land for £9,000, a little more than a year after buying it for £3,200. He had suffered a hefty loss, having spent a fortune on restoring it.

Griggs was to dedicate the first proof of his famous Owlpen etching to Jewson 'who with one only purpose possessed himself of the demesne of Owlpen when, for the first time in seven hundred years, it passed into alien hands – and with great care and skill saved this ancient house from ruin'. The etching depicts the manor floating tall, delicate and sublime behind thirty-foot-high yews, beneath one of which, hidden from the house, two women converse intimately in dappled dark shadow and pale early sunlight – or is it in moonlight? If Owlpen's story was a romance, Jewson and Griggs were its conjurors, revealing its mysteries for a new generation. The haunting image caught the imagination of collectors on both sides of the Atlantic, distilling in visible form a symbol of English civilisation for those who had been separated during the war years from the country they loved. If Owlpen increased Griggs' fame, Jewson's work on the house was the culminating achievement of his life.

CHAPTER 20

Enter Violet Gordon Woodhouse

1927–1929

*'William came. Glad Eve didn't – dare say she is
annoyed with me for not asking them, but what's
the good when she's always at Lypiatt.'*
Dorothy Walker, diary

Throughout 1927 William was absorbed in his work and trapped by commitments – an Oakridge production of *Devonshire Cream*, a puppet show at the Tuileries in Paris, a dutiful July holiday with his mother in Norfolk and in August a lecture to the Drama League. Harley Granville-Barker, now President of the Drama League, had tracked him down through the League's Director and founder, Geoffrey Whitworth, 'I hear that you sometimes like professional private engagements with your puppet show … are you free early August, Saturday next? We have 60 people to entertain …' With the two most influential figures in contemporary theatre pursuing him, this was an honour indeed. Granville-Barker, known in stage circles today as the father of British theatre, was legendary in his time. A playwright at seventeen, a successful actor at twenty-three, he was running the Royal Court Theatre at twenty-seven. From 1904 to 1907 he produced more than thirty-seven new plays (several of them by Bernard Shaw) and was the inspiration behind the regional repertory movement. He had ushered in a style of production that still approximates to our ideas of the best in modern plays and in contemporary Shakespearean theatre.

But with only ten days' notice, William regretfully turned down the offer. Under no circumstances could he cancel the late July treat

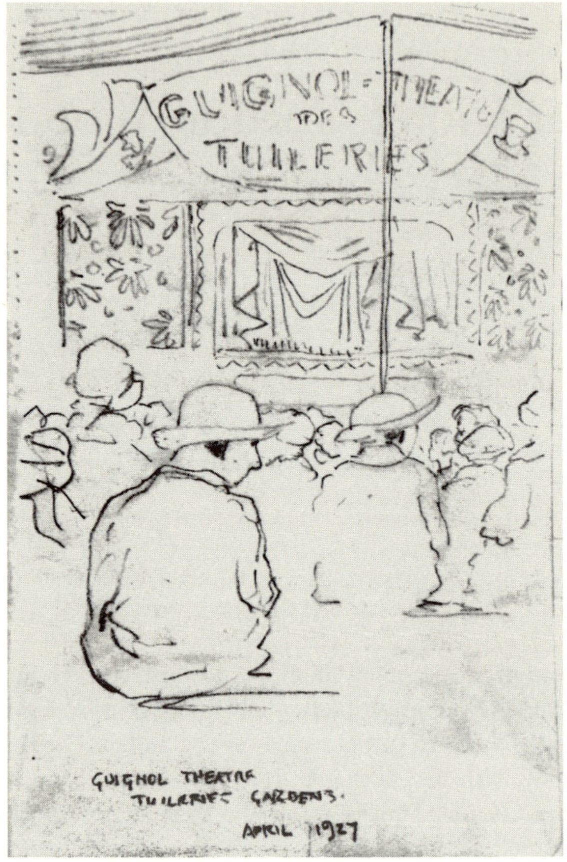

William took time off to watch the Theatre de Guignol in Paris before his own puppets performed. Eve is in the audience (backview), 1927

for his eighty-year-old mother. The two set off for what turned out to be a grey and cold holiday in Norfolk. But in Old Hunstanton village and in King's Lynn, he spent hours drawing carthorses and a new type of wagon he had not seen before.

In Europe his reputation continued to grow: John Drinkwater had been commissioned by the *Evening Standard* (15 December 1927) to write on the Berlin theatre. After covering six plays in six days, he ended by giving a dismissive review to Karl Scharton's slapstick marionettes at the Kunstler Theater and launching a paean of praise for William: 'if England only knew it, she has in William Simmonds a master the greatest in all England, who can make [puppets] incomparably more beautiful than anyone else in Europe.'

The even stream of life in the Sapperton Valley might have continued peacefully without interruption, at least until the onslaught of the next war. But Eve was on the brink of a seismic emotional upheaval. There had been no sign of unhappiness in her during their twenty years of marriage. How much anyone but herself was aware of the situation, no one knows.

In 1928 Eve began to keep an annual leather pocket diary with a tough steel latch. Like William's, hers held no intimate outpouring but recorded events factually – often leaving gaps of weeks between entries. Over the next eighteen years, she was to record her every encounter in Gloucestershire or London with the musician Violet Gordon Woodhouse and her three surviving 'husbands': her official one Gordon Woodhouse, Bill Barrington and the perpetually love-lorn soldier Denis Tollemache. The fourth, Max Labouchère, had died of his wounds just before the end of the Great War.

Eve had long watched Violet from afar with reverence at concerts she had given during the war. But in spite of having lived close by – just three miles from Sapperton – for five years, she had never formally been introduced. She had avidly bought Violet's gramophone recordings and had been to her concert at the Art Workers' Guild, envying her close relationship with Dolmetsch. For years before the war, Violet's charm and charisma, her unusual private life and her *ménage à cinq* had been much talked of in the Simmondses' London circle. To the musical, she was simply a genius.

The Woodhouses's acquisition of Nether Lypiatt Manor in 1923 had coincided with further food for gossip about them, this time caused by a Woodhouse family melodrama that made headlines in the national press. Voilet's husband Gordon had inherited the family fortune following the double murder of his two sisters. The killer was their butler, an ancient retainer who had returned traumatised from the war and shot them both at short range in the passage. To Violet's great dismay, he would not be reprieved but would be hanged in Gloucester.

Under these shocking but enriching circumstances, Gordon was freed from post-war financial pressure and was able to provide the setting for which his adored Violet was destined. The austere, under-furnished seventeenth-century Nether Lypiatt Manor was transformed into a resplendent jewel by Violet's original, idiosyncratic taste, her choice of furniture, paintings and *objets d'art,* her growing library and her damasks, chintzes, carpets and embroidery. At the centre of the house, the pale grey panelled drawing room doubled up as a music chamber, a focal point for lovers of early English music from every corner of Europe. By the time she and the Simmondses became friends, Violet had virtually withdrawn from playing her harpsichord – or any of her seventeenth-century instruments – in public. From now on she preferred to perform in the private settings for which these instruments and the early music were originally intended.

The first entry in Eve's diary came on 8 January 1928: 'Mrs Woodhouse and Mr Barrington called in am.' In William's studio Violet was shown an exquisite piece of netsuke-size ivory, *Pony Grazing,* destined for the Manchester Museum, and some wood-sculptured horses, *Farm Team,* intended for the Royal Academy. Hanging on a line of rope in a corner, she noticed the puppets that she had seen from a distance at the Blows' Christmas party. There, in their gossamer-light costumes, with their finely carved features painted in expressions that were fixed but at the same time seemed alive, they had moved Violet to tears and to laughter. At close quarters she was reminded that they were again just static, rather forlorn puppets awaiting resurrection through William's magic touch.

Back in the cottage, Violet was surprised to find Eve's Dolmetsch virginals and the Arts and Crafts purity of style in the sitting room with its Sidney Barnsley settee and its Barron seat and cushions – all orchestrated by Eve. When Violet saw the beauty and originality of Eve's embroidery, her acquisitive side sprang into action. Could she have a piece? Would Eve make her some clothing?

Eve, in spite of her handsome appearance, felt ungainly beside the petite Violet. Never had she seen anything like Violet's hair, or her clothing – the quality of the materials, her coat, dress, hat and shoes, so imaginative, artistic and unconventional. She was spellbound, too, by her porcelain complexion, her wit, her vitality and her warm curiosity. The presence of the Hon. Bill Barrington, however, unsettled her. His intensely blue eyes and evident appreciation of Eve caused her to blush. He was *'bel a faire peur'* – as Violet's niece once remarked.

Next day, with Violet's chauffeur at the wheel, Gordon, Bill and Violet swept the Simmondses off to Cirencester to see *Cinderella* (an outing to the cinema headed the list of Violet's ways to unwind from her daily four-hour regime of music practice). Invitations to lunch and dine at Lypiatt with exciting guests soon followed.

If the Rothensteins lived in a certain style, Nether Lypiatt and its gardens were for Eve a world apart in bohemian glamour. Bill, clearly a talented horticulturalist, oversaw the garden and farm, Gordon oversaw the housekeeping and Denis Tollemache, Dolmetsch's musical soulmate, came and went with a degree of independence. Violet's hold on women was as irresistible as her hold on men. She reserved a special place in her household for those who might free her to devote herself more perfectly to her music. For the moment this was filled by Mary Stanton, a quiet and cultured woman, who had given up home and husband to come and live at Lypiatt in happy servitude, running errands, answering the telephone, organising professional appointments – in short, fulfilling Violet's every practical need.

When neither entertaining nor practising, Violet was addicted to making expeditions all over the Cotswolds and soon conscripted her new friends to accompany her. On her birthday, 23 April, having discovered the Simmondses had never been to Bath, she asked them to accompany her there for the whole day. They were shown the architectural gems in various parts of the town, then went on to Angel's antique shop, to Baynton's secondhand bookshop and to lunch in the Grand Pump Room (later in the year she took them to her harpsichord concert in Bath Town Hall). The day ended with a visit to a film, and once back home at Lypiatt, Violet entertained Bill and Gordon by playing on the harpsichord from memory all the tunes they had heard that afternoon in the cinema. In his own quiet way William was growing as devoted as Eve to Violet; they had taken to each other instinctively. For him, she was becoming, without fanfare, part of their life.

In late spring Eve's diary entries increased in frequency, as if reflecting something important in her emotional life. As the months passed, the expeditions did not always include the entire Nether Lypiatt entourage – or William. Eve's diary notes her long walks in the woods with Bill Barrington, and expeditions alone with him to his gardening friends further afield: to Lawrence Johnston at Hidcote, and his burgeoning new eleven-acre garden, whose creation had been Bill's inspiration for his work at Nether Lypiatt. Closer to home near Chalford, they walked in Harley Butt's steep, hillside arboretum and saw his garden built on Arts and Crafts principles, another seminal influence on Bill.

On 20 December 1928 a symbol in Eve's diary appears out of the blue: 'Mr B. came into tea ✱.' Invitations to Nether Lypiatt grew more frequent. Eve's acceptance of the Woodhouses' invitation to spend Christmas with them put William in difficulties, as it meant he had to turn down the annual invitation to Christmas with the Rothenstein family in London. But Rothenstein, who disguised his ill health as much as possible, magnanimously masked his disappointment. 'We sang songs in your honour …', he wrote, '[your present] has made my heart sing all day … I see affection in the exquisiteness of the finish, in the intimate, tender, poise of the head and of the forelock crossing the face …' His children would have been sad to know that Violet had usurped what by now they regarded as their traditional Christmas rights with a *Calico Castle* puppet performance in the drawing room. A New Year's Eve party followed at Lypiatt. 'Heard Big Ben strike 12.00. Cherry brandy. Drank each other's health,' Eve wrote. At the end of January, she stayed at Lypiatt 'while William was away'.

Once full of blank pages, Eve's diary filled up; the entries became cramped and congested on the days when she saw Bill. It seems that Eve never quite told the truth even to herself. Nor could she: mesmerised by Violet, and simultaneously falling deeply for Bill, she was not able to think straight. Uncertainty crippled her. Had Violet cooled, she wondered, not daring to imagine she had an inkling of what was going on. Sensitive to life's every nuance, of course Violet did. For the moment, however, she did not consider Eve a threat. If Bill had to be pulled back from straying, Violet would do as she had done once before. On 30 January Eve recorded that V 'returned to London' – with all her men.

Time expanded and contracted abnormally. In her little candlelit bedroom, Eve could not put down what happened, nor was there any need. Her symbols, so proudly cryptic, would retain their hidden meaning all her life. Everything she had shared with Bill seemed hollow. His most trivial doing or saying, or not doing, swarmed around in her mind. She walked right round him, viewed him from every angle and in every light, storing up the memories against the long blank periods ahead.

She tried to return to the wood where he had kissed her, evoking the feel of early evening among the oak and beech, the shadows, the layers of leaves shutting out the sky, the bronze mosses at the foot of the trees, the floating sound of their voices, that explosive cry of the cuckoo, the disquieting ache of their walk back in single file through the trees, shuffling the dead leaves, stiff, self-conscious, imagining how she should have behaved.

Doubt and disappointment overtook her. Silence. No word, no message. The pitiable and one-sided truth. All might now be broken and nothing could repair it. A few yards away in the barn studio, William was working on his *Owl* late into the evening. In despair she closed the diary and shut the window against moths; recording the confusion in her heart, she lay awake wondering.

On St Valentine's Day, her control broke. Louise Powell was uncontactable and, in any case, out of the question. Eve would ring Sunni (Dorothy Larcher), however far her house in Hampstead was from Brompton Square. London was where she had to be. Eve found the two working overtime on new commissions and in difficulties over the inadequate water supply for dyeing their materials.

She pressed them to move to the Cotswolds. Wondering at Eve's low spirits, they gave her lunch and took her off to the new Arnold Bennett film *Piccadilly*, where Eve silently hoped she might bump into Violet, Bill, Denis – any one of the Lypiatt group.

On Eve's return home, an envelope in unknown handwriting dropped through The Frith letterbox. Eve's diary noted: 'Letter from Bill to William saying he will come over to see us on his return.' Later still another for William: 'Nice long letter from V. for William's Birthday.' Evidently it would be through William that Bill and Violet would communicate with the Simmondses. The stage had been set by Violet with consummate skill. The uncomfortable possibility dawned on Eve that Violet might value William's charm and artistic talent, together with his natural reticence, more than she valued Eve's own qualities. As for Bill, William soon discovered that Bill's range of interests was not confined to horticulture, garden design or the Lypiatt farm. He was also a keen amateur artist and had begun to seek William's advice on his drawings, framing, watercolours, paper models and cut-outs. His unannounced visits to William's studio and his disconcertingly unexpected summonses for discussions over meals at Lypiatt (always, of course, including Eve) were time-consuming. But William would without fail give him his full attention, however much it disrupted his work.

Oblivious of Eve's turmoil, William was as preoccupied by his work as ever. He was dividing his time between his Oakridge studio, monthly Art Workers' Guild meetings and occasional puppet performances. Emery Walker had booked him for the Guild's Christmas puppet show at Lincoln's Inn, but turned the honour into a mixed blessing: 'The lovely Old Hall', he said, would be open to the public for the first time but the Benchers 'were not acquainted with the immortal performances of your company [of puppets].' They would need persuading. Could William please obtain endorsements from heavyweights in the art world such as Sydney Cockerell, Professor Rothenstein, Sir George Clausen and Charles Aitken, Director of the Tate Gallery. At least there would be little difficulty with Aitken. He was negotiating to buy *Farm Team* for the Tate and the horses were to be given pride of place in the main gallery. If William had not been the reticent character he was, he might have added the Prime Minister to the list. Ramsay MacDonald, as much at home in artistic as in political circles, admired what was most modern – and for the moment he was particularly taken by the Sapperton circle. At the recent Burlington House exhibition, he had spent two hours in the Arts and Crafts rooms, studying the Biddulphs' new tapestry for Rodmarton Manor and William's two horses that were 'surrounded by admiring groups of people all day'.

Alone at Oakridge on 5 March 1929, Eve wrote 'Mr B walked over in the evening but did not stay.' Two days later, he did. Suddenly, the symbol increased from one to two: ✿ ✿. Eve was in emotional turmoil. Bill came with a message from Violet. Within days Eve was back in Hampstead, armed with an invitation to Brompton Square. For the next ten days Violet's white-hot attention focused on Eve – intermittently followed by cool indifference. Bill was nowhere to be seen.

They spent lunch, tea and dinner alone together. In the mornings Eve sat beside Violet while she practised. In the afternoons Eve was taken shopping; they went to galleries, to the theatre and, of course, to the cinema – the new Douglas Fairbanks part-talkie film, the *Iron Mask*, and Louise Brook in *Pandora's Box*. She was advised on her reading – the lesbian composer Ethel Smyth's *Streaks of Life* and *Impressions that Remained* and the homosexual Osbert Sitwell's *England Reclaimed* were recommended. And then in late April, after a film to Brompton Square, 'back to supper with V … Awake until 3.30.'

Violet's intermittent but intense concentration on Eve continued at fever pitch. During periods of coolness, Violet would pass Eve on to their mutual friend Dorothy Walker, another of Violet's star-struck devotees. Eve went off to the Walkers' annual party at Hammersmith to watch the boat race, only to bump into Violet later in the day, when she finally got her first sight of Bill for two weeks: 'Boat Race with D Walker. Had fine view sitting on the roof at the Walkers. Tate in afternoon, met V and Bill there!'

Missing Eve after her long absence, William came to London on 24 March to take her to the Rothensteins to meet Max Beerbohm. But the next day Eve shot off back to Violet for lunch and to help choose her a coat at Bradley's, followed by dinner and a film. A day or so later it was Violet's turn to entertain Max Beerbohm to tea – and to include Eve.

With the London whirlwind over, this emotionally see-sawing pattern repeated itself all over again in Gloucestershire. At parties at Lypiatt over the Easter weekend, Eve found Violet flanked protectively by Gordon, Bill and Denis Tollemache; and when she found several of the Sapperton clique also at Lypiatt for tea one day, she was annoyed with them for usurping her territory. The crush, with the Jewsons, Paynes and Powells, was, she remarked in her diary, only 'quite nice'.

At the end of the week, Bill broke away to turn up at The Frith for tea. Violet was reportedly ill. Overpowered by her pent up feelings, Eve experienced two wonderful days with Bill, albeit chaperoned by Denis during the day and by William at night. At some point the dam broke. In her dispassionate code she wrote 'to Lypiatt for Breakfast but V. ill with headache. Walked in the woods with Bill. Went to Tewksbury after lunch with Bill and Denis. Denis bought a jug for me. Stayed the night.' The next day, on 24 April 1929, the three were off to Bath, Wells and Glastonbury: 'beautiful sparkling spring day. Very happy ✱ ✱.'

Just as she and Bill had re-established their 'understanding', Eve's sense of joy evaporated when she found that Violet had once again attained the emotional upper hand over her: 'half expected V to tea', or a bleak 'V did not come … she must have forgotten; then V was unwell … depressed … she had a cold.' As often as not Violet's maid Bessie would ring with an excuse or, worse still, there was no message at all. On 30 May Violet 'did not come' to the tea Eve had lovingly made for her. Next day Eve expected her to call 'but she did not'.

Instead Eve listened disconsolately on Violet's gift of a wireless to the election results, which led to a hung Parliament. This was the first election in which women were allowed to vote. Next day, 1 June, a postcard came from Violet postmarked Stroud: 'suppose she has now returned to London', and two weeks later, 'V's broadcast. Heard her very clearly but not loudly. Telephone fixed. Rang up Bill. He came over for an hour.'

Although it was never mentioned among their friends, the Simmondses were struggling with their finances. They decided that their best hope of some sort of income would be to take on as many puppet bookings as they could. Most importantly, William had to create one or two new cameo plays with different scenes and characters and, above all, some more music. They worked out their terms for private bookings at a professional price. At £60 for a show, this hardly differed from a decade before and would not cover transport, which was often a problem. It would be best if they could find the right place in London for a long stint. The only person with a car in Sapperton was Harold Barnsley's son Edward, who helped out generously when he could. Together they would lug the stage up on to the car roof and load the puppet boxes into the boot, and he would drop the Simmondses as far afield as they wanted.

Throughout the summer the new puppets caused excitement and commotion wherever they went, honoured and feted all over the English countryside. Harley Granville-Barker rebooked them for a performance at Netherton Hall, his seventeenth-century house in Devon. He had fallen wildly in love – in the Italian manner, as Bernard Shaw acerbically remarked – with an American millionairess and writer called Helen Huntington. Now happily married, they were living a life of regal seclusion, attended by fifteen servants including liveried footmen. Barker was writing his definitive work on Shakespeare but had also involved himself with local affairs, having converted a small building on the estate for use by the village club. The Simmondses were invited for dinner.

Next day, the stage was set up in the club barn, and the puppets performed for two hours to a very 'enthusiastic audience'. The innovations were a hit. The new puppets were entirely different from William's previous ones. The figure of the tormenting, tauntingly cold, beautiful Estella, whose spirit William lifted from Dickens's Estella in *Great Expectations*, radiated self-possession and mystery. At the touch of only four puppet strings she could perform every form of pirouette on her extraordinary horse – a long-backed, white, luminous Lippizaner-like creature, another addition to his new *Circus*.

William could not afford to linger and within two days he and Eve were back in Oakridge. Closer to home the puppets were equally feted – at Lypiatt, Rodmarton, Daneway and Sapperton, at Lifford Hall in Broadway, in Yorkshire at an Arts and Crafts house (disconcertingly also called Netherton Hall) built by J.D. Sedding

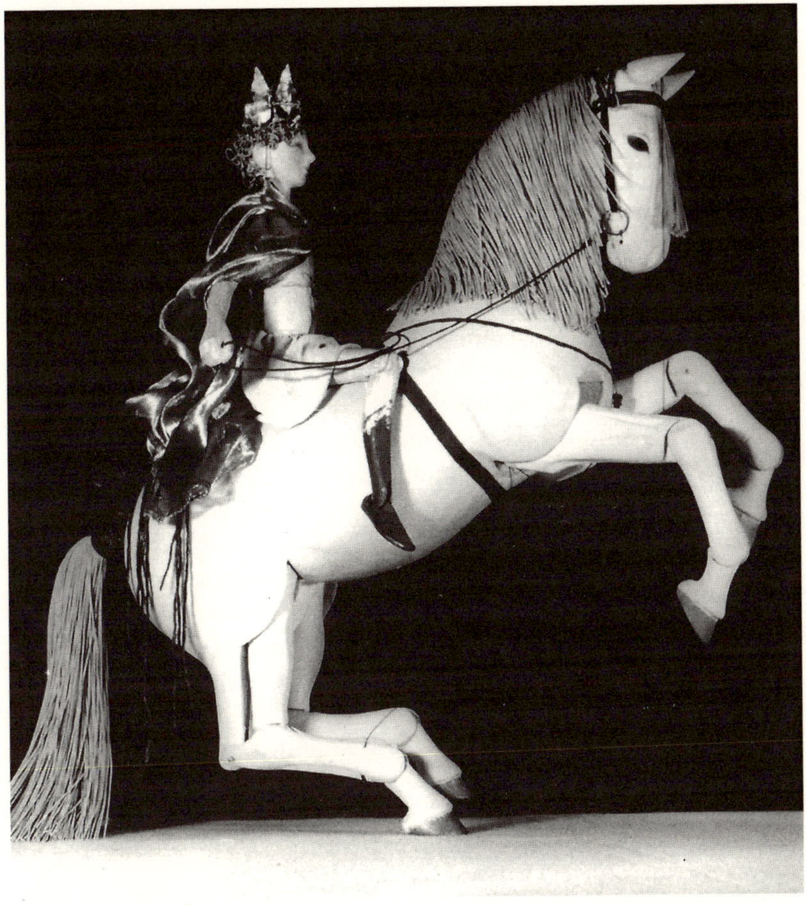

The puppet Estella on Snowball in the play *Circus*, after being dressed by Eve. Compare with plate 15

and finally back to the Blows at Hilles, a favourite annual fixture for William. The cool panache of Detmar's Cotswold house, an embodiment of Arts and Crafts philosophy, was on a smaller scale than Rodmarton. Its great hall with its impressive fireplace, elegant windows, tapestries and wooden ceiling, neither too grand nor too small, was accoustically perfect.

As committed as anyone to William, Detmar promised to find the right place for a London marionette season. These were still the sunlit years of his friendship with Bendor Westminster, and his influence on the fabulously rich Duke was absolute. As his *homme d'affaires* (and no longer a practising architect), he was manager of his estate and all his buildings in Belgravia and Mayfair.

Of the suitable Westminster properties at Detmar's disposal, there was the small racquets court in Grosvenor Mews or a larger room in his offices at 53 Davies Street, where the Duke's daughter's coming of age party had been held the previous year. But best of all, could be 30 Upper Brook Street, soon to become the Grosvenor Estate Office and temporarily unoccupied. The Duke, already a fan of William's, needed no persuading. Would William and Eve care to take the house for a two-week season in November?

During the autumn, Eve's turmoil continued unabated. There had been several summonses to London from Violet – with highlights such as *Porgy and Bess*, the comedian George Robey at the Royal Albert Hall and Charlie Chaplin's new film *The Gold Rush*. At Lypiatt Violet dangled, and sometimes cancelled at short notice, invitations to meet Ethel Smyth and the Sitwells or eccentric outings to visit friends' houses – and on one occasion to see 'a delightful dancing monkey at Waterlane House'. Then on Eve's birthday came the cut-off: '... rang Violet and asked her to come. She did not. Bill came and stayed to tea.' On 7 November Eve spent all day with Bill. Whatever passed between them, the pleasure was clouded by the feeling she was out of favour with Violet. She noted in November: 'Have written to V to tell me what is the matter.'

* * * * * *

Plans for the Upper Brook Street assignment needed care and attention. With Eve often off colour, feeling dizzy or complaining of headaches and throat infections, William enlisted two young assistants to relieve her on the puppet shows. The reliable Casty Cockerell, niece of Sydney Cockerell, born and bred into the Arts and Crafts world, would change the sets and receive the puppets when William had finished with them on stage. A more complicated aide was the self-educated artist and violinist Barnett Freedman, a kind but volatile character, rarely in good health and often short of money. He could be prickly and liable to shout if angry. The son of a poor East End Russian Jewish emigré, he had learnt to read and write music, play instruments, draw and paint in a hospital ward where he had been confined to bed between the ages of nine and thirteen. He would help Eve to provide the musical accompaniment for the shows.

William had Rothenstein to thank for Barnett Freedman. For three years Freedman had tried and failed to win a County Council scholarship to enable him to study at the Royal College of Art. Finally, he presented his portfolio of work to Rothenstein in person. Impressed, Rothenstein got him a stipend of £120 a year and Barnett began his studies in 1922, as a contemporary of Henry Moore, Eric Ravilious and Edward Bawden. Freeman's talent flourished and he went on to become one of England's finest colour lithographers and black-and-white illustrators.

From now on the two Simmondses, Casty Cockerell and Barnett Freedman would be a team. Casty wrote later, 'what we were doing was almost unique in those days … there were perhaps two other puppet theatres in England at that time … William worked all the puppets single-handed including the controls … the actions they were required to make were achieved with great accuracy …' The team's debut would be in the Duke's house in Upper Brook Street. This grandest of central London addresses was a godsend. To ensure comfort and good sight lines in the honey-coloured, panelled ballroom with its Waterford glass chandeliers, Harrods was brought in to construct an auditorium with raked seats. Evidently the recent crash on Wall Street had not dented the Duke's style. Detmar's aristocratic wife, Winifred, immersed in the Arts and Crafts world to which her husband had introduced her, was as enthusiastic about William as he, and offered to give a preview party to introduce the marionettes into the highest echelons of London society. After several days spent overseeing the set-up, the Simmondses were ready for her *salon de thé* on 25 November.

The marionettes shone and news about them spread fast. William noted that the matinees were sometimes 'Quiet and appreciative', but the 8.30 pm evening performances were 'noisy, full … very enthusiastic … crowded … great success'. But midweek Detmar Blow delivered a bombshell. Giving two days' notice, he asked William to drop everything and do a puppet show at Eaton Hall, the Duke's country estate in Cheshire. William, always worried at the damage caused by unpacking and packing the fragile dolls, let alone cancelling the full house on Friday night, thought it impossible.

Overnight he changed his mind: the Duke's important weekend guests needed entertaining, his generosity must be repaid. After all, he had lent him the Brook Street house. Moreover Detmar had been somewhat insistent. Next day the diary noted: 'Rang up Blow and suggested a plan by which we could get the puppets to the D. of Westminster.'

After the show ended, servants sent down from Eaton Hall worked until midnight dismantling the stage and helping William pack the fifteen marionettes into a heavy trunk. Next morning he, Eve, Casty and Barnett reached Euston Station in time to catch the 9.30 am train.

Even for the most blasé, arriving at Eaton Hall for the first time was an astonishing experience. A double avenue of trees stretched from the outskirts of Chester to the largest private house in England ('it's not a house, it's a town', wrote the Duke's third wife Loelia Ponsonby). The central part of the building was in the style of a French château and beside the chapel soared a clock tower the size of Big Ben.

Traversing several courtyards, from which buildings fanned out in all directions, the Simmondses' party reached the central quadrangle in which stood a vast bronze horseman with a falcon on his wrist. They entered the main house through a modest front door into an unimposing antechamber with footmen at every turn. To their right a red carpet stretched down the longest passage they had ever seen, leading to the marble-floored, tapestried Great Hall, a vast gothic space from which rose a staircase with suits of armour arrayed on every step like soldiers. Among all this stood Rubens's *Adoration of the Magi*.

It was in the ground floor ballroom, cleared of furniture and permanently ready for dancing, that they were to set up stage. Their supper was a snatched affair. In the unlikely event that they had been invited to dinner, it would have had to be all four of them or none – and Barnett was socially impossible. He had no time for authority, no respectable clothes and made no effort to disguise his origins: 'You don't want to go 'ampstead. It's an 'orrible place!' he told William.

The Eaton Hall routine allowed no drinking, and especially no cocktails, before dinner, but once the meal began rare wines were produced from the Duke's famous cellar. In his youth, the Duke had fought in two wars, winning a Distinguished Service Order (DSO), and counted among his closest friends a number of fellow warriors including Winston Churchill. Late in the evening, after a six-course banquet, the guests trickled into the ballroom, their number swollen by neighbours, together with their own house parties, invited in for the after-dinner entertainment. The recent chatelaine of Eaton Hall, the Duke's flamboyant, long-standing mistress Coco Chanel, had been replaced by a new fiancée, the shy Loelia Ponsonby, who was escorted by Churchill to her seat next to him in the front row.

The insecure and nervous Loelia had been forewarned that Churchill might be difficult. On his previous visits, when there was no dancing, the entertainment would be the village organist playing semi-classical music on a cathedral-sized organ in the Great Hall, or a performance from the little comedian Harry Tate or the popular 'Prime Minister of Mirth', George Robey, whose favourite attire was a clergyman's outfit minus the collar. Robey's speciality was pickpocketing. On one of Churchill's visits he had enraged him by unfastening the statesman's braces while he concentrated on holding on to his silver cigarette box. Churchill had threatened to leave. This night might be difficult. All the audience saw at first was a miniature stage set on a rostrum.

Like many actors, whatever the size of the auditorium, William could sense the movements and reactions of his audience. That night's guests were mellow – even, according to William, enthusiastic – though he saw that Churchill had fallen asleep. He was not surprised. His hero's political star from the tank days had undergone a roller-coaster ride, falling with the Gallipoli debacle, then rising again with his return to Lloyd George's wartime coalition government, falling again when he lost his seat with the downfall of the Liberals in 1922 and rising yet again when he returned to the Conservatives and was made Chancellor of the Exchequer in 1924. Now his reputation had crashed for a third time with the failure of his economic policies; England's return to the gold standard led to strikes, recessions and the defeat of the Conservatives in the 1929 election.

The first show was followed by another to the Duke's household staff. 'Bed at 1.00 am. A considerable success,' William wrote. Next day, back at Durrant Hotel, 'dead tired', he and Eve did a quick turn around back to Upper Brook Street for the Saturday matinee and evening show.

By Eve's account the next few days were if possible even fuller, with many people coming for a second and third time. Among the newcomers were Ethel Smyth, the Eumorfopouloses, May Morris, the painter Ellis Roberts and Violet's theatre-designer friend Norman Wilkinson. There had been no sign of Violet until on 14 December, the last night, the Rothensteins came in force and Violet appeared with her full cortège: Denis Tollemache, Gordon, Bill and Mary Stanton.

CHAPTER 21

William, Violet and Rothenstein

1929–1933

'I do get bored by Eve's talk,
and I would like to listen to William.'
Dorothy Walker, diary

William and Eve spent ten days over Christmas 1929 with the Rothensteins at Airlie Gardens, broken by a visit to Mrs Abbey at Chelsea Lodge and a token tea to exchange presents with Violet and Bill in Brompton Square. The Rothenstein way of celebrating was a present-giving ceremony on Christmas Eve and a festive dinner on Christmas Day in the large studio at the top of the house, with a 36-pound turkey displayed on a table glistening with crackers and candles. Not daring to overload William and Eve with a puppet show, they ended the evening with charades. Rothenstein, still under strict doctor's orders, sat quietly looking on.

Back at The Frith, Eve waited three days before Bill made contact. There had been no New Year's Eve celebration at Lypiatt and he was once more in the house without Gordon, Violet or Denis. After a lunch at Lypiatt, a walk to Eastcombe and tea back at The Frith, she helped Bill with his 'paper cut-out portraits'. The symbol reappeared in her diary. The pattern of insecurity started all over again: a longing to see Violet, whose affection and approval she craved, and never knowing when she would next see Bill. This became more painful thanks to his unexpected romantic gestures.

One day, finding no one at home, Bill left a basket full of pansies and plants on The Frith windowsill. Another day, 'hardly expected

Bill but he came. Fires all smoking and somehow rather a miserable time. Bill left about four o clock. I started reading "The Country of the Pointed Firs" to cheer myself up …' The reprint of Sarah Orne Jewett's late Victorian novel, described by Henry James as a 'beautiful little quantum of achievement', had again become a best seller with a new generation of readers. Eve was hypnotised by the story of the narrator's fluctuating relationship as she first settles down with another woman, then removes herself to a room of her own on a voyage of self-discovery. '… Must send it to V', she wrote. The emotional turmoil lurched on. If William was aware of it and hurt, he showed no sign.

Margaret Biddulph booked William for another puppet show at Rodmarton and asked him over to see the newly completed Norman Jewson chapel on the west of the house and the space that she had in mind for the performance. 'First visit there for some years – the atmosphere less genial than ever', William wrote, 'the furnishing of the new rooms, rather aimless and scattered but the large room very fine in itself.'

In spite of useful commissions of embroidery from Margaret, Eve was now less interested in the Biddulphs. Violet had so captivated her that she wanted to be available for whatever she might suggest. From their first encounter, Violet let it be known that she loved embroidered clothing. For dresses and coats Eve had been assigned an advisory role and was grateful for the introduction to the London couturier *Venturette*. She would await a summons to meet Madame Tost at Lypiatt for a fitting, followed by a second meeting at 21 Beauchamp Place. In equal measure, however, Violet loved presents. Little did Eve know when she proudly produced the first embroidered gift for Violet's birthday that she would be doing the same on Christmases and birthdays for years to come. Her career was impaired by her dedication to Violet. But that is how Eve wanted it.

When Eve was asked to Rodmarton for a final puppet discussion, she complained ungratefully of a most uncomfortable journey in the Biddulphs' Ford van, and an 'all rather chilly' tea at Rodmarton. She was surprised that Rothenstein continued to accept invitations there even during his convalescence. Her elevated sense of self also resented being patronised, especially now that she was ensconced, albeit precariously, in the glamorous Woodhouse set. She did not take kindly to Margaret's peremptory request to William to 'please come and tell our youth who works in our carpenters' shop how to operate the

Punch and Judy show – such an asset in the village to have a resident with an aptitude, and a chance for the boy himself'.

But Margaret was as dedicated as Claud to building a vibrant community around Rodmarton, and Eve knew it. Perhaps she was put out that she would get no help from Barnett Freedman, whose star was turning. He had been commissioned to illustrate Siegfried Sassoon's *Memoirs of an Infantry Officer* and was preoccupied by his forthcoming marriage. At least Casty was available.

On the day all was forgiven. The helpful carpenter set up the stage and covered the seats with rugs to create 'a very presentable Theatre'. The Biddulphs were 'charming ... gave a very nice tea party after'. Moreover, it had been a useful prelude to their London bookings. Some of the puppets had become worn and needed painting and mending. William thought Clown should be started again from scratch.

They were now better prepared for Charles St John Hornby's two parties at Shelley House in February. William was almost embarrassed by the reaction of the audience. Sir James Barrie, author of *Peter Pan*, sought William out to say he had never enjoyed anything in the theatre so much and even the dour editor of *Punch*, Owen Seaman, expressed his delight with uncharacteristic enthusiasm. This encounter also gave William a chance to catch up with news of his old comrade Shepard, who had joined *Punch*'s inner circle after the war, having shot to fame as the illustrator, on Seaman's strong recommendation, of A.A. Milne's *Winnie the Pooh* books.

Next morning the puppets went on to 2 Swan Walk to rest up with Esther Waterhouse for her party a week later. Widow of one of the last Pre-Raphaelite painters John William Waterhouse and the model for his famous *Lady of Shallott* (which perhaps inspired William's 1906 book illustration of Ophelia), she worked the Simmondses hard. With no mention of how the evening went, William merely remarks, 'Bed at 2.30.'

Just as the economic situation was developing into the worst depression in British history, the Simmondses' money problems appeared momentarily to lessen. To William's relief 'a very generous cheque' arrived belatedly from the Duke of Westminster via Detmar. He also sold his ivory *Pony Grazing* for a satisfactory sum to Manchester Art Gallery, and a cheque (albeit smaller than expected) was in the post from the Director of the Tate, who had finally confirmed the gallery's long-drawn-out acquisition of *Farm Team*. He apologised that limited finances made it impossible to offer more. Admittedly, William's pieces were more likely to be bought by museums than by individual collectors, so this sort of apologetic refrain might be expected to continue, but with the puppet shows still much in demand, he booked his first driving lesson; if all continued well, he might buy a car. To have his own vehicle for puppet transportation would make all the difference.

Barron and Larcher were also thriving. Strengthened in their resolve to leave London by Eve's steady encouragement, they had taken the plunge and, to Eve's joy, had bought a Georgian property called Hambutts near the Blows in Painswick, moving in on Barron's fiftieth birthday during a terrific snow storm. From now on, despite the ten miles separating them, the four friends would be continually in and out of each other's lives. There were outbuildings and a walled garden across the road that with Eve's help Barron would fill with plants and shrubs. Most important of all was the abundant water supply, enough to enable them to expand the business and experiment with different printing techniques. Both women designed their own blocks but Barron led the dyeing process and managed the business side of things. William suggested two of the Gardiners from Sapperton to help out with the mahogany blocks and Edward to design any furniture.

Far from drying up after the move, the number of clients was increasing. A big commission came from Girton College in Cambridge the following year and they found strong backing from the Little Gallery – a new London gallery off Sloane Street that was to become very influential. Muriel Rose, who opened it in 1928, soon became a central figure in the promotion of the artists and craftsmen of the 1930s. Word about this remarkable woman and her gallery spread rapidly. Her first show was devoted to landscapes by Thérèse Lessore, now married to Walter Sickert. Londoners, including Queen Mary, flocked to buy from her, drawn by its originality, which mirrored that of the work exhibited there. It had 'an atmosphere of its own ...', wrote *The Times*, 'its modern interior with its plain floor, plain walls and plain surfaces leaves the paintings, pottery and sculpture to take pride of place ... the modernity of the designs grows out of geometrical, sober colour to a happy medium between naturalism and abstraction'. Typical of Muriel Rose's triumphs was her sponsorship of the Welsh craftswomen who were re-establishing an old tradition of quilting and patchwork, culminating in her winning

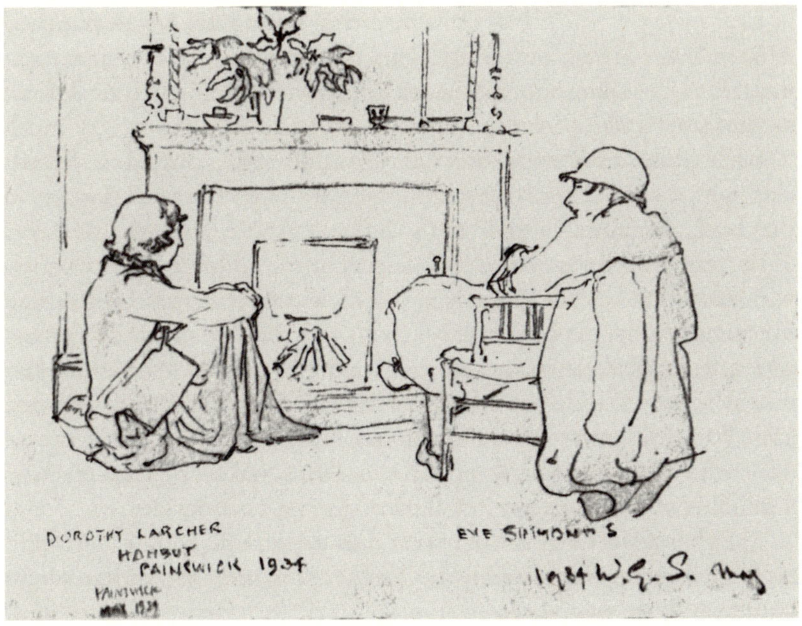

William's drawing of Eve with Dorothy Larcher at the house Dorothy shared with Phyllis Barron in Painswick, 1934

them an order from Claridge's for the bedcovers for their new Art Deco wing.

Throughout the 1930s the Powells, Larcher and Barron and her former assistant Enid Marx, Paul Nash, Edward Bawden and William (and to the smallest extent Eve) all flourished with the Little Gallery. Indeed, but for the fame reflected on the Bloomsbury painters from the writers in that charmed circle, Muriel Rose would perhaps be considered today on a par with Roger Fry as a champion of the visual artists of the interwar years. She was also extremely generous, and always ready to help her brood. When William was desperate to get almost unobtainable tickets to see Richard Teschner's rod puppets in Dragon Prince at the London Film Society, Muriel somehow managed to get them for him.

In Teschner's expressive Javanese creations, subtler and more beautiful than those of the Italian Teatro dei Piccoli, William felt for the first time that he was meeting his peer. Three years younger than William, Teschner had been an illustrator, painter and sculptor in turn-of-the-century Prague before committing his life to puppets. After the war he had moved to Vienna to devote himself to new techniques, his revolutionary 'theatre of figures' producing images of great drama and suggestion.

Eve's trump card with Violet was Eve's longstanding, close friendship with Larcher and Barron. Violet had loved Barron's designs in the Royal Academy exhibition and as soon as she could, Eve took her to see the new house and workrooms. The outbuildings were purring with activity. The converted stable block was now a studio with room for bales of linen, cotton and silk, and a dye house to hold the massive vat that Barron needed for expanding her range of colours. Her muted palette trademark in the 1920s was blue, iron, rust and oak gall. Within minutes Violet left orders for neck scarves and scooped up yards of material she wanted for cushions and seat covers. Lypiatt would become a showcase for Barron and Larcher designs.

Eve's staccato diary entries were still densely peppered with symbols, registering fluctuating joy and depression interspersed with habitual short references to Violet's and, to a lesser extent, Bill's moods: 'V more cheerful … V depressed … Bessic telephoned … V. upset … Pung [Pekinese] ill … she did not come.' Well into March 1930 on what seems to be a red-letter day, Eve was alone at The Frith one afternoon when Dorothy Walker, Sydney Cockerell and an American collector appeared, asking to see William's latest work. Feeling somewhat unprepared, she took them to the studio to show them his five wooden panels for the Cecil Sharp Memorial House destined for the opening later in the year. Bill suddenly appeared, summed up the situation and invited them all to Lypiatt for tea. For a brief moment Eve played hostess with Bill. Staying on after everyone had left, she helped him with some collages in Violet's private sitting room. She got 'home at 10.45. ❋ ❋ ❋ '. The symbols had increased to three.

The intense happiness was dashed almost immediately. The episode was followed a longer silence than ever. On and on it went. Eve became desperate: 'Expected Bill to ring up but think he must be away …' Bill again brought a bunch of flowers when Eve was out 'stuck in all the knockers … a very rare … Meadow Sage called *Salvia Pratensis*.' Invited for a walk alone with Violet, Eve was left 'terribly depressed'. This was swiftly followed by another entry: 'V and B both rather depressed.' Every now and then an elongated cross appears in Eve's diary – a symbol of suffering or was it a prayer?

William was immersed in his work. But even at the coldest time of year he did not abandon his walks, observing the fluctuations of wild-life in field, woodland and hedgerow. After twelve years in Oakridge, he was familiar with the sounds, shapes and scents of every small-holding, could mark the change in each meadow, in each tree. In wind, rain and storms, at dawn or in the falling dusk, he could sense what animals feel when they sniff the air. He never startled animals. The fox, the timid hare and the secretive badger – each seemed to know instinctively that he was part of their own world. In Siccaridge Wood he heard 'a slight sound and standing still saw a fine tawny owl in a holly tree only six feet from my face'; when he learnt of a cart-horse foal due to be born within the week in Miserden, he was back to draw it on its first day of life. He noted a new influx of fine geese in Edgeworth. More disconcertingly, he found a dead heron across the valley at Battlescombe, hanging by its head on a hazel tree – the second such he had seen in the valley.

Given his affinity with the natural world, it was surprising that William took on the honeybee and apiculture so late in his life. In June 1933 he visited a friend in Stroud who packed female workers, hundreds of drones and a queen bee into a travelling box. Back in The Frith garden, the colony was placed beside William's new hive overnight, and on the following day he had his first lesson in trans-ferring bees to a hive without getting stung. The litany of failure and success became a daily record in the diary, with intimate draw-ings that accompanied the notes. When the bees swarmed into Eve's espalier apple trees, he would try to understand the swarm's move-ment and meaning, their complex social life, the division of labour and the young queen's miraculous nuptial flight. He recorded the dangers of storms, and the sheer joy of ideal weather. His favourite book on bees was Maurice Maeterlinck's *Life of the Bee*, in which the author's part-poetic, part-scientific prose pays tribute to the bees' complex feats of architecture and their intrinsic sense of self-sacrifice. He came to believe the honeybees constituted one of the most orderly communities in the world – a humbling lesson to the human race.

If William had to go to London, it would only be to attend the monthly Art Workers' Guild meetings in Queen Square or to select pieces of wood from his trusted supplier in Clerkenwell. But Eve, with or without him, began going to London often at Violet's sugges-tion. When Mary Stanton was unable to be there to organise Violet's life for her, Eve filled the function of 'lady in waiting' admirably. But hovering in the background, now that her father had died, was Dorothy Walker, another potential candidate for the role. Star-studded notes recorded whom Eve met and where she went with Violet: to see the *Morning Post* music critic John Francis Toye or the film director George Cooper, to studios to see the work of Norman Wilkinson and the war artist Eric Kennington, whose *Gassed and Wounded* William and Eve had first seen and admired in 1918. Kennington was now working on a Thomas Hardy statue and allegorical reliefs for the Shakespeare Memorial Theatre.

On these visits, if his work allowed, William accompanied them; and in her heart Eve knew it was William Violet really wanted to be with. When Picasso came to see Violet, there was no question of Eve coming without William, and again when the Russian prima ballerina Tamara Karsavina came to Lypiatt, Violet made sure William could take a break from his workshop. She never tried or wished to divert him from his work, but sought his company when they were both free. It was not just the calming and steadying effect of his imperturbable serenity that Violet appreciated, he seemed to see only people's virtues, and through his discerning and sensitive observations made them feel that they were being admitted into his inner world. The quiet grace of his disposition – or as Rothenstein put it 'his beautiful character' – drew friends together in his presence, and made each of them feel a better and more intelligent person. All of them felt this: Bill, Gordon and Denis as well as Violet. Violet's affection for William was obvious in the care she lavished on a birthday celebration each spring, which contrasted with the last minute, token birthday tea, which was usually the best Eve could run to.

They shared a passion for the electric cinema; over the years the Simmondses and Violet, Gordon, Bill and Denis must have seen all the great films of the 1930s. And there was also the fact that William, in his usual quiet and unassuming way, had a cultivated and scholarly disposition. He went with Violet to visit the antiquary and Shakespearean expert Oliver Baker at a time when the market for genuine portraits of Shakespeare was booming, and optimistic misidentifications were frequent. Baker wanted William's opinion on the controversial, anonymous oil portrait that was on show at the Stratford Theatre Gallery, and also on the Droeshout engraving in the *First Folio*. Comparing the two, William found the engraving unskilled and roughly executed and undoubtedly the later of the two. It looked

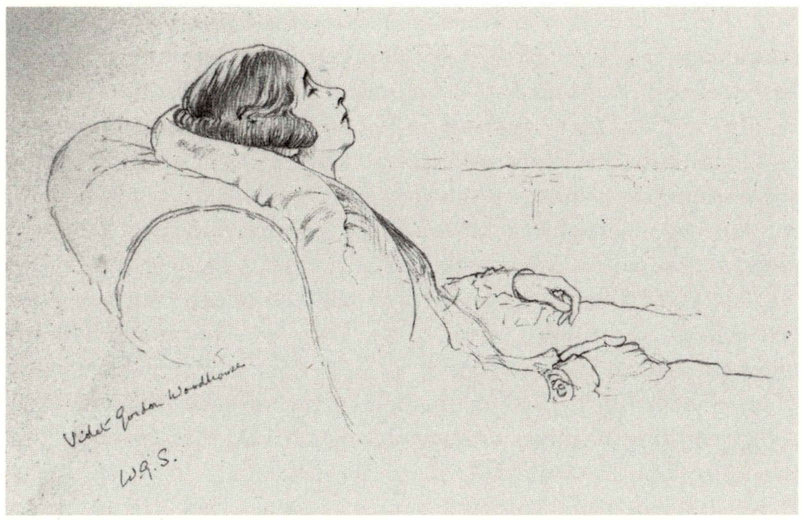

William's sketch of Violet Gordon Woodhouse asleep in the armchair at Nether Lypiatt, 1930s

as if Droeshout had made an outline of Shakespeare's head from the oil painting. The biographer Sir Sidney Lee, who had edited the *First Folio*, and the nineteenth-century scholar Richard Grant White both had a poor opinion of the engraver. William also went out of his way to accompany Violet to see another colleague from his Royal College of Art days, now a disciple of the Arts and Crafts movement, the silversmith Omar Ramsden in his studio in Fulham.

Violet's reverence for her hero Nelson led her to take all her men, plus the Simmondses, to the National Maritime Museum in Greenwich to meet with a naval historian. The museum possessed a mass of Nelson portraits and its archives contained the world's largest maritime historical collection, with a comprehensive range of rare manuscripts, books, charts, maps and pamphlets. Denis took William aside to persuade him to sculpt a miniature of the great man in time for Violet's birthday. Direct portraiture had never been his forte, but he took it on and his sixteen-inch wooden sculpture – a full-length statuette – turned out to be a masterpiece. Nelson's uniform, medals, epaulettes, posture and features reflected William's meticulous attention to detail and his ability to distil character and form into the essence (see plate 26).

The annual insecurity over invitations for Christmas at Lypiatt continued: Eve went to Lypiatt to say goodbye around 1 December, dreading the household's possible departure to London for two months, only to leave without an invitation from Violet. On a visit to the dressmaker Venturette and at Miss Rose's Gallery in April, she bumped into Violet by chance and was invited to tea in Brompton Square, where she found Bill acting strangely: 'he had a cold … could not come to the cinema … but he seems happier than when we last met.' Clearly Violet had gained the upper hand. Leaving Bill behind, she swept Eve off to see *Congress Dances*, a romantic German musical comedy film of Tsar Alexander travelling through Europe incognito and being assailed by a charming Viennese glove seller who throws flowers and a visiting card into his carriage. The inevitable love affair follows.

In Gloucestershire William's puppet bookings kept Eve in contact with the hallowed circle. A highlight would be the Blows' concerts, when Violet would perform on the harpsichord soon after their annual Christmas party at Hilles. In 1931 Winifred was entertaining in ever-greater style. The hall was decorated with a vast Christmas tree and there was a lavish supper, followed by two successive marionette parties. Casty and Barnett Freedman (and his new wife), back in full force for the big shows, were put up in a Painswick pub and William wrote: 'V. good audience … but a little girl tried to walk into the show to tell the puppet scene shifters her name – had to look severely at her and frighten her out.' The following night there was another 'very good audience, with Charles and Margaret Gere, Lord Clifford, and the poet James Villiers'.

Detmar, charming as ever, slipped a cigar into William's breast pocket as he was leaving, which back home that evening he cut in half to smoke in his armchair. Detmar's friendship and loyalty were rock solid. When William's alabaster *Foal* failed to sell that year at the Academy, Detmar insisted on displaying it in his Davies Street office. He had also hinted that another Eaton Hall puppet performance towards the end of the year might be in the offing. Winifred Blow followed up, to discuss plans and to settle the date. Neither she nor any of Detmar's friends had an inkling of the tragedy that was to befall Detmar. Only Loelia Westminster, the perpetrator of Detmar's future downfall, knew that.

Rothenstein, deprived of painting out of doors by his doctors, had begun writing about his past. He sent William an advance copy of his new volume *Men and Memories*. At a low ebb one evening, Eve read it from cover to cover. William was eulogised, and two flattering paragraphs were devoted to Violet. Confessing to being unmusical, Rothenstein wrote of his admiration for her, describing the one time that he had been invited to hear her play at Lypiatt: 'Even for me, a precious experience, not only to hear, but to see; to watch her sensitive fingers range over the keys ... a rare pleasure ... silvery sounds, like whispered music, enchant my ear.' He used the occasion to pay tribute to William in language that would later be plagiarised by Osbert Sitwell: '[her] taste in music is carried into all her possessions, her furniture, her books, china and pictures, and there, too, are some of William Simmonds' fine carvings in wood and ivory', and ended by saying that the two Simmonds's carthorses at the Tate were 'among the most notable piece of true sculpture there'. On the facing page he inserted a photograph of the piece he had championed over several years, William's majestic *Farm Team*.

Of Eve there was no mention. In Rothenstein's third and last memoir he finally refers to her, albeit without mentioning her remarkable gifts as a botanist. With little interest in Eve and less in gardens, he praises her economically as 'an exquisite artist, an embroideress and musician'. He lays more emphasis on her cooking skills, but the compliment is patronising and backhanded: 'moreover she can bake her own bread. A loaf from her is the kindest gift I can receive. Yet her bread, she declares, is baked in the usual way, only she gets her flour from a neighbouring flour mill.' Eve deserved an entry of her own; she was a fine artist in three fields. But few wrote about her in any detail either before or after her death. With her sense of decorum and propriety, she was overshadowed by her husband's originality and charm. At least Alfred Powell understood the poetry of her garden; his postcard to William one December said it all: 'How is Eve's Garden of Eden? I hope a few flowers still, reminding of Paradise!'

Even if Eve was put out, she held her head high at Betty Rothenstein's two wedding parties in March at Airlie Gardens. The puppets were asked to perform both nights and Eve noted a fresh convert in the Irish lieder singer and friend of Elgar Harry Plunket Greene, who shared the Simmondses' love of folk music.

Without Eve, William went to a dinner held in Rothenstein's honour to celebrate the knighthood bestowed on him by the Prime Minister, Ramsay MacDonald. To his pleasure, he found himself seated next to the architect Lionel Pearson, famous together with

Charles Jagger for the war memorial at Hyde Park Corner. The realism of the huge howitzer gun and brilliantly sculpted over-life-size corpse, the rejection of traditional sentimentalism in the attempt to portray the true nature of battle were all daring for the time. A speech was given by the warden of New College, Oxford, and a letter read out from Max Beerbohm, who could not be there.

* * * * * *

William persuaded Eve to consider taking on another public puppet show in London. His motive was not only pecuniary. At the age of fifty-five, his confidence since the Brook Street performances had received a boost from his friends – in particular from Rothenstein, who, with all the confidence of a successful impresario, pestered William to perform once more to the wider metropolitan audience. He had come to believe that the two art forms in which William excelled were interlocked: sculpture might be William's deepest form of expression, but equally exquisite, in their way, and equally expressive of him as an artist, were the poignant haunting wooden dolls that gazed on the world with something of William's penetrating spirituality. As a one-man director, designer, poet, librettist, musician and manipulator, William was now at his zenith.

But in loyalty to Detmar, he would not consider Brook Street again. When the Simmondses had performed their second show for the Duke at the end of 1931, there had been no sign of anything amiss. Winifred had come to The Frith to discuss final details and all had gone according to plan. But unknown to Detmar's friends, trouble had been brewing soon after the Duke's marriage to Loelia Ponsonby. Detmar had got on well with her predecessor, the Duke's mistress Coco Chanel; they shared tastes and friends and appreciated each other's artistic genius. It was on Detmar's introduction to Phyllis Barron that Coco had commissioned cushions and curtains from her for her French château. The Westminsters' marriage had been in difficulties from the start and from the start, too, Loelia took against Detmar as one of the 'hangers on, toadies and ingratiating, oily sycophants' who never left Bendor's side, as she put it in her memoirs. Seldom left alone with her restless husband, she determined to loosen the hold of his advisers.

She particularly targeted Detmar, as the most trusted of the Duke's friends, and had been undermining him in every way she could. By her account, he accompanied Bendor everywhere, steered him away from business conversations and ensured that documents needing his attention were always presented to him at the last minute. After months of growing suspicion, the three found themselves becalmed together one day on the *Cutty Sark*, sailing from Scotland to Liverpool. To pass the time, Bendor asked to take a look at his papers. To his surprise he found he was being asked to sign away 99-year leases in Mount Street for no capital payment and a peppercorn rent.

There could have been an innocent explanation: most of the properties were much in need of modernisation, and it was customary among London's larger landowners to keep the freehold and give long leases in return for extensive work to bring houses up to date by installing plumbing and electricity. But Loelia's moment had come. She knew that others connected to the Grosvenor Estate were jealous of Detmar's imaginative architectural innovation and his unique hold on the Duke's affection. For twenty years, through the war and the Depression, he had run the estate superbly and adapted it skilfully to a changing world. Lesser talents and backward-looking trustees found his mastery hard to take.

After summoning a solicitor to look into the situation with one of the trustees, the Duke succumbed to Loelia's jealous malice, accusing Detmar of defrauding the estate. Bitterly hurt, Detmar resigned and collapsed into a deep depression. To begin with few of the Blows' wider circle of friends knew what was amiss. But Loelia made sure to spread the word and soon the Blow family was shunned by society. They and their friends have maintained to this day that Leolia's fabrications were the sole reason for Detmar's departure and in this tragedy of betrayal the female Iago had triumphed. Unable to clear his name, and sunk in despair, Detmar would be dead, his heart broken, within five years.

CHAPTER 22

Detmar Blow Destroyed

1934–1939

*'… that fantastic, natural, artificial, yet intensely moving world
of Mr William Simmonds' puppets, whose outer universe is,
this year, the Grafton Theatre … shows us great things in little,
and has a curious affinity with that longing of the human heart
for a simplicity that shall contain all complexity'*
Harriet Keen Roberts, *Grafton Theatre* magazine, 1934

In the end William chose the Grafton Theatre – or rather its Director chose him. Judith Wogan had seen the Brook Street show and had written straight afterwards asking if he would consider presenting 'such beautiful things as your puppets' in her theatre. William explained that a single show would not be worth his while. After prolonged negotiations she agreed to reduce her rate to £25 a week for a Sunday performance for her Theatre Club. Well aware of the financial risk from his experience at the Stroud Festival, William took the plunge and signed up for a fortnight starting in late November 1934.

He began work on a longer version of *Circus* and a new play centred on a Victorian family, *Mahogany Suite*, which was to become one of his most famous puppet plays. Of course, he had to shoulder expenses for ticket sales, advertising and attractive images for journalists, and to find a cameraman who could capture the puppets' spirit and characters. This time he set about photographing them himself in his workshop, using the light from a petrol lamp. To his admirers the results were excellent, producing images reduced to their most simplified form, yet at the same time so detailed that one could see the figures' tiny delicate hands, with all their lines and veins; and the circus horse, performing his sedate gallop, the hooves turned up to reveal its inner thrush (see plate 15 and page 215).

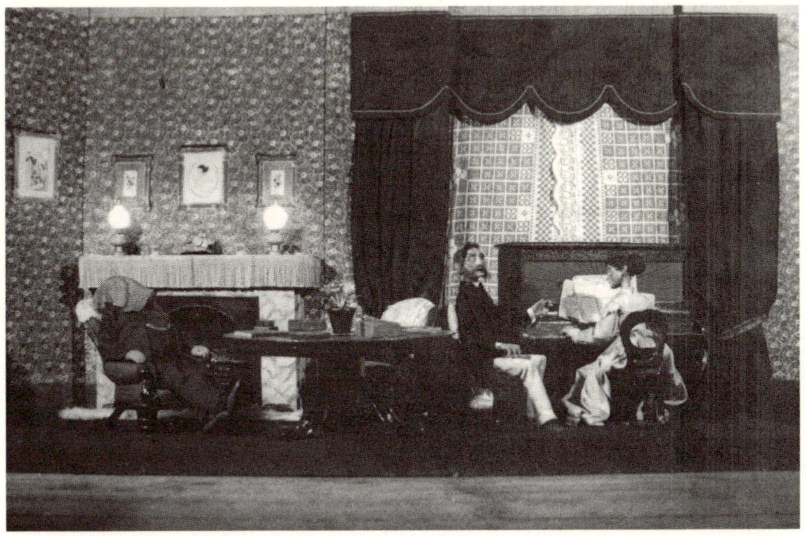

The parlour scene in the Wimpole Street skit *Mahogany Suite*

Maybe William had let slip the sources for his inspiration. One of the more literary theatre critics who came to Oakridge before the show opened, described William's Victorian parlour in *Mahogany Suite* as having been influenced by a morality tale, *L'Amie Inconnue*, by the eighteenth-century writer Maria Edgeworth, where the central character, Angelina, defies convention to run away and discover 'the higher species of friendship'. Surely, too, the critic mused, parts were a gentle parody on *The Barretts of Wimpole Street*, a recent box-office hit starring Charles Laughton. In William's little play 'Mr Barrett of Wimpole Street sat asleep by the fire, waking with a start, whilst the cat asleep on another chair rose with all its fur on end to miaow at the music ... beside the fireplace ... were photo albums and glass case ornaments ... it is a gem – the puppets must be seen to be believed.'

It would be a challenge to fill the theatre for a fortnight. Loyal as always, Muriel Rose sold Grafton Theatre tickets to all her clientele coming into the Little Gallery. Determined that William's venture should succeed financially, Violet combined a house-warming party in her new flat in Porchester Terrace with the promotion of the show. *Tatler* wrote of Mrs Gordon Woodhouse's party: 'nothing like the Marionettes has ever been seen in this country ... Mr Simmonds has an astonishing power of reducing an emotion to its essence.'

Ethel Smyth, whom William had known through Violet for some time, saw the puppet show at Porchester Terrace and wrote beautifully to him:

Coign, Woking
June 20th 1934

Dear William,
I wrote to Violet asking if – when – I might come and see you and try and tell you what a strange haunting absolutely unique impression your art leaves in one's life – yet not unique, for it joins hands with all the various other impressions the art of others have left. And of the most disparate characters – all one feels about England and Drake – the troubadour visions, very un-outlined ones, that have been with me since youth – and that the sway of strolling love & music – that intoxicating little figure gives form and substance to: (this, I think is one of your most wonderful achievements) – As for the woodland scene all the time I thought of Flaubert's 'St Julien L' hospitalier' – surely one of the most wonderful stories in the world and of which the feeling you invoke is direct heir.

I long so dreadfully to see that scene again, and for two people I know who were not present to see it. It is a bore being too deaf now to hear the suggestive tinkling that I feel certain must have been like all the rest – like the foot-work of the fat white aproned lady – and the foot work of many others of your company – just right.

Will you thank Violet and the two men for the whole great evening. I was too tired (am doing a devastating rheumatism cure) to depart as I should have liked to do – I never said goodnight to Gordon and Bill except in spirit. There are times in life when all you can do is melt away in a taxi. My love and gratitude to your wife.

Yours ever with more admiration and more intensely alive gratitude than is decent to express.
Ethel Smyth.

After the opening, *The Times* wrote that *Mahogany Suite* was permeated with the 'wit and humour of the luxurious sentiment of the last century'. But it was the *New Statesman*'s reviewer who most perfectly expressed the essence of William's art: 'In other puppet shows marionettes imitate or parody human life. Mr Simmonds' puppets lead a withdrawn exquisite life of their own, a life which we share as we watch them, but to whose patterned and rhythmical loveliness, we can hardly hope to aspire.'

There were usually one or two devotees who would make it their business to help William succeed in London, but this time two of his most active supporters were ruled out by events beyond their control. Poor Winifred Blow was out of action. After Detmar's humiliation, Loelia Westminster had ensured the Blows' social ostracism. Detmar's friends, however, stood by him, appalled by the way the Westminsters had treated him. When Sydney Cockerell wrote calmly to the Duke asking for an explanation, he received an icy reply from a lawyer. Detmar was now in an American clinic and suicidally depressed.

As for Rothenstein, however much he willed William on, his energy was depleted and his time at the Royal College of Art was coming prematurely to a close. With less income, and less success in selling his paintings, he had become more subordinated to Alice's wishes (particularly after she had inherited a substantial sum of money after the death of her friend Lady Herringham). They moved from Airlie Gardens to a flat in Hampstead, where she continued to live in grand style with maids in black-and-white uniform.

There was always Sydney Cockerell, who would come several times with an extravagance of different friends. But William's new champion was Ellis Roberts's wife, Harriet. She was mesmerised by the puppets and wrote in a letter to Eve, quoting Yeats (and perhaps cribbing a phrase appearing in the *New Statesman*'s rave review dated 24 November 1934), that 'they are caught in the artifice of eternity'.

Harriet took it upon herself to badger a remarkably eclectic group of friends to discover for themselves what she had personally experienced. When H.G. Wells was unable to come to her first night dinner, she sent him the promotion leaflet and wrote that she was 'struggling to find words to say what I thought of the show …' The man who described himself as the Don Juan of the intelligentsia, as flirtatious as ever in his seventies, told her in his funny, lisping, clipped voice: 'I'll go if you say it's so good.' Once she got him there, she reported back to Eve that Wells had enjoyed the puppets so much that he went twice and promised to pass the word on how charming they were. Then she persuaded Desmond MacCarthy to include William's puppetry in one of his BBC literary broadcasts, a coup that led to ticket sales doubling.

Possibly the most important and influential potential admirer ensnared by Harriet was her friend Margot Asquith's son, Anthony, the up-and-coming film director and collaborator of Terence Ratti-gan. She wrote to Eve: 'how cruel and outrageous I feel to ask but could William possibly do *Circus* and *Mahogany Suite* on the last matinee on December 5th … is this the last straw … an outrageous request but I am bringing Anthony Asquith who is keen on the idea of a film.'[1]

After the Grafton Theatre fortnight, the puppets were much sought after and there was a flurry of new bookings. After a good article in *Country Life*, an invitation came from the University Club in Edin-burgh asking William 'to bring the Little People' to follow on from the Munich Marionettes. And the Wills family, who lived close by at Miserden Park in Gloucestershire, wanted a teatime party and a late 9 pm performance for the village. Their seventeenth-century house, in part rebuilt by Lutyens after a fire, overlooked the valleys and woods next to Daneway and Pinbury through which William often walked. On his first exploratory visit with Peggy Wills, a warm and friendly widow with five children, he found the Victorian drawing room-cum-hall as ideal as the one at Hilles. At one end there was a raised floor forming a natural stage, large enough for the proscenium and the spinet. On the day, even with help from Casty Cockerell and Barnett Freedman, Eve was exhausted by the strain of performing twice in one night and retired to bed straight afterwards. The five skits were long-established favourites, nothing new like *Mahogany Suite*, but William had probably overtaxed her so soon after the Grafton Theatre fortnight.

Eve's exacting notes on the scores for the eight characters' move-ments and their songs show the precision and concentration needed from her and her two assistants, operating without the unifying pres-ence of a conductor. To take but one skit, *Harlequinade*: during the 'Greensleeves' overture, Harlequin enters and is soon joined by Col-umbine; they dance to 'Oranges and Lemons' (see page 166). There follows a clown cavorting to 'Old Mother Oxford'. Next, the pup-pets Pantaloon, Ghost and Elephant perform sequentially dancing the Halfe Hannikin and singing 'Hey, boy and up we go'. The show ends with Randy Horse in the finale followed by Troubadour and Pink Lady acting to the music of *The Triumph* and *Serenade*. Eve's notations on the remaining four skits – *Woodland, The Circus, Scene Shifters' Shift* and *Seaport Town* – are remarkable. These extraordi-nary marionette performances, with technical demands as complex as those of an operetta, albeit in miniature, would have been hard to operate without her. The less-committed Casty Cockerell and Barnett Freedman were important, but their contribution was minimal compared to Eve's.

Eve recovered in time for the next booking in the Goldsmiths' Hall. The Assembly Room had been lit by silver candelabra on the tables, and from the ceiling hundreds of candles hung in big lustre chandeliers. Incongruously, after the show and tea, there was dancing to a jazz band. Next day William took Eve to the Royal Academy to see the largest display of Chinese art ever exhibited in Europe, chiefly organised by William's patron George Eumorfopoulos, who had travelled to China to select the pieces. Rumour had it that he had lost much of his fortune during the 1931 crash and was negotiating to sell part of his collection to the V&A and British Museum for £100,000.

Four days later they were off again on a far longer visit to the Cadburys at Wast Hills in Birmingham. To add further strain and annoyance to Eve, Casty and Barnett arrived only minutes before the first show started. Next day harmony was restored on an outing to Birmingham Art Gallery to see the rural sculpture collection donated by the Quaker artist and collector Estella Canziani. Their last evening show ended with a packed audience.

* * * * * *

Eve's see-sawing between desolation and euphoria continued as before. Throughout her bouts of hypochondria and mild illness, William never failed her. To outsiders their devoted partnership appeared solid. William would happily take her in his Riley to Lypiatt, where she would 'walk alone with Bill round the fields and the garden and return home late after tea' or go on a garden outing further afield. Then came more frequent bleak references to Bill being ill, or away, until a strange entry noted her lunching alone with Gordon at Lypiatt. With no mention of Bill, except for one last, desultory, single symbol, Eve increases her visits to London to see Violet and listen to her practise with the British violist Lionel Tertis for their two concerts in 1935 at the Wigmore Hall. Even then Bill is never there, nor again when she is invited to the theatre. In 1936 Eve's leather diary no longer has a steel clasp; it is all but blank. In 1937 it stops for good.

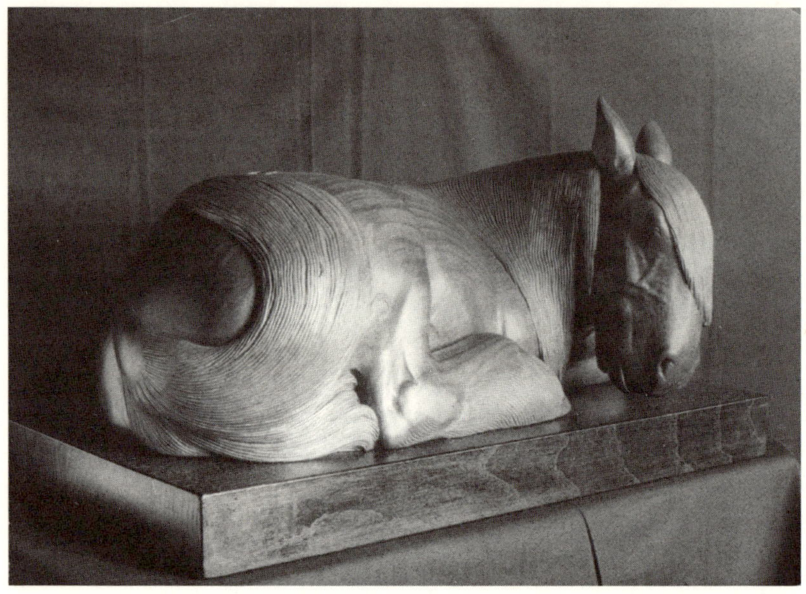

Old Horse at the Royal Academy exhibition

William kept carving. After the death of Violet's two adored dogs, he made a beautiful boxwood Pekinese to comfort her (see plate 23). This glorious creature, with its thick splash of tail, its squat, assertively placed paws, its knowing black eyes and its flash of ebony in the ears, took pride of place on the carpet in the Lypiatt drawing room, from where it gazed up at Violet. She also bought a smaller version of William's *Cat with Marble* (the original having been acquired by Carlisle Art Gallery), on which he had experimentally scorched a fur pattern into the pine on the cat's back (see page 5). He sold his *Farm Team* and a cheque for £139 15s. 5d. arrived from Muriel Rose, who reported that William's postcards printed by the Tate were selling like hot cakes in her gallery, and also in the Tate itself (see page 185).

When William's eighteen-inch piece *Old Horse* appeared at the Royal Academy, one fan wrote to him perceptively: 'You avoided realism, touched Idealism until you came to the head – where expression is almost human … In his eyes foreknowledge of death … It still haunts me.' To another admirer, this quiet, impassive creature communicated the approach of death, reminiscent of Shakespeare's seventh stage of man: 'The last scene of all … that ends this strange eventful history ... sans teeth, sans eyes, sans taste, sans everything.'

Painters and sculptors of animal subjects had been categorised demeaningly as 'animaliers' – a title that seems to suggest that animals could never possess the depth and spirit of the human soul. Those familiar with the Parthenon frieze or the horses of the eighteenth-century artists George Stubbs and Antoine-Louis Barye know otherwise. But it was not only the subject matter that was belittled. There was a prejudice against small sculpture, a feeling that it was not to be taken seriously. In recent times the rediscovery of Netsuke sculpture has done something to redress the balance, as perhaps has the influence of environmentalism on our view of animal habitats. Such classification never worried William. He was his own man. He had a profound understanding of the animals and birds living and breathing close beside him in the Cotswolds. They, and the natural world as a whole, were his spiritual life.

* * * * * *

The German Arts and Crafts movement remained strong in the 1930s. William had befriended Harro Siegel, the German puppet master, when he came to visit The Frith during his tour of Europe with his handmade puppets. He had revelled in 'the skill and animation of William's art, the sheer-deep joy of watching his puppets ... It is such a great thing: to behold mastership; to watch the ease and lightness, which only can emerge from long labour and experience ... to make ones means of expression so smooth and flexible, that they fit tight like a glove, which seems so easy to the beginner, and is such a hard thing to the more experienced.'[2] Siegel's academic ambitions were rising fast. In 1936 he was appointed to the Staatliche Kunstschule of Berlin as Professor for Education in the Arts, and until 1943, was artistic collaborator at the Reichsinstitut für Puppenspiel. Strangely the friendship continued almost up to the beginning of the war: in November 1938 Siegel stayed in a pub in Sapperton to visit William, and he came again in January 1939, when he was brought over to tea at The Frith by the progressive educationalist George Trevelyan months after William had sent his *Hare* to the prestigious 'Berlin Arts and Crafts Exhibition'.

The politically sensitive Rothenstein had been alert to the dangers of Hitler's rise to power as early as 1931 and to the increasing attacks on Jews and the exodus of Jewish artists, writers, businessmen and intellectuals from Germany. Now that he had taken back the tenancy of his cottage, he was spending longer periods at Oakridge, dropping in to see William and listen to the news on his wireless. He had no wish or need to be in London. Despite long absences during his illness, the village and its world had remained his spiritual home, a current connecting him to a life he had all but lost. He wanted, too, to be close to William and to reignite their old friendship. At one of his lowest ebbs, he had written to William while convalescing: 'There are many things I want to do with you, and see, and talk over with you. May we ride the smooth and rough waters and anchor side by side again next year … Rachel too wants to walk through wood and fields with you again.'

In some of the Cotswold villages the sense of danger was strong enough by the summer of 1935 that the possibility of another war was already envisaged.[3] To William and Eve certainty came much later.

CHAPTER 23

Initial Years of the Second World War

1939–1941

'The chilling sound of a warplane spiralling to earth …
A parachute floated past the classroom window at Oakridge
School … as a plane came down, scraping the bell tower.
The children were told to get under their desks.
Transfixed, they watched and waited.'

On 22 August 1939, at tea with Beatrice Hornby, William and Eve listened to 'the very grave statement by Chamberlain. All very depressed and alarmed.' The shocking news of a pact between Germany and the Soviet Union brought home to William for the first time the danger of Britain's situation. He wrote in his diary, 'a great surprise. Emergency measures being take.'

Although the Molotov–Ribbentrop Pact contained secret protocols, one thing became obvious: Hitler was cynically clearing the decks for further hostilities near Germany's borders, starting with Poland, whose territorial integrity had been guaranteed by Britain. War seemed inevitable. And Russia would be no help.

Rothenstein visited with Alice and three of their children to discuss the future. Despite his poor health and age, if war were declared he would be offering his services again as a war artist. His idea was to draw portraits of various types of airmen for use as historical records by the Air Ministry. Gloucestershire had eighteen military airfields, most of which were in the Cotswolds, far enough from France to deter the Luftwaffe's fighter escorts and near enough to Birmingham and Bristol to enable the RAF to deploy them quickly against German bombers. These would provide Rothenstein with a rich cast of pilots, maintenance staff and engineers.

More politically engaged than twenty years ago, William too was determined to contribute. He and Hornby checked through the fifty pages of Air Raid Precautions from the Home Guard instructions and finalised their plans. There were several airports as well as numerous satellite airfields and landing grounds around Oakridge, which meant that the area was particularly vulnerable to attack. Those in Bibury, Barnsley Park, Southrop and Fairford felt alarmingly close. The expectation that the Luftwaffe would get through even the strongest defences led them to act fast to form a committee for the five neighbouring villages. They had to create patrols, recruit observers and messenger boys, and print signs for First Aid posts. The telephone in Hornby's house would be used for reporting back to headquarters.

The first management committee meeting in the village hall did not go well:

'Hornby and I very angry at finding signs of a ring in the committee … Mrs Hunt blunt while she led their attack … new optional plans discussed.' Fortunately, since there would be frustrations enough without Mrs Hunt's help, the quarrels blew away on the outbreak of war and did not reappear.

The Simmondses' wireless was a magnet for the anxious friends who poured into The Frith to keep abreast of the escalating crisis: 'all very disturbed about effect of the news on the young men of the family …', William wrote. 'News all the weekend is very black … Germany apparently determined to make war although declaring peaceful intentions. Word has it that the emergency hospital organisations in London are preparing for a million casualties in the first month of war if it comes.'

On Friday 1 September, William wrote in capitals: 'GERMANY INVADED POLAND THIS MORNING … Children being evacuated from London and all large towns today and probably for three days.' In the evening the Simmondses and the Rothensteins listened to Chamberlain's announcement that all men from eighteen to forty were to do service. Next day: 'Germans ordering air raids on Warsaw and other Polish towns … they seem to have taken one town … no part of the line being held against them.'

As a wave of evacuees poured into Cirencester station for dispersal into villages, Eve rearranged her spare room beds in case her excuse – that she had to house her niece Hermione – failed to satisfy the billeting officers. In the event she escaped without having to take any evacuees. After orders to black out all windows, she took down her curtains and went shopping in Stroud for material. Everything there was sold out, even post cards, due to the rush of children writing to their parents in joy or misery about their new homes. She searched in vain for thick black cotton in Lewis & Godfrey's haberdashery department and settled for a dark blue material, only to find it was not dense enough and had to be doubled up and sewn on to the blinds. Every villager had blocked out the smallest chink of light against the possibility that Reichsmarschall Hermann Göring was about to launch the Luftwaffe against the villages of Gloucestershire.

On 3 September the news they had dreaded came through on the Simmondses' wireless: 'This morning at 11.15, after the expiration of our ultimatum to Germany to withdraw troops from Polish territory, the Prime Minister declared the British Empire to be at war with Germany.'

Eve retired to bed with a cold for ten days. On 22 September she took her first walk for some time to Sapperton to see Mary Jewson, who was 'very tired after her heavy role of receiving and allotting children into neighbours' cottages. Most of the children sent there are ill.'

Lunching at Lypiatt, Eve found Violet overwrought at the news that her nephew, John Gwynne, had joined the army and was leaving for France. Her footman and gardener were keen to sign up, too. Violet detested war with a deep passion, but despite her anger she committed herself to do her bit for the country. She had brought all her instruments from London for safekeeping. For the next three years, until she broke both her wrists in 1943, she travelled throughout the country, braving the blackouts to perform fundraising concerts and live broadcasts for the BBC.

To calm her nerves in pre-recording rehearsals she often asked William to be with her. In preparation for her clavichord Bach recital for the BBC in 1940, he went to Lypiatt to hear her practice. On the day of the recording in Bristol, attended by her extensive household, he sat alone with her during the test rehearsal in the studio annex. Like Rothenstein, she appreciated William's imperturbable serenity and above all his judgment.

William devoted concentrated attention to his Home Guard Air Raid Precautions (ARP) duties. The possibility of invasion was all too real. When equipment did not arrive, ingenious as always, he found ways to make gas masks, splints, stretchers and a detailed map of villages for which he took responsibility. In Cirencester he contacted the Pioneer Corps, now installed in Bingham Hall, and helped them re-instate the dormant Rifle Range, a legacy from the First World War. The Air Ministry gave him the go-ahead for a camouflage scheme for aerodromes and landing grounds.

January and February 1940 in Oakridge were among the coldest in living memory. For weeks, snow and a heavy frost covered the land:

> The thickest coating of ice I have ever seen … walking through grass is like walking through glass and in the long parts makes a great noise. Large tree trunks are snapping off and can be heard in all directions. Four branches fallen in our meadow … Larches in our copse drooping with the load and swaying from side to side slowly, looking very mournful, but less broken than the beech.

Then the larch tops broke. Late at night William heard the noise of falling branches, then a crack and a splitting sound, followed by a noise like falling shingle as one heavily loaded branch crashed down. Every telephone line was down 'in great loops to the ground or broken and hanging round the poles like chandeliers …' William's notes continued: 'Animal tracks in the snow from mice and rabbits: the rabbits! This weather … that's heaven for them, they eat bark from the trees and it seems to fatten them. Rabbits get fat!' He bought a loaf of bread for the starving birds. When he went to give winter food to the bees he found them all dead.

Practical life centred round putting lamps under the frozen supply tank in the attic and in the larder and washhouse. The cold permeated William's studio: 'Too cold to be in the workshop … I have no sufficiently active job', so he finished his pair of ebony-eyed pine rabbits in the kitchen. After receiving £20 for Mrs Bowman's gravestone, and more funerary commissions in Bisley and Painswick, he remarked wryly that his only work now was designing for the dead. Earning a living was suddenly a struggle. Barron and Larcher were also hard hit. They were selling their car, moving into their workshop and hoping to let Hambutts.

* * * * * *

In May 1940 Winston Churchill became Prime Minister and immediately set about reinforcing the ARP. His Foreign Secretary, Anthony Eden, broadcast an appeal for volunteers for local defence. Within twenty-four hours 250,000 men between fifteen and sixty-five had joined up. A month later the ARP had increased to a million, now to be known as the Home Guard and designated by Churchill as an auxiliary of the regular army.

May saw a dramatic series of events in Europe as the Germans invaded and defeated France and the Low Countries. By the end of the month the British army had its back to the sea. William wrote almost daily on the developing disaster. On 3 June he recorded 'the bulk of the British Army have got away from Dunkirk, a terrible ordeal for everyone engaged. Heroic calm under fire & bombs. Especially Red Cross horses on the open beach.' On 14 June, the day Paris fell, he and Eve lunched at Lypiatt with Violet's now wounded nephew, who was soon to return to his anti-tank force unit: 'he spoke of sleeping in the woods & Nightingales singing all night in spite of bombs … they even sang in London after bombardment.'

The diary entries give an eerie sense of the encroaching enemy as a collaborationist French government is formed at Vichy and the Germans invade the Channel Islands. William notes German and British plane losses and records his day and night telephone duty reporting back to Home Guard headquarters. After accounts of bombing in Wales, Scotland, Northern Ireland and the South West, the entries record events closer to home: 'Five German planes brought down. Vibration awakened me … Driffield is bombed with delayed action bombs, horses and cattle killed but no people.'

Finally, bombing came to his doorstep. 'At about 2.15pm heard gun fire and anti-aircraft shells. I saw shell burst up high in the North and a parachute coming down through rolling misty clouds towards Oakridge Lynch. Then another coming down near Tunley … crashed below footpath on Wear Farm Oakridge Lynch.' The chilling sound of a warplane spiralling to earth was an inexhaustible subject of discussion among the villagers and destined to linger long in their memories. A parachute floated past the classroom window at Oakridge School that day in July 1940 as a plane came down, scraping the bell tower. The children were told to get under their desks. Transfixed, they watched and waited.

Eventually, the headmaster, who was part of William's Home Guard unit, returned to the schoolroom with a gun in his hand and told them to get back to their lessons. He was unaware that his daughter had gone out to the airman to find out if he was all right. When he answered in German she went to her father, who disarmed him, gave him a drink and waited for the Aston Down airfield commander to make the arrest.

William's report also noted a fight between a Spitfire and a Junkers 88 bomber. The British pilot had crashed in flames on Oakridge Common. Of the German crewmen, three had bailed out and survived; one of them was later arrested by the Sapperton policeman. The fourth, whose parachute had failed to open, was found dead, hanging from a tree in Tunley Wood.

Mrs Hornby, who had from day one kept a pitchfork behind her front door 'in case a German might arrive in the garden', was no longer mocked. The village became the centre of attention as people flocked to see the German plane parts. One of the Gardiners began to charge for the sight. Within a fortnight he had collected £40 for the Red Cross.

Rothenstein's offer to the Air Ministry had been gratefully accepted. Despite the strain of travel he was in high spirits, drawing portraits of airmen all over England as well as Scotland and Wales. He was fascinated as much by the determination and skill of the maintenance teams as by the courage of the pilots and their crews. Maybe, too, respite from Alice's carping about his friends was some compensation for the discomfort of his journeys.

On his flying visits home he impressed William by appearing at his door in full uniform. His son John had transferred the Tate Gallery offices to the Oakridge family sitting room and installed a secretary in the village. He told William that his *Black Mare*, owned by his now impoverished Greek patron Eumorfopoulos, had been sold at Christies. He had left a bid on behalf of the Tate but it had gone beyond his budget.

William did not yet know it, but his diary was recording the turning point of the Battle of Britain. Incensed and baffled by the RAF's resistance, the Germans abandoned their attack on airfields and turned on the civilian population in an attempt to destroy Britain's morale. On 7 September 1940 air raids began in full force: 'First heavy air raid on London. A great deal of damage done, 306 people, killed, 1,337 injured. Fires on Thames, Docks, Offices, Hospitals ...' Later in the week, 'Buckingham Palace bombed again and hit by 5 bombs ... Oxford Street, Selfridges wrecked.'

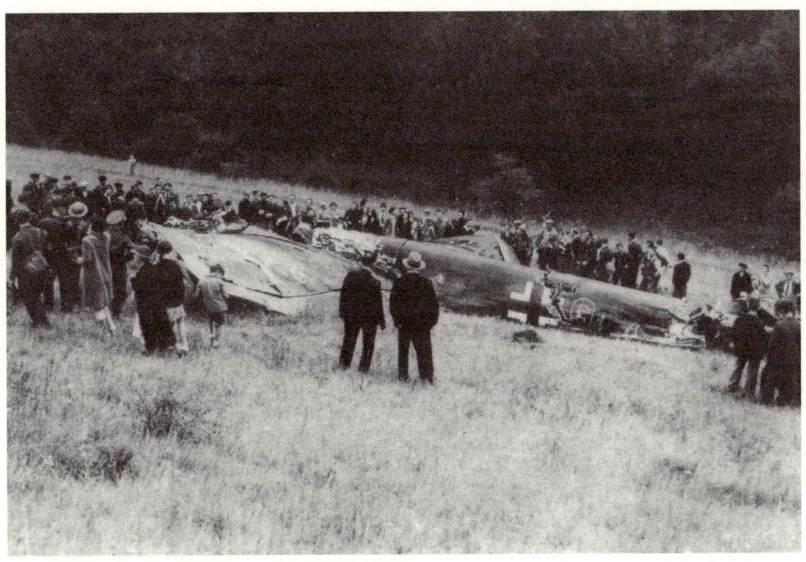

German bomber, Junkers Ju 88A, crashed in Oakridge Lynch in July 1940. The pilot parachuted out, floating past the classroom window of the village school to land in the garden yard

By the end of the year London had been bombarded 'almost nightly'. William recorded, 'Great damage done but the people show great courage … air raid fighters and firemen heroic work under terrible conditions. 32 churches destroyed or made unusable.' William continued his dispassionate notes on the devastating loss of historic buildings: 'London fighting nightly bomb attacks … the last on Sunday when Fire Bombs destroyed the Guildhall, Trinity House, St Bride's Church and many of the city's most treasured buildings all in the centre square mile within the walls. So ends this year of war.'

Hitler had given up hope of invading Britain, but the fear of invasion was replaced by fear of starvation as German U-boats and capital ships, epitomised by the great battleship *Bismarck*, threatened to put a stranglehold on the Atlantic shipping lanes.

At last, like a sign from heaven that all was not irredeemably lost, came the news that *Bismarck* had been hit and then sunk. On Monday 26 May William noted its sinking by torpedoes 'from "Ark Royal" seaplanes after a chase of 1,000 miles'. With a sense of joy and relief, he for once relaxed his Home Guard duties. He established a new stock of bees and took time off to help Violet practise, calm her nerves and be with her at Lypiatt during the recording of her BBC Empire Concert. But the bombs continued to drop. On 14 June he wrote: '6 bombs on Painswick. I must have slept through this before the telephone warning reached me.' He and Eve were anxious for Barron and Larcher but when they visited them next day they found them safe. Four of the six bombs had demolished cottages, killing two people and injuring others, one of whom was not expected to live. Bombing continued near Gloucester for another three days.

When William Hornby developed back pain in July 1941, William took over his Home Guard duties. Gas masks had to be disinfected and new arrivals of steel helmets to be fitted with linings and distributed to the fireguard teams. He set up a Spotters' Club and devised weekly tests for the boys. He gave rifle instruction and talks on food production, bomb disposal and 'enemy aircraft and airborne troops'. He attended a course of gas lectures in Stroud and advisory committee meetings in Gloucester. For his own sanity, he made a meticulous record of British and German plane losses. In spite of the intensity of the Home Guard work and Eve's ill health, he continued carving in his studio and looking after his bees. There were moments of leisure too. Stroud cinema premiered Chaplin's *The Great Dictator*, soon followed by a replay of *The Gold Rush*. At the Gimson sale in Sapperton, William bought some small pieces of furniture and a 'nice little Italian picture'. Always there were friends – the Jewsons, Barron and Larcher, and Violet, now settled at Lypiatt for the duration of the war together with Bill, Gordon and the desperately ill Dennis. During the war years he saw more of her than ever before.

CHAPTER 24

Latter Years of the Second World War

1941–1945

'Cripps conferred with William before giving a prime-time BBC broadcast: we must, Cripps insisted, help Russia with armaments, raw materials from our mines and food from our fields, and do with less for ourselves ...'

After the bombing of London, there had been an exodus to the Cotswolds, with the most notable arrival in the Sapperton Valley being that of the Cripps family. Having bought a house in Far Oakridge virtually sight unseen, the politician Sir Richard Stafford Cripps had only one day to visit the property before being dispatched by Churchill to Moscow, but within a week his wife Isobel and their three daughters had exchanged teatime visits with Eve. It would be another year before he and William became friends. A rich, evangelical Christian with a reputation as a formidable lawyer and controversial MP for East Bristol, Cripps held extreme left-wing views. In Socialist circles during the 1930s he had been a noted force, urging strikes against munitions factories, suggesting that defeat by Hitler would be 'No bad thing' for British workers and advocating an anti-Fascist Popular Front with the Communist Party and the Independent Labour Party. When Churchill formed his wartime coalition government in May 1940, he had appointed him Ambassador to the Soviet Union with a brief to negotiate some form of neutrality with Stalin, recently allied with Hitler in his non-aggression pact. Then a year later, came Hitler's massive summer attack on Russia. Seeing that if Russia survived, the war could still be won, Churchill ordered Cripps back to Moscow to offer Stalin unreserved British support.

The remainder of 1941 saw further military and naval setbacks to Britain's friends and allies. After the Japanese bombing of Pearl Harbour, on 7 December, the United States declared war on Japan. Four days later Hitler declared war on the United States.

On New Year's Day 1942 William wrote that in spite of a temporary lull – 'possibly because of the Russia campaign' – he expected renewed bombing in the spring. As if in defiance of the desperate war situation, he gave five New Year puppet parties for his local friends, which now included the Cripps family. Almost immediately Cripps found a mutual rapport with William, scarcely less strong than that between William and Rothenstein twenty years earlier. He had been brought up in Gloucestershire, was devoted to small-time farming and was breeding an ancient line of ram on his land at the nearby village of Filkins. An instinctive admiration for the Arts and Crafts movement had led him to decorate his private rooms in the Moscow Embassy with Soviet handicrafts. He was a (not very accomplished) amateur carver and had become a connoisseur of Chinese art.

William's hard work for the Home Guard in the villages was, of course, admirable in Cripps's eyes. When Moscow was being bombed, he too had done his share of fire-watching as a volunteer for the Russian ARP. Eventually the Soviet government had ordered him not to take unnecessary risks and he had resigned himself to taking a book, a pipe and his beloved dog Joe (named after Stalin) down to the Embassy air raid shelter. Now home, having resigned as Ambassador to the Soviet Union, he was a man with a mission: to persuade the British that however miserable their situation, it was nothing to the hardship suffered by the Russians.

To win the war, said Cripps, far greater sacrifice was needed. Personal interests and comforts had to be put to one side. The snow and cold of the British winter was not the cold of Russia, thirty to forty degrees below zero. He had witnessed at close quarters the starvation, courage and self-sacrifice of Soviet soldiers and the civilian population, and was angered by what he saw as the indifferent response of the British to Russia's predicament. We must, he insisted, help Russia with armaments, raw materials from our mines and food from our fields, and do with less for ourselves. Methods of production had to be increased. He was shortly due to give a prime time BBC broadcast and conferred with William on what he would say.

The effect of Cripps's eight-minute talk was dramatic. The 'Postscript to the News' programme made famous by J.B. Priestley in

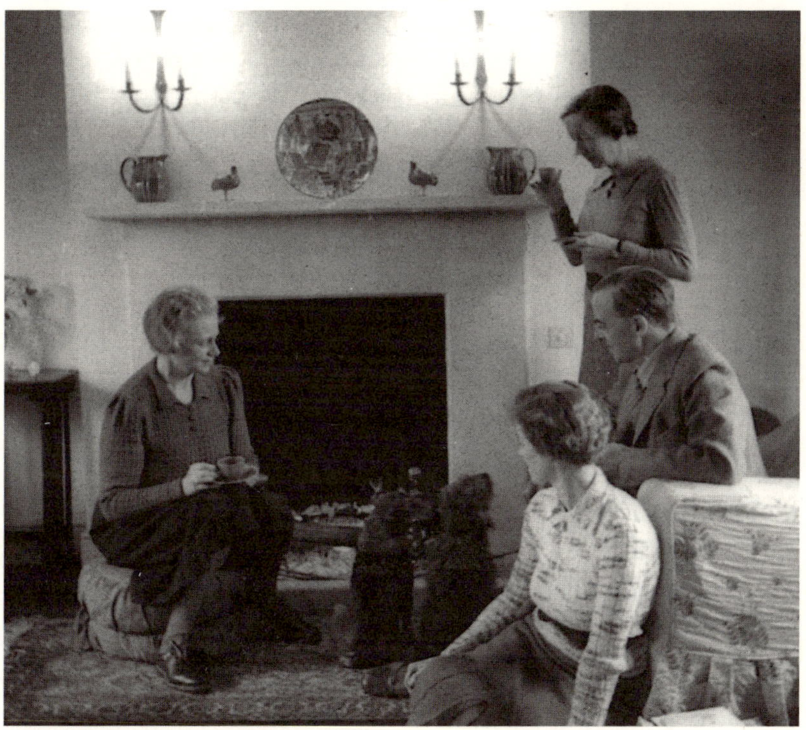

When Richard Stafford Cripps and his family moved to Oakridge in 1941, they immediately became close friends with William and Eve

response to Nazi propaganda reached an audience of several million. In cool, crisp tones but with a touch of charm, Cripps admonished the British people about their indifference, the lack of urgency that he had felt since his return. He even took a swipe at the Home Guard:

> you've known the tragic horrors of prolonged aerial bombardments … your homes and possessions destroyed – but you have not experienced the brutalities and savage violence of the Nazi invaders. Many of you are members of the Home Guard and have to train and watch; but you've not yet had to turn yourselves into Guerrilla fighters behind enemy lines, certain that you would die a death of torture if you were captured … you've not been starved, stripped of your clothing in the bitter cold of the open streets and forced to work day and night as slaves of a foreign country, building roads

and fortifications to defeat your own countrymen … Hitler may be strong enough to renew his attack with success in the spring … Each hour of work that you lose, each day that you do less … makes our total effort less effective and lets down someone somewhere who is offering his life to save for you all the things that you value in life, whether it be in Africa, Malaya, Russia, China or elsewhere … your individual effort is your personal responsibility … This is a total war that demands total effort. Victory will hang in the balance as long as men and women hesitate to play their part …

Churchill promptly appointed Cripps to the War Cabinet and made him Leader of the House of Commons as a symbol of national and Allied unity. Cripps was not a man who made friends easily, but he and William were by now constantly in and out of each other's houses. William offered to mend one of his valuable Chinese pottery figures and Isobel commissioned him to make some doll's house furniture. Cabinet members were exempt from petrol rationing and whenever the Crippses went shopping they took the Simmondses with them.

Rothenstein had pushed himself so hard that it was surprising he had not collapsed sooner. His portraits of the RAF pilots and aircrew had involved arduous travel to distant places, sleeping in cold, makeshift buildings and eating irregular meals of dried eggs, dried milk, spam and a barely edible South African fish called snoek. In the autumn of 1942 he ended up in hospital for two months. Back in Oakridge, heavily protected by Alice, he came across a pot of honey lovingly left on the doorstep by William: 'so secretly', he wrote, 'that it was only discovered later. You are a rare friend indeed for how many years now I have had your affection.' He had been too weak to get to his London exhibition of airmen portraits – and was miserable that not one had been sold. When William was allowed to have tea with him, he found him chairbound, confined to reading and writing letters.

At this critical juncture of the war, with the German armies' advance slowed or stalled in North Africa and Russia, Churchill's trusted ally Field Marshal Smuts, Prime Minister of South Africa, was due to broadcast to the nation on the BBC. On 21 October William closed the first aid meeting early to listen to the speech on his wireless. He was not disappointed. Smuts, eloquent and intelligent, paid generous homage to the bombed House of Commons and its indomitable political master: 'Irreplaceable treasures of a thousand years of almost uninterrupted progress and culture and peaceful civilisation have disappeared forever ... But one thing is not lost; one thing, the most precious of all, remains, and has rather increased. The soul remains.' He honoured Churchill as 'the embodiment of the spirit of eternal youth and resilience, the spirit of a great, undying nation in one of the greatest moments of history ... The stage is set for the last, the offensive phase.'

Two days later Smuts's words turned out to have been prophetic: news came of a massive attack by Generals Alexander and Montgomery on the Afrika Korps at El Alamein, dubbed by Churchill 'The Battle of Egypt'. After twelve days of bitter fighting Rommel was in full retreat. Three years of hostilities had at long last led to the first major victory on land. A week later US forces, with British naval help, invaded North Africa on the western Mediterranean coast. Overnight Churchill's fortunes revived. Speaking at the Mansion House on 10 November, he was able to say, 'Now this is not the end. It is not even the beginning of the end. But it is, perhaps, the end of the beginning.'

In Oakridge there was unbridled celebration. The sound of church bells cascaded from the church tower into the hills and valleys. A parade of civil defence members marched down into the village, led by the school's special constable, then William, followed by his wardens and senior fireguard officers.

Before the end of November came an even greater turning point. On the 22nd, writing once more in capitals, William recorded the catastrophic failure of the German attack on Stalingrad: 'RUSSIAN SUCCESS AGAINST THE GERMANS AT STALINGRAD BY FLANKING ATTACKS.' The German 6th Army was surrounded, leaving over 200,000 men trapped.

With North Africa now being cleared of enemy troops, Russia safe from defeat and the United States making its power felt, the sense grew that things had begun to swing decisively in Britain's favour. Churchill was later to reflect: 'Before [Alamein] we never had a victory: after [Alamein] we never had a defeat.'

William and Eve navigated Christmas 1942 invitations between competing friends. Over lunch at Lypiatt, William gave Violet the most affectionate of presents, and one that is surely one of his masterpieces: a minuscule dormouse, sitting upright, two inches high, carved from a scrap of pine salvaged from the Chalford walking-stick mill. The simplicity of the little animal's squat form, its tail curving round on to its stomach, the almost human fingers clasping an over-size nut, the expressive eyes peering out, had the delicacy and shining polish of a Netsuke ivory carving. And its flat back of smooth fur seemed unremarkable until, touchingly, two tiny ears at the top caught the light (see plate 7).

Back in Oakridge in time for Christmas tea with the Crippses, William was showered with presents by the three daughters. A few days later he took Eve to a second Christmas tea with the Rothensteins. It seemed everyone he knew had become creative again. 'My first bit of puppet making since war broke out', William told Violet, Bill and Gordon during their visit to his studio, '… nothing new, but revised leg movements for Fat Lady in the shop scene.' Sadly for Violet her morale plummeted after falling on an icy patch in the garden. She broke her right wrist and then her other wrist when she slipped on the linoleum going into the hospital. William eased her pain by designing a special splint contraption for both arms to keep her fingers straight and unstrained.

Eve at last caught the patriotic 'Dig-For-Victory' mood, turning most of her garden over to vegetables. The experiment was not an unqualified success. After planting her first batch of seedlings, she discovered two cows in her garden causing 'far worse damage than badgers'. At Lypiatt Bill had been ordered to plough most of the grass fields and had a barn well stocked with corn.

Shopping, in any case, had become near impossible. All large cars were commandeered as ambulances or military vans and petrol for private use was stopped altogether, except for designated 'Official Users'. The famous theatre composer Ivor Novello was gaoled for four weeks for misusing petrol coupons – a dramatic message that nobody was immune from prosecution. William stored his little Riley in the shed and now became totally reliant on the Cripps family for transport: if Stafford was at home they would go in his chauffeur-driven car to Stroud not only to shop but also sometimes to see a film. The cinema's latest offering, *In Which We Serve*, based on the true story of Lord Mountbatten's destroyer sunk during the evacuation of Crete, provided all the enjoyable excitement of wartime heroism. Noël Coward produced the film, wrote the screenplay, composed the score and starred in a leading role, along with John Mills, Celia Johnson and Richard Attenborough.

* * * * * *

To William the war came to appear at once more all-consuming and more distant. Dark rumours spread of unspeakable German atrocities towards Jews. There were reports of massive tank battles on the Russian front and of engagements between the Japanese and the Allies in the Far East. Closer to home, the news was of ceaseless bombing of Germany and of a successful campaign to protect Britain's Atlantic supply lines from attacks on German U-boats. Cripps had been made Minister of Aircraft Production in November 1942. Despite his religious ideals, he held no misgivings about 'Bomber' Harris's policy of strategic bombing of enemy cities and industrial districts regardless of the loss of civilian life or the reduction to rubble of Europe's cultural heritage. William records briefly the collapse of the German armies at Stalingrad, the surrender of Rommel's Afrika Korps, the Allied invasion of Sicily and Italy's withdrawal from the war, but the destruction of Europe's civilisation casts a pall over his diaries and often silences them.

For some time there had been tension verging on hostility between Alice Rothenstein and Eve. What it was really about is not clear. Alice seems to have accused Eve of 'causing trouble' with her son Billy and to have urged the Woodhouses to break off relations with the Simmondses.

In January 1944 a sick Rothenstein hobbled over to William's house in the hope of reconciliation. But William was ill with flu and Eve took it upon herself to let Rothenstein know the hurt Alice was causing. In a sad letter to William, Rothenstein skated between marital loyalty and apology for his wife's behaviour:

6 January 1944

My Dear William,

I hope you have got over your attack of flu. I missed you when I came down with Duffy, but was glad to see Eve.

… I am always hoping that Alice's mood will change – I believed once or twice that it had, but it is not so as yet, that is clear from what Eve told me. Husband and wife are two people and not one; none of us know the inner life of any two and the need to keep a working partnership in being is a strong sense among many (most?) married people … I do regret the days when among friendly doors, yours was the friendliest, opening always to my knock. I had indeed hoped that by coming at times to ours you would overcome and heal the rift, so I was the more distressed to hear what Eve told me …

Ever yours dear William,

William R

It took William several drafts before he produced a satisfactory reply four days later. With heartfelt openness he wrote of the affection he felt for his friend and how comforted he was to hear of Rothenstein's feelings about the breach: 'the waste of the precious years.' With so much suspicion and complaint in the air, he felt powerless to repair the state of affairs. He too remained loyal to his wife: 'What the real trouble is about I can only guess and that Eve had set Billy's friends against him is quite without any truth … few can admire Billy, his warmth and his wit more than Eve does and this is plain to everyone … perhaps we were expected to break with one friend [for example Violet] at the bidding of another but this only spreads trouble.'

Knowing how ill his friend was, the rift was all the more painful for William. He had caught sight of Rothenstein as with great effort he delivered the letter and glimpsed him going up the meadow, 'a knight with two supporters … resting in a field'.

In January 1945 Rothenstein was bedridden again. He asked William to visit him. William sat by his side for half an hour: 'all the company he is allowed now – his only visit since I was there a week ago.' Rothenstein was well aware of the course of the war – the Allies' landing in France, the recognition of Charles de Gaulle as head of a provisional French government, the move to Berlin of a floundering, enraged Hitler to direct operations from his bunker. Nonetheless, V2 rockets continued to hit Britain at the rate of about eight a day. The concentration camps had become fairly common knowledge in the summer of 1944 with the Soviet army's entry into Poland, but neither William nor Alice could bring themselves to tell him on his deathbed of the horrors revealed by the liberation of Auschwitz on 27 January.

On 10 February Rothenstein begged William to stay longer, 'he was looking v weak and depressed. Alice present all the time and over talkative. He said at last "Alice do let me talk to William … I am quite content to sit with William without talking".' Four days later William wrote that his friend was dead, 'to my great loss'.

Rothenstein was buried in the graveyard of St Bartholomew's, Oakridge's parish church. His coffin was borne down the steep path by Fred Gardiner and three other village craftsmen. Max Beerbohm gave the address at his memorial service in London and spoke of him as 'a giver with both hands in the grand manner'. Relations with Alice never softened. In July she wrote a letter to William: 'someone's asked whether you were living with us … John was puzzled and looked up in *Who's Who* and found that you had given Far Oakridge as your address omitting your house – as we have never had any other address other than FO since FIRST we came MANY years ago to Iles Farm.' Over eight pages, she told him to alter his entry: 'Max Beerbohm used to make such fun of "Far Oakridge" when he stayed with us in the war – wrote a poem in fact.'

William was having none of it. Alice's next six-page letter, in an ever-larger scrawl, often with barely six huge words to a page, declared:

I don't want to embarrass you but Far Oakridge has been our address for years before the last war. It is absurd for you now to use it – when your own house has a name and a lovely one – I can't suddenly invent a new name for ourselves – nor do I wish to – but since it was brought to my notice I cannot ignore it … Alas I cannot alter our own – NOR would I.
Yours ever,
Alice R.

She and the Simmondses never met again.

CHAPTER 25

William's Final Years

1945–1968

'The calm still centre of the movement'
John Gwynne on William Simmonds
to the author, 1979

On 8 May 1945 the Allies accepted Germany's surrender, bringing the war to an end. William did not join in any crowd celebration. The European war's desecration, the broken landscape, the dust and rubble, much-loved buildings maimed or destroyed – thirty-two London churches gone, sickening damage to the Houses of Parliament, the Royal Academy, Burlington Arcade, the obliteration of the Arts Club – all this seemed, at times, enough to drown out all sounds of the past.

But if after the war some of William's friends fell into depression, he never buckled. Well into his eighth and ninth decades, in spite of the scarcity of raw materials, he intensified his own work. Each piece was sold immediately to a private patron on condition it could first be viewed at the annual 'Royal Academy Winter Exhibition'. When the new President and fellow sculptor Sir Charles Wheeler greeted him on one occasion, he seized William's two hands in congratulation, telling him how especially pleased he was that William should remain loyal to the Academy. William replied that it was *the* place to be and that 'all artists should be thankful that such a beautiful gallery is at their service'.

At the same time William applied himself to saving and renewing the fragments of the England he loved. He set out to encourage the 'little platoons', as Burke had famously referred to them – the societies of volunteers on whom civil society ultimately depends. He increased his support for the Society for Protection of Ancient Buildings, the Council for the Preservation of Rural England, the Campden Trust founded by Fred Griggs, the Gloucestershire Guild of Craftsmen in Painswick (of which Phyllis Barron was now Chairman), the Rotary Club and, to a lesser degree, the National Trust. He exhibited his work in the Stroud Festival, in the Cheltenham Group of artists and, of course, each year in the Royal Academy. He gave encouragement to those who turned up at his door: the progressive educationalist G.M. Trevelyan, R.M. Jones, Griffiths Jones, the Mitchel family and Alan Durst, whose book on ancient and contemporary wood carving strongly featured William's sculpture; and William gave talks and interviews on Gimson and Barnsley, on the Arts and Crafts movement, on his own work – anyone and anything to help the cause. The monthly London meetings at the Art Workers' Guild had always been for him the intellectual powerhouse where he continued to exchange ideas and theories. He was there each month.

The mythical status his puppets had attained in the 1930s went on growing. In 1945 Jan Bussell, now writing a serious text on marionettes, included William's troupe in his book, embedding him into the ancient tradition of street-kiosk theatres that had thrived under so many different civilisations – in India, Tibet, Burma, Africa, Persia, China and Japan; the Turks, Italians and Spanish, the ancient Greeks, Romans and Egyptians had their puppet shows long before the beginning of theatre with human actors. It was tantalising for the general public that William's performances were so rare, to be seen only (after some persuasion) at The Frith or in the Jewsons' sitting room, and sometimes, just sometimes, in Sapperton Village Hall – if the village parents begged hard enough.

A late-flowering friendship began when Olaf Baker, the best-selling children's author, saw William's puppets in the 1950s. He shared his affinity with animals. The hero in his *Shasta of the Wolves* was a boy who lived with a wolf cub and communicated with it through body language and voice, and gained insight into the animal's mind until he was almost half a wolf himself. Baker wrote William a fan letter after seeing his puppets, lamenting that they were no longer accompanied by Eve at her Dolmetsch spinet but on the gramophone:

For years, I have wanted to see the puppets which had come out of Faeryland … and do their little jumps and leaps and wanton wiles! You are a magician! What with your sculpture, your ivory carvings and other achievements in art, I don't feel it is FAIR that so many gifts should have been bestowed on one single person! There is that old Leonardo da Vinci who as we're so tired of hearing, did everything possible for human ingenuity or genius! But was he capable of making DOLLS to open for us the portals of fairyland, or indeed of heaven? … certainly NOT! Let the Mona Lisa smile! If she had been fortunate enough to see your puppets, that smile would have broken into such a laugh of delight as would have ruined her grin for good and all!
Olaf Baker

Another champion for William was Violet's friend Beryl de Zoete, scholar and practitioner of dance and theatre, who wrote from Gordon Square, the house she shared with the orientalist Arthur Waley. Beryl wanted help on her Heinrich von Kleist translation:

Possibly you may like to glance through my translation of Kleist's Marionette Theatre (the illustrations are NOT of my choosing). Young Beichan is getting on but how I wish it were with your puppets. I recently saw *Antiparnasso*. Orazio Vecchi's music which is enchanting and the Lanchester puppets. I enjoyed it greatly, but they simply don't begin to compare with yours. We have [seen] Violet's black cat. How beautiful it is. She has given me a photo of it.

There was a sense of distance with Violet, which William had not experienced before. Her way of protecting herself from the havoc wrought by the war had always been through music. This time the catalyst was Osbert Sitwell's younger brother, Sachie (Sacheverell), who had discovered a Scarlatti sonata and begged Violet to play it for him. Together the two uncovered beautiful and unknown pieces and the shared excitement gave a new meaning to their lives.

After a long gap Dorothy Walker, now monitoring all Violet's calls, had invited the Simmondses to hear Violet play for Sachie in her new Mount Street flat. Then silence for several more months until, in March 1947, Eve rang Mount Street and Dorothy issued an invitation to tea the next day. It was almost immediately cancelled, leaving William to celebrate his birthday lunch with Eve at the Imperial Hotel in Stroud without Violet for the second year running. Then a Christmas invitation came, and he was touched that she was proudly displaying his ebony cat that she had bought at the 'Royal Academy Exhibition'. This would be his last Christmas lunch with her.

Violet was now gravely ill. In early May 1947 she asked to see William and Eve. There seemed to be some improvement and her condition was stable enough for Bill and Gordon to take her to Brighton. As he had done with Rothenstein, William wrote full of optimistic encouragement, disguising his sadness. In January 1948 Violet died. William and Eve did not go to her funeral in Sussex but went to the memorial service in London and afterwards to lunch in Mount Street with Bill and Gordon.

After six months Bill gently reappeared in Eve's life – at first accompanied either by Dorothy or Gordon, then with him alone. As of old she had lunches at Lypiatt and 'walked in garden with Bill'. From now until he left Lypiatt, she continued to see him and Gordon as much as she saw Barron and Larcher. On 15 April 1950 she wrote in capitals 'GORDON DIES' and went over to pick flowers with Bill for the grave where he would be buried beside Violet in Folkington in Sussex. Never before – not even after Violet's death – had Eve expressed overt sorrow in her diary. It was the end of an era that had brought magic into all their lives and Gordon had been the quiet master of its ceremonies.

Following Violet's wishes to the letter, Bill moved swiftly out of Lypiatt and bought a house in Sussex. Writing to William in 1951 (it seems he did not write to Eve), he looked back nostalgically: 'at a _lovely_ past ... reminded of the lovely times we had on darling V's birthdays with all the excitement of seeing her opening all of her presents. I think you and Eve never had a failure there. All of us did occasionally but [she] never let us know it.'

With a tinge of bitterness, he attempted to stir William up against Violet's nephew John (my father) and sometimes targetted Eve as well: 'I wonder what happened to all your lovely carvings at Lypiatt ... Where is the black cat and the 3 or 4 other cats. I often envy the owner of the ash cat with the ball ... oh heaps of other things.'

'Did Eve ever get the embroidered caps and other things she made ... or did everything go in jumble sales? I wish I had taken lots of things but they were left with everything else to John.'

In 1951 came the Festival of Britain, a huge event that was to bring both Simmondses, at the peak of their careers, to wider public attention. The idea had first been proposed when the end of war was in sight in 1945 to Cripps. No doubt the huge success of the Arts Council's 'Modern Crafts Exhibition' tour of America and Canada had been noted. A shipload of invaluable art had been sent across the submarine-infested Atlantic in the hope of strengthening the Americans' respect and kinship for Britain now that they had entered the war.

No one could have been better placed to oversee her country's contemporary modern art movement than Muriel Rose. In creating a set of British rooms for the American show, she had to choose and assemble materials, curtains, upholstery, book illustrations, pottery and furniture, even cutlery (no sculpture, so William was excluded). Just a few names from the spectacular range of artists – Eric Ravillious, Vanessa Bell, Eric Gill, Edward Bawden, Graham Sutherland, Ben Nicholson, David Jones, Reynold Stone, Albert Rutherston, Catherine (Casty) Cockerell, Michael Cardew, Arnold Dolmetsch, Duncan Grant, May Morris, Barron and Larcher and, of course, William Morris, and from among the weavers, textile printers and embroiderers Eve, Ethel Mairet, Enid Marx – give an idea of the quality and vibrancy of the work.

There was a sense of excitement too. A 400-seat state-of-the-art cinema, a Telekinema that could screen 3D films and a 2,900-seat concert hall. Sir Malcolm Sargent and Sir Adrian Boult conducted the concerts that opened the festival. As a small child, I was taken to the Pleasure Gardens, where hundreds of open-air amusements awaited.

The Arts and Crafts movement made its mark in the festival at the several exhibitions that were held outside London. The artist-craftsmen were shown at the Montpellier Rotunda in Cheltenham, where an 'Exhibition of Cotswold Craftmanship' was held in July 1951. Homage was paid to the stars of the 1920s and 1930s – the Barnsley brothers, Ernest Gimson and many of the Sapperton fraternity – with due respect paid to the genius of William Morris and his daughter May. Here William exhibited thirteen carvings, Eve two embroideries.

After several winters of hardship and often being cut off by snow, the Simmondses moved up the hill to a cottage in the centre of Oakridge Lynch called Wells Close. Now that both Alfred and Louise Powell had died – Louise in 1956 and Alfred in 1960 – William's close friend Gerald Carter, the weaver, had taken over their house in

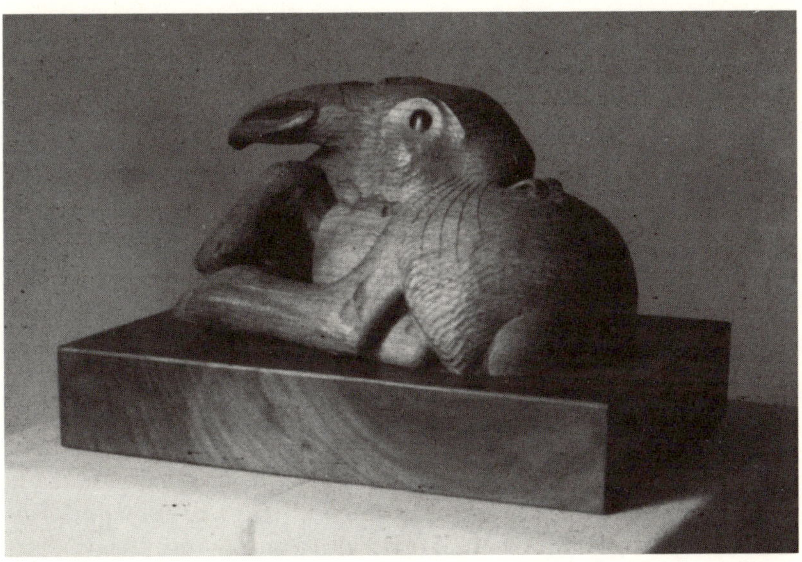

Young Hare, 1959

Tunley. Both Gerald and his daughter Bella helped William (who was now without a car) in every way. In the walled garden a stone hut was turned into a suitable workshop and Eve began planning a herbaceous border. Her eyesight had deteriorated too far to continue any embroidery. But even at Wells Close the long winters proved hardly less testing. Wiliam would open up his workshop in the early morning in minus twenty degrees Celsius and after lighting the oil fire had to wait two hours until the temperature reached minus ten and he could begin work. He had no intention of living any other way than through his sculpture. The puppets had been supplanted completely.

Each Easter and Christmas holidays my brother and I continued to visit the Simmondses. We always brought our whippet in the hope that one day William might sculpt him, but he never did. In 1962, during another cold winter, we battled our way through ice and snowdrifts to their cottage. Temperatures had plummeted during the Big Freeze as it came to be called. Rivers, lakes, even the sea froze. 'I hope', William said to us, 'to do smaller things in other materials ... .' At the age of eighty-two, when his hands became too arthritic to handle a chisel and to work in wood, he signed up at Stroud Art School to learn how to make figures in clay.

When the teacher Tony Davies heard William was coming, he confessed to Gerald that he was verging on being frightened. How on earth could he take on the teaching of someone who was a Royal Academician artist of originality and brilliance and whom he held in high esteem? But in spite of their vast age gap, they formed a strong rapport. Tony was astounded by the speed in which William could transform drawings into three-dimensional reality. William only needed one demonstration of how to work with clay before he had grasped both the technique and the possibilities of the material.

As I grew up, I saw less of William. But in our way we remained close. My mother sent me to Italy to study drawing with 'Signorina Simi' – I do not remember her real name, which no one ever used. She was the daughter of a Florentine painter who was influenced by the nineteenth-century artists of the Macchiaioli School. Like the Pre-Raphaelites and William as a student, they did much of their work outside to capture natural light, shade and colour. As with William, they found their inspiration in nature. After six months with Signorina Simi, I signed up to Chelsea School of Art, and after that to the Slade. Once a rival to the Royal Academy where William had trained, it now bore only a fleeting resemblance to what it had been in William's day. The plaster casts were in storage, allegedly smashed and disposed of in the 1980s by the Slade Director Bernard Cohen. We still drew and painted from life class models. In the theatre design classes (an exhilarating experience under Nicholas Georgiadis), when we had to design the sets for an assigned play, we were told to use large brushes, to dip, splash and splatter, to free ourselves. We were not taught architectural mathematics, even though they were essential for the working drawings needed for building the sets.

In 1966 William completed his last sculpture in wood – an eighteen-inch long *Young Donkey*, a Nubian burro sometimes called a Jerusalem donkey, which according to Christian belief carried Jesus on Palm Sunday for Christ's entry into Jerusalem. The breed is distinguished by a strongly marked cross on its back. Going to the place of Jesus's Crucifixion, he turned his back on the sight, but out of love and loyalty stayed until all was over; he could not leave the Master whom he had carried. God caused the shadow of the cross to fall across the donkey's back. Aware of his own approaching death, and knowing this was to be his last piece of sculpture, William dug into the hickory-wood handle of his chisel to use the wood for the donkey's eyes and then threw the rest of the tool away. The sacred and devotional Christian story was surely a consolation and inspiration to him.

To this day it reposes on a plinth in the hall of the historic Arts and Crafts Cotswold Farm, near Duntisbourne Abbots, owned by Iona and Mark Birchall. It is a strangely compelling piece. Feet stretched out in front of him, he looks serenely over his shoulder towards those who pass by. 'Whoever comes through this hallway', says Iona Birchall, 'is unable to control the urge to stroke the animal.'

That year, in the depths of another arctic January, Eve succumbed to what seemed a serious illness (but was as always undiagnosed). Far from well himself, William tended Eve for ten days without help. But it was not Eve who died first.

In 1968 a large one-man Simmonds exhibition in Cheltenham was in preparation. It was to include drawings William had made in the 1920s and 1930s in the Cotswolds and on journeys to Wales and France. In another section would be his early and recent ivory, wood and stone carvings and pottery, as well as his early book designs and paintings.

But in the early summer, William, took to his bed to rest at doctors orders, setting himself up with a tray to continue work on a ship and its rigging in light wood, cardboard and string. Gerald Carter felt William was strong enough to be left while he took a short holiday with Bella. But within a few days he was dead. He was buried near Rothenstein in the graveyard of St Bartholomew's Church, Oakridge Lynch.

Postscript

Eve lived on for another twelve years. She carefully protected William's work by giving as much as she could to museums. At the end of her life the memories of friends that she most cherished were of Dorothy Larcher and Barron. Bill was, of course, never mentioned. Of Violet she nursed a noticeable resentment. In an interview (which she knew full well would be quoted in print), she described how she had begun making bonnets for Violet's birthday presents from 1927 onwards:

> I counted that over the years I must have made about sixteen, and some of them much more elaborate … They were always kept in a drawer in her bedroom at Lypiatt, but she died in London and quite what happened to them I have never known … the woollen one she always wore going to Bath in the winter. The other little one was always worn in the garden. As far as I know there was no-one who cared about them – except Violet's maid.

Eve's niece Hermione, who had moved in to help during William's final illness, stayed on at Wells Close to look after her aunt. Hermione found her difficult to live with and she herself had no interest in the Simmondses' work. After Eve's funeral and her burial close to William's grave, Gerry Carter came across a bonfire in Wells Close's garden. He rushed in to save letters, diaries, photographs, and more; Bella has kept this Simmonds treasure trove safe to this day.

Notes

Chapter 2

1 Auguste Rodin wrote of the sheer joy he felt in the natural, elegant kindness of Lanteri's teaching, which he said had 'liberated him from ignorance'.

Chapter 3

1 Cowper letters, Royal Academy Library, London.

Chapter 6

1 William obeyed. This painting, *A Sheepfold* (watercolour, 1906), is now owned by the Laing Art Gallery, Newcastle-Upon-Tyne.

2 He had yet to make his name with his legendary illustrations for *Winnie the Pooh* and *The Wind in the Willows*.

Chapter 8

1 Derived from the Italian *Commedia dell'arte*, by the eighteenth century the English *Harlequinade* emerged as a popular story or folk tale. After a chase through the woods the hero, often possessing magical powers, finally reveals himself as a Harlequin and the other characters reveal themselves as to who they really are.

2 His first drawing, the Fovant miller's wagon, which along with hundreds of later images provides a unique historic record of British wagons, is now in the Museum of English Rural Life, University of Reading.

3 £100 would be equivalent to £25,000 in today's money (2018).

Chapter 9

1 Indigo was among the oldest natural plant dyes known to ancient civilisations but challenging to work with. Initially, when Barron's cotton or linen fabrics were removed from the dye-bath, the chemical change did not come out as she wished. To Eve, the results could not have mattered less. She found the Matisse-like shapes and geometric designs beautiful and avidly took scraps from whatever appeared.

Chapter 18

1 Barron was sharing the gallery with her one-time mentor Ethel Mairet. In 1916 Barron had read Ethel's scholarly book, *Vegetable Dyeing*. It had become Barron's second bible (the first being Edward Bancroft's book written in 1794 which she recommended 'everyone should read as a novel'). She had taken the plunge to send Ethel samples of her work for her opinion. The response was electric. Would Barron join her in her forthcoming London exhibition 'bringing everything you have done'? From then on Ethel had ensured that Barron's genius saw the light of day, first in fairs and markets and, as she became fashionable, in numerous small London galleries.

Chapter 19

1 Lawrences's murals were seen in Villa Mirenda in 2014. They no longer exist.

Chapter 22

1 More annoying still, from today's perspective, is the failure of William's puppets to be seen on television. In late December 1938, Jan Bussell, famous for his broadcast of Karel Čapek's book on robots, wrote from the BBC to ask if William would consider bringing the puppets to London to be filmed in the BBC studio. William was cautious and it never happened.

2 Letter to William Simmonds from Harro Siegel, Berlin, 26 March 1935.

3 The Quenington Village minutes in July 1935 reflected fear of Hitler's new German bombers, combined with Britain's own large-scale RAF expansion, was spreading 'Air panic' throughout the country. Quenington wanted to make it clear they would support Prime Minister Stanley Baldwin's efforts to protect the peace – but Baldwin's announcement that he would be establishing county Air Raid Protection units did nothing to calm nerves. The Chairman of the Parish Council proposed '… that a resolution be sent to the League of Nations, or National Peace Council, stating that we do not want war'. This was followed by the entire population of 300 villagers signing a Peace Ballot endorsing the Parish Council.

Sources of Quotations

Private Papers

British Library, London: the letters of Alfred Powell

Cheltenham Art Gallery and Museum: Dorothy Walker's diary and personal correspondence

Royal Academy Library, London: the letters of Frank Cadogan Cowper

Tate Archive, London: the diaries of William and Eve Simmonds and the majority of personal correspondence

Chapter opening quotations for chapter 6: Lucas, E.V., *Edwin Austin Abbey (1852–1911)*, vol. 2, Methuen & Co, London, 1921; chapter 12: Largo, Mary, *Christiana Herringham and the Edwardian Art Scene*, Lund Humphries, London, 1996; chapter 14: papers in Hoover Institution at Stanford University; chapter 19 Tate Archive

Further material

Works by William Simmonds can be found in public collections throughout Britain, including Gloucester Folk Museum (puppets); Gloucester City Museum (woodcarvings); Tate Britain (woodcarvings and watercolours); Tate Archive (photographs and private papers); Laing Art Gallery, Newcastle-upon-Tyne (watercolours); Crafts Study Centre, University of the Creative Arts, Farnham (puppets); Cheltenham Art Gallery and Museum (woodcarvings) and the Museum of English Rural Life, University of Reading (sketches and photographs).

Select Bibliography

Anand, Mulk Raj, *Conversations in Bloomsbury*, Wildwood House, London, 1981

Bennett, Daryl, *Liberty's furniture (1875–1915)*, Antique Collectors' Art Club, 2011

Boyd Haycock, David, *A Crisis of Brilliance*, Old Street Publishing, London, 2009

Brockington, Grace, *Above the Battlefield, Modernism and the Peace Movement in Britain 1900–1918*, Paul Mellon Centre, Yale University Press, London 2010

Carruthers, Annette, *Edward Barnsley and his Workshop, Arts and Crafts in the Twentieth Century*, White Cocklade Publishing, Oxford, 1992

Douglas-Home, Jessica, *Violet, The Life and Loves of Violet Gordon Woodhouse*, Harvill Press, London 1996

Drury, Michael, *Wandering Architects: In Pursuit of an Arts and Crafts Ideal*, Shaun Tyas, Stamford, 2000

Durst, Alan, *Wood Carving, A Studio Handbook*, Studio Vista, London, 1938

Evans, H.A., *Highways & Byways in Oxford and The Cotswolds*, Macmillan and Co., London, 1905

Frayling, Christopher, *The Royal College of Art, One Hundred and Fifty Years of Art and Design*, Barrie & Jenkins, London, 1987

Fry, Roger, *Vision and Design*, Pelican Books, London 1920

Gellér, Katalin, *The Art Colony of Gödöllö (1901–1920)*, Gödöllö Municipal Museum, Gödöllö (Hungary), 2001

Gimson, Ernest, *His Life and Work*, Shakespeare Head Press, Stratford-Upon-Avon, 1924

Gosling, Lucinda, *Great War Britain, The First World War At Home*, The History Press, Stroud, 2014

Greensted, Mary, *The Arts and Crafts Movement in the Cotswolds*, Sutton Publishing, Stroud, 1993

Harries, Meirion and Susie, *The War Artists*, Michael Joseph, London, 1983

Harris, Alexandra, *Romantic Moderns*, Thames and Hudson, London, 2015

Harrod, Tanya, *The Crafts in Britain in the 20th Century*, Yale University Press, London 1999

Hilton, Timothy, *The Pre-Raphaelites*, Thames and Hudson, London, 1970

Jewson, Norman, *By Chance I Did Rave*, published privately, 1973

Kimball, Roger, *Art's Prospect: The Challenge in an Age of Celebrity*, Ivan R. Dee, Chicago 2004

Legge, Sylvia, *Affectionate Cousins: T. Sturge Moore and Marie Appia*, Oxford University Press, Oxford, 1980

Lewis-Jones, June, *The Cotswolds At War*, Amberley Publishing, Stroud, 1992

Lewis, June, *Walking the Cotswold Way*, David & Charles Publishers, Newton Abbot, 1986

Lucas, E.V., *Edwin Austin Abbey (1852–1911)*, Methuen & Co, London and Charles Scribner's, New York, 1921

MacCarthy, Fiona, *Anarchy & Beauty, William Morris and His Legacy, 1860–1960*, National Portrait Gallery Publications, October 2014

Masefield, John, *The Box of Delights*, Egmont, London, 2012

Massingham, I.J, *Shepherd's Country, A Record of the Crafts and People of the Hills,* Chapman & Hall, London, 1938

McCormick, John, *The Victorian Marionette Theatre*, University of Iowa Press, 1938

Mee, Arthur, *The King's England, Gloucestershire*, Hodder & Stoughton, London, 1938

Parry, Linda (ed), *William Morris*, Philip Wilson, London, 1996

Owen, Richard, *Lady Chatterley's Villa*, Armchair Traveller, London, 2014

Rothenstein, William, *After Fifty Man and Memories*, Vols I and II, Coward McCann, New York, 1932

Rothenstein, Elizabeth, *Stanley Spencer*, Phaidon Press, London, 1945

Russell, Gordon, *Designer's Trade: Autobiography*, George Allen & Unwin, London, 1968

Saumarez Smith, Charles, *The Company of Artists, The Origins of the Royal Academy of Arts in London*, Modern Art Press, London, 2012

Shakespeare, William, *Tragedy of Hamlet*, with illustrations by W.G. Simmonds, Hodder & Stoughton, London, 1910

Spalding, Frances, *Roger Fry, Art and Life*, Granada Publishing, London, 1980

Speaight, Robert, *William Rothenstein, the Portrait of an Artist in His Time*, Eyre & Spottiswoode, London, 1962

Weir, Jane, *Walking the Block*, Templar Poetry, Matlock, 2008

White, Jerry, *Zeppelin Nights, London in the First World War*, Bodley Head, London, 2014

William Morris & Kelmscott, The Design Council, London, 1981

Peter, Wohlleben, *The Hidden Life of Trees*, Greystone Books, Vancouver/ David Suzuki Institute, 2015

Whitfield, Paul, *A World of My Own (1923–1941)*, Endymion Publications, London, 2012

Acknowledgments

I would like to thank Mary Greensted, for suggesting to me that I write the Simmonds biography and for her generous guidance. And my special debt of gratitude to Agnieszka Kolakovska, for helping in so many ways to complete the book; also to Professors Robert Grant, Colin Leach, Roger Scruton and Tanya Harrod for lending me her notes and material. And to Caroline Brooke Johnson, Ocky Murray and the team at Unicorn Publishing Group, Veronica Faulks and Victoria Miller.

To friends and colleagues who gave ideas and information, I give much thanks to Jane Eve, Jacqueline Sarsby, Virginia Ironside, Christine Wood, Iona Birchall, Phillip Mansell, Chris Stephens, Michael Daley, Xan Smiley, Anne de Courcy, Sara Payne, Caroline Swash, Philip Smith, Christopher Woodham, Rachel Bailey, Charlotte Mitchell, Mary Haines, Peter Charlton, Irene Dworkin-Brendel, Max Rothenstein, Lucy Rothenstein, Kirsty Hartsiotis, David Murray, Professor Roy Foster, Nicola G. Bowen, Nicholas Spencer, Andrew Gimson, Mary Walsh, Charlotte Gere, Penelope Curtis, Simon Biddulph, John Biddulph, Thomas Gibson, Lucy Abel-Smith, Mary Rhodes, Max Hastings, Rebecca Jewell, John Beer, Alan Powers, Fiona Fraser, Guy Baxter, Gian Douglas-Home, Belinda Cadbury, Martyn Wyatt, Maud Craigie and Helen Smith.

Thanks too to my two grand-daughters, Selina and Lilah Douglas-Home for their acute observations on the sculpture and to my brother Martin Gwynne for his memories and encouragement.

For invaluable help with research, I thank once more Maggie Evans, Rachel Saunders and David Mallinson, especially for his patience and invaluable skill in photographing Simmonds pieces often in unusual places and at unusual times, and to Bella Peralta for information and for uncovering more and more unclassified material in her beautiful studio, and for giving permission to reproduce the photographs.

Finally, to my late husband, Rodney Leach, who despite his initial scepticism on the Arts and Crafts movement, saw the point immediately chapters emerged and gave me constant encouragement.

For archive material, I thank the V&A Theatre Department in Blythe Road, London; the Royal College of Art; the Tate Archive and Chris Stevens; the British Library, London; the Wilson Cheltenham Museum; Emery Walker's House in Hammersmith; the Wilkinson Archives, Gloucestershire City Museum; the Oakridge Community Archive; the Hoover Institution at Stanford University and the Harvard University Archives. With special thanks to The London Library for help and inspiration during my lifetime.

Picture Acknowledgments

Every attempt has been made to trace accurate ownership of the copyrighted visual material in this book. If any unintentional omission has been made, please notify the publisher who will correct it in all subsequent editions.

Artworks by William Simmonds: © the artist

Front cover: © Gloucester Museums Service; endpapers: © Jessica Douglas-Home; page 4 private collection, photos: David Mallinson; page 10 Tate Archive; page 13 *Illustrated London News*; page 20 private collection; page 36 Tate Archive; page 49 Bella Peralta; page 69 Tate Archive; page 74 private collection; page 80 Tate Archive; page 89 private collection, photo: David Mallinson; pages 103, 112, 114, 115 Tate Archive; page 117 Magdalen Evans; page 134 Bella Peralta; page 135 Gloucester City Museum; page 158 Bella Peralta; page 166 private collection; page 169 Tate Archive; page 174 Douglas Hayward Puppet Archives; pages 183, 185, 188, 196, 198, 206, 215 Tate Archive; page 225 Bella Peralta; pages 229, 235 private collection; page 240 Chantry Bequest, Tate Archive; page 249 Oakridge Community Archive; pages 253, 265 Tate Archive; plates 1, 2, 3, 4, 5, 9, 17, 18, 19, 29 private collection; plate 6 Yale University Art Gallery, New Haven, CT; plates 7, 8, 26, 27, 28 private collection, photo: David Mallinson; plates 10, 11, 12, 13, 14, 15, 16, 22, 23 Tate Archive; plate 24 Tate Archive, courtesy of David Murray; plate 19 Bella Peralta, photo: David Mallinson; plate 20 Crafts Study Centre, University of the Creative Arts, Farnham.

Index

WATERLA...
Junker crashed in footpath at WEAR FARM and alive airman floated into School garden.
Crash SITE
OAKRIDGE LYNCH
Parachuting down. Alive German Pilot!
Dead German Parachutist
OAKRIDGE
CANAL